Seeking Employment in Law Enforcement, Private Security, and Related Fields

J. Scott Harr

Kären M. Hess

West Publishing Company
St. Paul   New York   Los Angeles   San Francisco

DEDICATED TO THE PURSUIT OF DREAMS

We look forward to hearing from our readers who call with the exciting message, "I got the job!" This book is for you. Good luck!

We also wish to provide a special dedication to Geneva Middleton, our dean, and to Henry Wrobleski, coordinator of the law enforcement department, who provide an exceptional learning experience for law enforcement and private security students at Normandale Community College.

A note on the artwork: Officer Joe Guy relieves the stress of police work by drawing. We thank him for his contributions which add a light touch to a serious subject.

ACKNOWLEGEMENTS

We wish to personally express appreciation to the law enforcement and security professionals who have helped prepare this text. We greatly appreciate the research assistance provided by Normandale Community College media specialist, Pam Reierson, to whom the Minnesota law enforcement community owes a debt of professional gratitude, as do we.

We also wish to thank the contributors to this book which is richer because of their personal sharing: Brian Benick, Officer, Plymouth Police Department; Jim Chaffee, Director of Security, Walt Disney Pictures and Television; Jim Clark, Chief, Eden Prairie Police Department; Dennis L. Conroy, PhD, Sergeant, St. Paul Police Department; Timothy E. Erickson, Education Coordinator, Minnesota Board of Peace Officer Standards and Training (POST); Joe Guy, Officer, Roseville Police Department; Scott M. Knight, Sergeant, Chaska Police Department; Molly Koivamaki, Senior Crime Prevention Specialist, Eden Prairie Police Department; Robert Meyerson, Trooper, Minnesota State Patrol; Linda Miller, Sergeant, Bloomington Police Department; Marie Ohman, Executive Director, Minnesota Board of Private Investigators and Protective Agents; Richard W. Stanek, Sergeant, Minnepolis Police Department; Timothy J. Thompson, Director of Human Resources and Corporate Relations, Minnesota Timberwolves, and Henry Wrobleski, Coordinator, Law Enforcement Department, Normandale Community College.

Thank you, too, to reviewers of the manuscript for this text: Frank P. Alberico, Joliet Junior College; William J. Halliday, Brookdale Community College; Robert Ives, Rock Valley College; Robert H. Burrington, Georgia Police Academy; Joseph Macy, Palm Beach Community College; Charles E. Myers; Aims Community College; and Carroll S. Price, Penn Valley Community College.

We also wish to acknowledge Christine Hess for her careful and accurate manuscript preparation, Diane Harr for her assistance reviewing the manuscript, and West Publishing Company editors Susan Tubb, Robert Jucha, and Diane Colwyn for their encouragement and assistance.

Finally, a profound thanks to our families for their patience and encouragement. From Scott, a special thanks to my wife Diane, daughter Kelsey, and son Ricky, with whom I have always shared my dreams.

FOREWORD

Abraham Lincoln once said, "Prepare yourself for the day opportunity presents itself, and you will be rewarded." The process of entering public or private law enforcement usually consists of several steps to "prepare yourself."

This book is a genuine contribution to the future of young Americans seeking employment in public and private sectors of law enforcement. It provides guidance and motivation.

This book, by J. Scott Harr and Kären M. Hess, has been heralded by many as being the best in providing information, guidance, and direction to those seeking a career in the public or private policing fields. The authors give applicants a realistic approach. Each chapter is presented in a factual "this is what it is all about" manner and represents thinking and research that conveys a positive approach and purpose.

The past and present dynamics of seeking employment projected into the future suggest great optimism for applicants who pursue job hunting with a positive attitude. This book goes as far as our knowledge takes it today. It is the best resource to appear in many years and gives applicants an enlightened, positive approach to job seeking in these highly competitive fields.

Henry M. Wrobleski
Coordinator of Law Enforcement
Normandale Community College

INTRODUCTION

"The longest journey begins with but a single step."--Anonymous

The purpose of this book is simple: to help you develop a job-search strategy to land your "dream" job. Webster's Dictionary defines *strategy* as ". . . a careful plan or method. . . the art of devising or employing plans. . . toward a goal." Your goal is TO GET A NEW JOB! Whether it is to enter into a profession or to advance within your current profession, it sounds so simple. After all, most of us have had no trouble getting work--flipping burgers, washing dishes, babysitting. Do not let this lull you into a false sense of security.

You have chosen to pursue employment in a field that has become exceptionally popular. Increasing numbers of individuals are acquiring the prerequisites necessary to enter police and security work. Some municipal police departments have received over 1,000 applicants for single job openings! Additionally, once in the profession, relatively few people leave, so jobs do not open up rapidly. Lateral transfers often fill new jobs with experienced individuals.

The days of walking into a law enforcement agency or a private security department with little or no preparation and expecting to be offered a job are gone. A carefully planned job search strategy has become more important than ever.

In addition to the vast number of applicants who possess the minimum qualifications for police or security jobs, many applicants have excellent experience. Applicants may have worked out of state as law enforcement officers or as private security officers. Military experience has also proven to be very beneficial in the job search, as has advanced college education.

In fact, some departments require applicants to have a bachelors degree. And some applicants have Masters Degrees, law degrees, PhDs, and a myriad of speciality certificates. In addition, many people have taken advantage of volunteer opportunities related to the field, such as police reserves, volunteer rescue/firefighting, and civilian police support jobs. Such work not only provides valuable experience, but also demonstrates that the individuals can be trusted in a field demanding unqualified ethics. In short, many applicants begin their job search with exceptional qualifications, making them most attractive candidates.

Do not get discouraged. While this information may be a bit overwhelming, it should not make you want to give up. You will eventually get a job. When and what that job will be depend on your job hunting strategy. While job hunting sometimes takes longer than anticipated and has occasional discouragements, it is also challenging, exciting, and eventually fruitful.

This book addresses both *law enforcement* and *private security* because they are complementary professions. A private security job can be a stepping stone into a police job. Many students majoring in law enforcement have jobs in private security. Even entry-level security jobs are becoming harder to obtain. Additionally, private security is recognized as an attractive field. Pay, hours, and assignments at the management level often are better than in the public sector. Conversely, a police job can lead to a position as a security director. Further, lateral transfers between both professions are occurring more often.

This book also addresses promotions. Traditionally, law enforcement and private security promote from within. The ability to advance through the ranks requires many of the same attributes that apply to the entry-level job seeker. But, it also requires an effective strategy. The skills discussed here apply equally to getting a new job in a new field and to getting promoted.

Keep in mind that this book was written for individuals throughout the country who seek employment in law enforcement, private security, or related fields. It is, therefore, general. Each state has different laws which you must be aware of, for example, laws regarding licensure requirements, use of polygraph testing, and the like. In addition, every employing agency will have its own individualized requirements, for example, what areas in a background investigation will be of particular concern, or what types of physical agility testing will be given. Find out what your state and the agency you are interested in require and expect of applicants.

Recognize that searching for a job actually is a job in itself. The first step is to develop a personal job hunting strategy. Always remember, however, your job hunt strategy should not control you--you should control it. A planned strategy will make the entire process more tolerable, successful, and even enjoyable.

To help you develop such a strategy and get the job you seek is the purpose of this book. The first section gives a general overview of the fields and options within them. The second section discusses preparing for your job search, particularly the testing portion and what employers look for. This is followed by a section describing specific job-seeking strategies to land your "dream job." The book concludes with a look at how you can succeed on the job once you get it and how it might change in the years ahead.

Throughout the book you will be asked to become actively engaged with the topic being discussed, to write down your ideas and plans. Such instances will be indicated by a row of asterisks: ************. You may want to keep a notebook handy for this purpose. The more you interact with the content in this book, the more you will get out of it, and the more effective your job-search strategy is likely to be.

Each chapter has a series of *Mind Stretches* to get you thinking about the topic as it relates to your particular interests and talents. Again, to get the most out of this book, *do* take time to work through these Mind Stretches, either mentally or in your notebook.

Each chapter concludes with *An Inside View* of the topic, written by someone in the field. These brief, personal essays are based on experience and give a variety of perspectives on what is or might be important in seeking a career in law enforcement, private security, or related fields, as well as learning how others have succeeded. Repetition occurs within these personal essays. Although the individuals were asked to write about their experience with the topic of the chapter, many felt compelled to add information and advice about other areas as well. As areas are repeated, you will come to realize how critical certain aspects of the job-seeking process are. Every contributor talks about them. You may also find some contradictions with what is said in the text. Use your own judgment as to whose advice you feel suits *you* best. Often no "right" answer exists.

Let your first reading be only the beginning. As you get into your job search, use the book as a reference. In addition, libraries and bookstores have a tremendous amount of information on the many important aspects of job searching. Keep practicing your skills such as working up great responses to those "most commonly asked" interview questions. Look at interviews that do not result in a job as opportunities to practice your interviewing skills. Continue to role-play interviews whenever you get the chance.

Experts say that most people will have between *five* and *twenty* careers--not just jobs, *careers*--during a lifetime. The job-hunting process is, indeed, continuing, so become skilled at it.

I am genuinely interested in your job search. I have experienced the excitement of being "the one" selected, the bitter disappointment and pain of not being "the one," and the frustration of being cut at an early stage of a hiring process as well as after making it into the finals. Believe me, I know what it is like. That is precisely why I have written this book. I want you to get the job you want in the field you choose.

I would also welcome comments about this book--what's helpful and not so helpful. And I'd like to wish you the best of luck in your job search. Here's to developing the skills and strategy that will get you the job you really want!

> *Having once decided to achieve a certain task, achieve it at all costs of tedium and distastes. The gain in self-confidence of having accomplished a tiresome labor is immense.--Arnold Bennett*

J. Scott Harr, 1992

CONTENTS

SECTION ONE
THE CHALLENGE

Before beginning your job search, you should fully understand what it is you are getting into. You've probably read startling statistics about the rate of change facing employees and the job market. Law enforcement and private security are being directly affected by these dramatic changes and will continue to be affected. Chapter One looks at what the career you're seeking entrance into might look like by the year 2001.

Chapter Two discusses careers in law enforcement and private security as they presently exist, how the two fields differ, what the requirements are for entrance into these fields, and specific advantages of each.

Chapter Three explores other careers within the criminal justice system that might be better suited for you. The field is vast and has many options other than law enforcement and private security jobs.

Chapter Four has you think about choosing a career and what factors to consider. It helps you look at the requirements for entrance into law enforcement and private security in light of your background, experience, and personal likes and dislikes.

If after reading this section you are convinced that a career in law enforcement or private security is for you, the rest of the book provides strategies and techniques to help get the job you seek. The fields of law enforcement and private security are demanding, and so is the road to employment in these professions.

You have made an important decision by taking this step to develop your job search strategies. Let's get started!

CHAPTER 1

EMPLOYMENT TRENDS:
THE WORLD OF WORK

Most of our adult lives are spent working. Taking into account commuting time, overtime, thinking about our jobs, and worrying over work, we spend more of our waking hours in the office, at the factory, on the road, behind the desk, than we do at home.--The Joy of Working, p.ix.

Do You Know:

* What needs all people have?

* What the "hierarchy of needs" is?

* What role work has in meeting our needs?

* How our labor force will change in the future? What effect this will have on work?

* What job areas will expand? What areas will not?

* What occupations are growing the fastest? Declining?

* How jobs in law enforcement and security will look in the future?

* What futurists predict about society and how this will affect work in the United States?

* What factor age will play in future work?

* What factor education will play in future work?

INTRODUCTION

Working *is* important. It provides you with income, to be sure. But work is so much more. Work helps to form your identity, and it makes a statement about who you are. In fact, according to well-known psychologist Abraham H. Maslow, work meets *all* five levels of human needs. Maslow developed a hierarchy of needs going from the most basic, physical needs, to the most complex, self-actualization needs, with safety, social, and esteem needs in between. These needs and their job-related counterparts in a *satisfying job* are often as follows:

* Physical: Good working conditions
                                 Rest periods
                                 Labor saving equipment
                                 Sufficient income
                                 Heating/air conditioning

* Safety: Safe working conditions
                                 Good supervision
                                 Job security
                                 Training in survival

* Social: Feeling of belonging to a "job family"
                                 Agency/department/organization spirit
                                 After-hour get togethers
                                 Picnics and softball games

* Esteem: Challenging job
                                 Promotions
                                 Titles
                                 Community recognition
                                 Awards

* Self-
Actualization: Opportunity for growth and development
                                 Discretion/decision-making authority
                                 Contributing to society/organization

According to Maslow, as needs are satisfied at the lowest level, people move up the hierarchy to the next level. Think for a few minutes about what's important to **you** in the career you select. Which level(s) of need will influence you the most? ********** (Get your notebook and jot down your responses.)

A study conducted by *Psychology Today* had participants rank what was important to them on the job. The factors they used follow. Rank them yourself, using a #1 for the most important down to #17 being least important.

____ The amount of freedom you have on your job.
____ Amount of fringe benefits you get.
____ Amount of information you get about your job performance.
____ Amount of job security you have.
____ Amount of pay you get.
____ Amount of praise you get for a job well done.
____ Chances for getting a promotion.
____ Chances for taking part in making decisions.
____ Chances to accomplish something worthwhile.
____ Chances to do something that makes you feel good about yourself.
____ Chances to do things you do best.
____ Chances to learn new things.
____ The friendliness of people you work with.
____ Opportunities to develop your skills and abilities.
____ The resources you have to do your job.
____ The respect you receive from people you work with.
____ The way you are treated by the people you work with.

How other people rank the factors is not important. You may be interested to know, however, that in the survey, "Chances to do something that makes you feel good about yourself" was ranked first and "Chances to accomplish something worthwhile" was ranked second. What *is* important is how *you* ranked them. Think carefully about your top rankings and how well they would be met in a career in law enforcement or private security. * * * * * * *

Work satisfies so many human needs that those who find themselves without meaningful employment usually experience a loss. If work is unfulfilling, your needs must be met elsewhere or anxiety, frustration, or even depression may result.

If you are unemployed, say in the case of an unexpected lay off, lives become seriously disrupted. Losing a job and being unable to find other work has driven some to such self-destructive behaviors as alcoholism and other drug abuse and even suicide. Truly, work is important as something positive to do to meet your needs, including not only money, but identity and self-esteem.

For these reasons it is important to give careful thought to what work you pursue. This book will help you decide what you want to do with your working life. You will have a chance to look at what is important to you and what you have to offer employers. According to Hage (1989, p.1D), "Career planning may deserve more time than most give it." Many people spend more time planning their next vacation than they do planning what they're going to work at for the rest of their lives. To do so is risky, because as Cornish (1983, p.5) suggests:

> Choosing a career has never been as difficult as it is today. There are far more occupations than ever before with new ones springing up every day, and the older occupations are changing radically. Add to that the fact that people are living longer and adopting new lifestyles, and it's no wonder that the notion of a lifelong commitment to a single career now seems a trifle quaint . . . .

> Choosing a career--and sticking to it--used to be a lot easier. In bygone times, a boy would naturally follow the occupation of his father, easily picking up needed skills while still a toddler. By the time he reached adulthood, he would be fully trained and ready to earn his living. A girl would learn the homemaking skills from her mother and by the time she reached her teens was ready to run a home on her own.

This situation has changed dramatically. Cornish notes that the Industrial Revolution in the mid 1800s started the change, a change from a rural to an urban society dependent on the match between humans and machines. Important changes that have taken place since then include the changing of several values:

Then	**Now**
A warm, secure family life	Soaring divorce rates
Participation in a great ennobling nation-state	Vietnam and Watergate
Hope of heaven in the afterlife	Weakening of the church

According to Cornish (pp.7-8), as "emotional supports shriveled," two new dreams replaced them--a dream of a successful career and a dream of a carefree, pleasurable life-style:

> In the career dream, the career would include a period of training during which one's true merit was established and one gained the tools to perform tasks that would win money and admiration as one moved steadily up the ladder of success. During this ascent, one would enjoy all the creature comforts, live in luxurious surroundings, consume gourmet edibles and potables, have an abundance of admiring friends and adoring lovers--just like the people in the television commercials . . . .
>
> But the romanticized dream of a successful career--a dream that blossomed in the 1960s--received nasty shocks in the 1970s. . . .
>
> Adding to the problem of economic recession was the arrival in the job market of the baby-boom generation and the enormous growth of higher education.

The romanticized dream of a successful career becomes even more problematic when it involves the fields of law enforcement and private security. Many people are intrigued with employment in either law enforcement or security because they want to be like the TV undercover police officer or private investigator they watch week after week. You must enter your career search with a much more open mind. Realistically, what *is* the job you are seeking?

A LOOK AT JOBS OF THE FUTURE--WHERE WILL YOU FIT IN?

As the twenty-first century approaches, interest has heightened in looking ahead at what our world of work might be like. Certain trends are pointed out repeatedly:

* The labor force will continue to grow.

* The total number of jobs will increase rapidly.

* The most rapid growth will be in jobs in the *service sector* (which includes law enforcement and security).

* Blue collar jobs will decline slightly.

* More education will be needed for more jobs.

* An alarming number of young people will not be qualified for the new jobs.

* More workers will be between the ages of 25 and 54.

* Women and the minorities will also account for a greater share of the workforce.

Growth in the Service Industries

According to Cooper (1988, p.443): "The service-producing industries are expected to provide almost the entire net increase in new jobs--some 20 million--by the turn of the century." Cetron (1984, p.10) also notes:

One of the easiest employment trends to spot is the projected growth in service industries and service industry jobs . . . . Service occupations steadily have grown to become the economic roots of the U.S. work force. According to the U.S. Bureau of Labor Statistics, more than two-thirds of the nation's employment growth during the past 20 years has come in the service sector and that trend is expected to continue.

According to the *Occupational Outlook Handbook* (p.6): "Employment is expected to continue to increase much faster in service-producing industries than in goods-producing industries. In fact, service-producing industries are projected to account for about 9 out of 10 new jobs between 1984 and 1995." This reference also notes (p.9) that service occupations within this broad service industry have an exceptionally bright outlook:

This group [the service industry] includes a wide range of workers in protective, food and beverage preparation, cleaning, and personal services and is expected to account for more job growth than any other broad group. Among the protective service occupations, correction officers are expected to have much faster than average growth because of the increasing number of inmates, and guards are expected to have faster than average growth because of concern over crime and vandalism.

Cetron (p. 41) also notes: "Lest there be any doubt about the vitality of the service industries as a part of the U.S. economy and as a major employer, estimates indicate they will support more than 88 percent of the American work force by 2000."

Similar impressive projections are made by Silvestri and Lukasiewicz (1989, p.43): "Employment in the service occupations group is expected to increase by 23 percent from 1988 to 2000. With an increase of more than 4 million jobs, it will add more jobs than any other major occupational group. Silvestri and Lukasiewicz (p.55) project the employment in the protective service occupations under low, medium, and high scenarios for economic growth as follows:

Occupation	Low	Moderate	High
Correctional officers & jailers	251,000	262,000	276,000
Firefighting occupations	307,000	321,000	337,000
Police and detectives	559,000	583,000	614,000
Police & detective supervisors	93,000	97,000	102,000
Police & detective investigators	64,000	66,000	70,000
Police patrol officers	403,000	421,000	442,000
Crossing guards	58,000	61,000	64,000
Guards	795,000	1,050,000	1,129,000
Other protective service workers	316,000	333,000	351,000
Detectives & investigators, except public	57,000	61,000	65,000
Sheriffs & deputy sheriffs	60,000	63,000	66,000

Need for More Education

A second trend is noted in *Workforce 2000* (1987, p.xiii):

> The new jobs in service industries will demand much higher skill levels than the jobs today. Very few new jobs will be created for those who cannot read, follow directions, and use mathematics. Ironically, the demographic trends in the workforce, coupled with the higher skill requirements of the economy, will lead to both higher and lower unemployment: more joblessness among the least-skilled and less among the most educationally advantaged.

This concern is shared by Cooper (1988, p.444): "The Labor Department predicts that more than half the new jobs created by the end of the century will require education beyond high school. Today, fewer than a quarter of all occupations require a college degree; by 2000, almost a third of the jobs will be held by college graduates."

As noted in *Projections 2000* (1987, p.35): "The projected growth of the broad occupational groups shows the increasing need for education. Occupations in which a large proportion of workers have college training are among the fastest growing. Occupations in which a large proportion of workers have less than four years of high school are generally among the slowest growing."

The Bureau of Justice Statistics (1987, p.1) notes the importance of education in state and local law enforcement agencies: "All state police agencies and almost all local police (99.7%) and sheriffs' agencies (97.5%) with 135 or more sworn personnel required new officer recruits to have at least a high school diploma. About 10% of state and local police agencies and about 6% of sheriffs' departments required at least some college education." In the security field, also, to become certified, education beyond high school is a requirement for all but the most experienced individuals.

The reality is that a high school diploma, while perhaps meeting the bare requirements for some jobs, will seldom be sufficient to assure career advancement opportunities.

KEEPING UP TO DATE

An excellent source to keep current on jobs and employment trends is the *Occupational Outlook Handbook*. Updated every two years, this career resource describes what workers do on the job, where they work, how much they earn, the training and eduction they need, and the job outlook for about two hundred occupations. It also includes a listing of sources of state and local job information. Check your local library.

You might also want to check with state agencies and employment offices as well as your state department of education, state job services agencies, and state labor departments.

REFERENCES

Bureau of Justice Statistics, *Profile of State and Local Law Enforcement Agencies, 1987,* Washington, DC: U.S. Government Printing Office, March 1989.

Cetron, Marvin. *Jobs of the Future: The 500 Best Jobs--Where They'll be and How to Get them.* New York: McGraw-Hill Book Company, 1984.

Cooper, Mary H. "Help Wanted: Why Jobs Are Hard to Fill," *Editorial Research Reports,* 2:9, September 9, 1988.

Cornish, Edward, ed. *Careers Tomorrow: The Outlook for Work in a Changing World* (selections from *The Futurist*). Bethesda, MD: World Future Society, 1983.

Hage, Dave. "Career Planning May Deserve More Time than Most Give It," *Star Tribune,* April 4, 1989, p.1D.

Occupational Outlook Handbook. Reprint: "Tomorrow's Jobs: Overview." Washington, DC: U.S. Government Printing Office. 1986-1987 edition.

Projections 2000. Occupational Outlook Quarterly. U.S. Department of Labor, Bureau of Labor Statistics, Fall, 1987.

Renwick, Patricia A., Lawler, Edward E., and the *Psychology Today* staff. "What You Really Want from Your Job," *Psychology Today,* May 1978, pp.53-65.

Silvestri, George and Lukasiewicz, John. "Projections of Occupational Employment, 1988-2000," *Monthly Labor Review,* November 1989, pp.42-55.

Workforce 2000: Work and Workers for the Twenty-first Century. Indianapolis, IN: Hudson Institute, Inc., 1987.

MIND STRETCHES*****

1. Imagine you have a crystal ball--what changes do you see in the world of work:
   -- 5 years from now?
   --10 years from now?
   --50 years from now?

2. What role do you think education will play in the future?

3. Do you think work will become more specialized or more generalized in the future? Why? How will your job goals be affected?

4. What do you think will happen to current age limitations on jobs? Why?

5. What jobs do you think will become more necessary in the future? Less necessary?

6. How do you predict the field of private security will change? Why?

7. How do you predict policing will change? Why?

8. Recognizing that our entire society is always changing, what importance will you place on continuing to change and grow yourself?

9. Is always striving to improve yourself important to you? Is there a danger in not continuing to grow and change?

10. Can you think of jobs that do not now exist but will within the next ten or twenty years?

"Professionalism?"

AN INSIDER'S VIEW

THE CHANGING FACE OF

PRIVATE SECURITY

Marie Ohman
Executive Director
Minnesota Board of Private Investigators
and Protective Agents

The security practitioner of the 1990s is faced with a challenging and continuously evolving new frontier. This new frontier manifests itself in tremendous changes in the existing service industry. Modern society needs to maintain an effective system to protect the public from wrong and also to deal with the multifaceted criminal justice system. Private security has become an integral part of our society's efforts to maintain a semblance of order.

A major change area is the evolving "face" of public law enforcement. The ability of the general public and business communities to rely on public law enforcement for prevention services, and for acting when prevention fails, has diminished. A key factor in that change is economic.

Attempting to provide services for a growing population with fewer dollars creates problems for traditional law enforcement agencies. The demands placed on public service force law enforcement administrators into deciding *not* what they need or would like to do, but just how much they can do with their limited resources. The areas of need left unaddressed, or instances where a special need is perceived, have begun to be taken over by private client dollars spent for private security services.

A 1985 study published by the National Institute of Justice and Hallcrest Systems, Inc., estimated the ratio of private security officers to that of public law enforcement officers to be 2 to 1. Recently, that estimate has been stated at closer to 3 to 1.

Private security forces have been and will continue to be a viable employer in our country's workforce. The stereotypical view of an elderly, gun-carrying security guard is slowly being replaced with that of a modern security officer who deals with all facets of protection from the traditional "observe and report" role to intricate knowledge of alarm and computer systems, thorough knowledge of security concepts, and expertise in safety and first-aid responses.

Private security will continue to be essential in society. From a philosophical view, as long as generations are raised in an environment of economic difficulties, materialism, and little accountability for actions, the necessity for maintaining order will be an absolute. A trend in government today is to look to the business world for answers to problems. Included in that trend is the reality that private security plays a vital role in protecting people and property in this country, traditionally public law enforcement's role. After many years of evolution, private security has gained long overdue respect as a profession.

CHAPTER 2
CAREERS IN LAW ENFORCEMENT
AND
PRIVATE SECURITY

The very first step towards success in any occupation is to become interested in it.--John Dewey

Do You Know:

* How most people learn about careers in law enforcement and private security?

* How accurately police officers think they are portrayed on television?

* The differences between public and private policing?

* What the requirements are for law enforcement and private security jobs?

* Which parts of the country offer more opportunities for employment in law enforcement?

* What the benefits of federal employment are?

* The growth potential of private security?

* The advantages of employment in the private sector?

* How public and private officers' salaries compare?

INTRODUCTION

To make informed decisions about your career, you must gather factual data. Some of this information comes from within. Do you possess the personal attributes needed to be an officer? Can you give orders? Can you take orders? Can you remain calm under stress? Can you treat people professionally and apply the law equally? Can you work the hours under the conditions required by the job? Can you control innate and acquired drives and impulses under various environmental situations, some of which may be ambiguous?

You also need to consider objective, external data. This chapter provides information about careers in law enforcement and private security. Much of what happens within these professions is not common knowledge. Consequently, many people considering employment in either field may find themselves relying on inaccurate data. Unless you have a personal friend or relative in either field, you are likely to obtain what you know about it where most people do: television or the newspaper.

Television may lead you to believe *police work* falls into one of two categories: downtown at night, driving from call to call with siren blaring and red lights flashing or investigating macabre crimes in obscure locations. Television may lead you to believe *security work* consists primarily of solving crimes the police cannot or will not deal with.

It Isn't So

Because of the popularity of police investigators, detectives, and private investigators, movies and TV shows about them abound. But their primary goal is to entertain, not to educate. Sensationalism is much more likely than realism. As Shepherd (1989, p.5E) says:

> In 18 episodes of "Miami Vice" last year, Crocket and Tubbs killed 43 people, five
> times as many as the entire Miami police force killed in the whole year. (On average,
> a Chicago police officer fires his gun, for any reason, every 27 years.)

To select a career based on fiction is to set yourself up for disappointment. No one knows better than those in the profession that television and the movies don't exactly "tell it like it is." A study by Penn and Schoem (1987), *Television and Police,* found that while a high percentage of the public considers the portrayal of police on television as accurate, only 14% of the New York City police officers interviewed thought this to be the case.

The uniforms, the cars, the equipment, the apparent prestige, and the legal authority and power combine to make for a romantic ideal. This is why the media loves to portray public and private detectives as such colorful characters. Don't be fooled. Take a hard look at these professions as you make realistic, informed decisions about your future career.

PUBLIC VS. PRIVATE

Because public policing and private security are closely related and because people employed in one field often become involved at some time in the other, start by looking at how the two fields basically differ.

A primary difference between public policing and private security, as the names imply, is who you work for. Who pays your salary? Individuals in public policing are paid with tax dollars and, consequently, are accountable to the tax-paying citizens, whether on a local, county, state, or federal level. They are, therefore, under constant scrutiny by both the public and the politicians charged with overseeing expenditures of public funds. Many people live complacently with the attitude that "serious crime could never happen in our town, so why spend increased tax dollars on policing?" Therefore, regardless of rank, no public peace officer will become rich from the job.

Private security positions, in contrast, are funded by business, industry, any entity in the private sector wanting protection beyond what public law enforcement provides.

Another basic difference between public policing and private security is the essential goals of each. Public law enforcement is quite reactive, operating as a service to the jurisdiction that pays for it. Ideally, it serves everyone within its jurisdiction equally, without a profit motive. People call and the police are expected to respond.

Private security seeks to prevent problems and limit losses for a particular private employer. It is pro-active. Whether a private security operation is *proprietary* (the security officers are actual employees of the company) or *contractual* (a company hires security officers from an independent security company), the private security profession is profit-oriented and serves the employer paying for such service.

A third basic difference between public and private policing is in the statutory power involved. Public police officers are an arm of the government and act with its full authority, including the authority of arrest. As stressed by Creamer (1980): "Police arrest powers are indeed awesome, and even while they protect society, they can destroy a citizen." Police may, however, be denied access to private facilities that are accessible to those facilities' security officers. Without a warrant, public police could well be denied access to an industrial facility that relies on its own security department to deal with such concerns as industrial espionage.

Private security officers have no more power than private citizens. However, as citizens, they can carry weapons, conduct investigations, defend property, and make arrests. And they may, in fact, *appear* to have more authority than regular citizens as a result of wearing a uniform, carrying a weapon, and having the approval of the organization to defend the property.

Competitors or Collaborators?

Frequently public policing and private security are viewed as being competitors. Additionally, many people in public law enforcement look down on security officers, calling them "wanna be's," that is, individuals who really want to be police officers but didn't make it. The negative view of private security officers is apparent in a statement made by a police sergeant in Georgia (Remesch, 1989, pp.32-33): " . . . to state that the only difference between a police officer and a security officer is the title 'security,' is like comparing a surgeon to a butcher since they both cut meat." Remesch (1989, p.33) notes:

> Much of the problem centers on the still-evolving nature of the private security industry. Like a grown sibling, the older, wiser, public police officer wants the private police officer to just follow his lead in the path he's traveled a million times. But like the younger sibling who has finally reached the age of maturity, members of private security are saying to their brethren: "We've grown up. Give us some respect."

Private security is growing. Burden (1989, p.92) estimates that 900,000 people are employed in private security, compared with about 650,000 public police. Remesch (1989, p.33) suggests:

> This drastic increase is the direct result of citizens who have decided to take an active role in law enforcement. The increase in crime in once quiet neighborhoods; coupled with the cutback in police budgets and services, has left citizens vulnerable, but rather

than pay more taxes for better services, the citizenry has chosen services from the private sector.

Competitors? This should not be the case. What is needed, as noted by a police captain from Baltimore, is cooperation: "We need cooperation because basically we all pursue the same goals. We all want to improve the quality of life" (Remesch, p.67).

The benefits of cooperation are illustrated by Segal (1989) in his article, "Too Many Cooks?" which describes how several agencies are working together to provide security and protection for Denver's Stapleton International Airport. Such cooperation is becoming more evident throughout our nation.

Another obvious reason for cooperation is that individuals often move from one field to the other. Some individuals use private security as a stepping stone into public policing. Likewise, some individuals in public policing enter private security, sometimes as a consultant, sometimes after retiring from public policing, and sometimes as a part-time job while working as a public police officer. Burden (1989, p.92) says: "The rent-a-cop business has grown steadily over the past 30 years as the fear of crime and the demand for police service have risen. Today, in some city precincts, there are more moonlighters than on-duty officers on the streets."

LAW ENFORCEMENT--UP CLOSE

The allure of being a police officer makes this profession extraordinarily popular. The public generally believes that being a police officer means wearing a uniform and pushing a squad car around town. Maybe some think of detectives, but few people outside the field have any idea of the variety of employment available. Consider the vocational spectrum shown with the following partial listing of positions, many obtained by reviewing the 1990 *International Association of Chiefs of Police Membership Directory*:

Arson Investigator
Attache
Ballistics Expert
Booking Officer
Border Patrol Officer
Chaplain
Chief of Police
Chief of Staff
Commander of Field Operations
Commissioner
Communications Officer
Community Safety Coordinator
Community Service Officer
Conservation Officer
Crime Lab Technician
Crime Prevention Specialist
Customs Officer
Data Processing Specialist
Deputy
Deputy Chief
Detective

Detention Officer
Director of Research and Development
Director of Scientific Services
Director of Standards and Training
Document Specialist
Emergency Management Coordinator
Evidence Technician
FBI Special Agent
Fingerprint Expert
Firearms Instructor
Forensic Scientist
Gaming Enforcement Agent
Gang Investigator
Inspector
Instructor
Intelligence Officer
Investigator
Jailer
Juvenile Specialist
K-9 Handler
Narcotics Agent
Operations Specialist
Patrol Officer
Personnel Specialist
Photographer
Pilot
Police Attorney/Legal Advisor
Police Psychologist
Police/School Liaison Officer
Police Surgeon
Polygraph Operator
Professor
Psychiatric Advisor
Public Relations Officer
Public Safety Director
Radio Communications
Records Management Director
Scientist
Security Specialist
Secret Service Agent
Serology Specialist
Sheriff
Street Crimes Specialist
Superintendent of Police
S.W.A.T
Traffic Officer
Training Director
Treasury Agent
Trooper
Undercover Operative
Undersheriff
U.S. Marshal
Water Patrol
Witness Protection Agent

Jurisdictional Opportunities

To begin your look at law enforcement, consider the basic areas in which you might work. Jurisdiction in this sense basically addresses both *where* particular agencies work and *what* their enforcement emphasis is. The primary jurisdictional levels are federal, state, county, and local law enforcement.

While law enforcement officers may enforce the law wherever they happen to be (for that matter, by power of citizen's arrest laws, so can private citizens), different levels of law enforcement agencies have different areas of responsibility. For example, while Secret Service agents are law enforcement officers, they do not do traffic enforcement. Similarly, local law enforcement officers are seldom called on for diplomatic protective service. The following descriptions of federal, state, county, and local agencies are from *Introduction to Law Enforcement and Criminal Justice*, (Wrobleski and Hess, 1990, pp.34-52).

Federal Agencies

Federal agencies include the Federal Bureau of Investigation; the Federal Drug Enforcement Administration; United States Marshals; Immigration and Naturalization Services; the Bureau of Prisons; the Bureau of Customs; the Internal Revenue Service; the Secret Service; the Bureau of Alcohol, Tobacco, and Firearms Tax; Postal Inspectors; the Coast Guard; and the military services.

The Federal Bureau of Investigation (FBI). The FBI is the primary investigative agency of the federal government. Its special agents have jurisdiction over more than two hundred federal crimes. They are responsible for general investigations, both criminal and civil, and for domestic intelligence dealing with the internal security of the nation. The FBI's four investigative priorities are organized crime, foreign counterintelligence, white-collar crime, and terrorism.

In addition to these numerous responsibilities, the FBI provides valuable services to law enforcement agencies throughout the country. The *Identification Division* is the central repository for fingerprint information; over 22,000 agencies contribute to and may obtain information from it. The *FBI Laboratory* is the largest, most effective criminal laboratory in the world. Its facilities are available to any city, county, state, or federal law enforcement agency in the country.

The *National Crime Information Center* (NCIC) is a complex, computerized, electronic data exchange network developed to complement computerized systems already in existence and those planned by any local and state law enforcement agencies. *Uniform Crime Reports*, another service provided by the FBI, is a national clearinghouse for United States crime statistics.

The Federal Drug Enforcement Administration (DEA). Narcotics agents seek to stop the flow of drugs at their source, both domestic and foreign, and to assist state and local police in preventing illegal drugs from reaching local communities. They become involved in surveillance, raids, interviewing witnesses and suspects, searching for evidence, and seizing contraband goods.

United States Marshals. The functions of most deputy marshals are more enforcement than investigative. They are responsible for (1) seizing property in both criminal and civil matters to satisfy judgments issued by a federal court, (2) providing physical security for United States courtrooms and protection for federal judges, jurors, and attorneys, (3) transporting federal prisoners to federal institutions when transferred or sentenced by a federal court, and (4) protecting government witnesses whose testimony might jeopardize their safety.

Immigration and Naturalization Service (INS). INS border patrol agents conduct investigations, detect violations of immigrant and nationality laws, and determine whether aliens may enter or remain in the United States. INS immigration inspectors are responsible for detecting people who violate immigration and nationality laws.

The Bureau of Prisons. The Bureau of Prisons is responsible for the care and custody of those convicted of federal crimes and sentenced to federal penal institutions. Correctional officers coordinate work assignments, enforce rules and regulations within institutions, and carry out plans developed for correctional treatment and modification of inmates' attitudes.

The Bureau of Customs. The Bureau of Customs has agents stationed primarily at ports of entry to the United States, where people and/or goods enter and leave. Customs agents investigate frauds on customs revenue and the smuggling of merchandise and contraband into or out of the United States. Customs is active in suppressing the traffic in illegal narcotics and works in close cooperation with the Federal Drug Enforcement Administration. Customs patrol officers maintain uniformed and plainclothes surveillance at docks and airports.

The Internal Revenue Service (IRS). IRS agents investigate willful tax evasion, tax fraud, and the activities of gamblers and drug dealers. The bureau has three divisions: Examination, Collection, and Criminal Investigation. Examination staff selects and audits tax returns of individuals and corporations. Collection staff includes revenue officers and field workers who contact delinquent taxpayers. Criminal Investigation staff includes special agents who conduct investigations, make arrests, provide armed escorts, protect other employees as well as government property, and assist Secret Service agents in protecting the president and other public officials.

The Secret Service. The Secret Service has two major law enforcement functions: to suppress counterfeiting and to suppress forgery of government checks and bonds. It is also responsible for protecting the president of the United States, the president's family members, the president-elect, and the vice-president. The *Secret Service Uniformed Division* protects the executive mansion and its grounds. The *Treasury Police Force* protects the Treasury Building and the Treasury Annex in Washington.

The Bureau of Alcohol, Tobacco, and Firearms Tax (BATF). The BATF is primarily a licensing and investigative agency involved in federal tax violations. The Firearms Division enforces the Gun Control Act of 1968, which deals with the manufacture, sale, transfer, and possession of restricted firearms in the United States.

Postal Inspectors. Postal inspectors enforce federal laws pertaining to mailing prohibited items such as explosives, obscene matter, and articles likely to injure or cause damage. Any mail that may prove to be libelous, defamatory, or threatening can be excluded from being transported by the postal service. Postal inspectors protect the mails and recipients of mail. They also investigate any frauds perpetrated through the mails such as chain letters, gift enterprises, and similar schemes.

The Coast Guard. The Coast Guard assists local and state agencies that border the oceans, lakes, and national waterways. They have been actively involved in preventing the smuggling of narcotics into this country.

The Military Services. The armed forces also have law enforcement responsibilities. The uniformed divisions are known as the Military Police in the Army, the Shore Patrol in the Navy, and the Security Police in the Marine Corps and Air Force. The military police are primarily concerned with the physical security of the various bases under their control. Within each operation, the security forces control criminal activity, court martials, discipline, desertions, and the confinement of prisoners.

State Agencies

Many federal agencies have state counterparts. State agencies with law enforcement responsibilities may include state bureaus of investigation and apprehension and state fire marshal divisions as well as departments of natural resources, driver and vehicle services divisions, departments of human rights, and state police and highway patrol.

State Bureau of Investigation and Apprehension. The Bureau of Investigation and Apprehension places investigators throughout the state to help investigate major crimes and organized criminal activity; help investigate the illegal sale or possession of narcotics and prohibited drugs; conduct police science training courses for peace officers; provide scientific examination of crime scene and laboratory analysis of evidence; and maintain a criminal justice information and telecommunications system.

State Fire Marshal Division. Designated state fire marshals investigate suspicious and incendiary fire origins, fire fatalities, and large-loss fires; tabulate fire statistics; and provide education, inspection, and training programs for fire prevention.

State Department of Natural Resources (Fish, Game, and Watercraft). Conservation officers investigate complaints about nuisance wildlife, misuse of public lands and waters, violations of state park rules, and unlawful appropriation of state-owned timber. Conservation officers also dispose of big game animals struck by motor vehicles, assist state game managers on wildlife census projects, enforce wild-rice harvesting rules, and assist in identifying needed sites for public access to lakes and streams. The department also issues resident and nonresident boat licenses and licenses for hunting, fishing, and trapping.

Driver and Vehicle Services Division. The *Motor Vehicle Section* registers motor vehicles, issues ownership certificates, answers inquiries, returns defective applications received through the mail, licenses motor vehicle dealers, supplies record information to the public, and in some states, registers bicycles.

The *Driver's License Section* tests, evaluates, and licenses all drivers throughout the state; maintains accurate records of each individual driver including all violations and accidents occurring anywhere in the United States and Canada; interviews drivers whose record warrants possible revocation, suspension, or cancellation; records the location of every reported accident; assists in driver education efforts; and administers written and road tests to applicants.

Department of Human Rights. The Department of Human Rights enforces the Human Rights Act, which prohibits discrimination on the basis of race, color, creed, religion, national origin, sex, marital status, status with regard to public assistance or disability in employment, housing, public accommodations, public service, and education.

State Police and State Highway Patrol. Some state police enforce all state laws; others enforce only traffic laws on highways and freeways and are usually designated as state highway patrols.

Usually *state police* do not work within municipalities that have their own forces, except on request.

Most *highway patrol* agencies enforce state traffic laws and all laws governing operation of vehicles on public highways in the state. They usually operate in uniform, drive distinctively marked patrol cars and motorcycles, and engage in such activities as (1) enforcing laws regulating the use of vehicles, (2) maintaining preventive patrol on the highways, (3) regulating traffic movements and relieving congestion, (4) investigating traffic accidents, and (5) making surveys and studies of accidents and enforcement practices to improve traffic safety.

County Agencies

The two main types of county law enforcement agencies are the county sheriff and the county police. Another officer of the county is the coroner or medical examiner.

The County Sheriff. Each sheriff is authorized to appoint deputies and, working with them, to assume responsibility for providing police protection as well as a variety of other functions including (1) keeping the public peace, (2) executing civil and criminal process throughout the county (such as serving civil legal papers and criminal warrants), (3) maintaining and staffing the county jail, (4) preserving the dignity of the court, and (5) enforcing court orders.

The County Police. The county police, not to be confused with the county sheriff and deputies, are often found in areas where city and county governments have been merged.

The Coroner or Medical Examiner. The principal task of the coroner is to determine the cause of death and to take care of the remains and personal effects of deceased persons.

Local Agencies

Local agencies include township and special district police and municipal police.

Township and Special District Police. Many townships have only a one-person police force similar to the resident deputy system frequently found in sheriff's departments in which one person must police vast, sparsely populated regions. This person serves as a "jack-of-all-trades" and is on emergency call day and night. This individual's home may serve as headquarters.

Municipal Police. This is what most people think of when they think of law enforcement. As noted by the Bureau of Justice Statistics (1989, p.1), in 1987 the United States had about 15,000 state and local general purpose law enforcement agencies operating in the United States, including almost 12,000 local police agencies and 3,000 sheriff's agencies. The average department has six to ten officers. The five basic roles of most police officers are to enforce laws, preserve the peace, prevent crimes, protect civil rights and civil liberties, and provide services.

Jurisdictions Compared

Each agency level has its own particular benefits. Federal work may be prestigious and dynamic, and also usually has the best pay and benefits. However, it also usually has higher standards and often requires relocating. Because of the large number of people employed by the federal system, the bureaucracy can be frustrating, with a possibility of feeling engulfed in the numbers. Federal benefits are excellent, however, and transfers within that system are available. On the other hand, likely transfers can substantially interfere with today's common two-profession families. Age may also be a drawback. You cannot be older than thirty-five at the time you are hired because of laws governing retirement in the federal law enforcement system.

Employment with local law enforcement has its own benefits, frequently associated with being part of a more concentrated law enforcement effort. One community benefit of having a local police department is local identity and control. Many officers enjoy being a recognized part of a smaller community. Smaller agencies may have fewer transfer or promotional opportunities, but may also permit officers to assume more responsibilities on the job.

Where Jobs Exist

Usually, the larger the geographic jurisdiction, the greater the number of employment opportunities. According to *The American Almanac of Jobs and Salaries,* (1987, p.1) "in 1985 more than 18 million Americans, almost 20% of the total workforce, were on the public payroll," with the following breakdown:

> 2.9 million civilians (non-military) worked for the federal government
> 2.0 million were in the military
> 3.8 million worked for state governments
> 2.4 million worked for municipalities
> 1.8 million worked for counties
> 5.1 million worked for towns, villages, and school districts

In considering where you might find your best employment potential, consider which governmental agencies have the greatest number of employees because with numbers go advancement potential. Remember, however, that it is also easy to get lost in the sheer numbers.

Local police departments offer over three-fourths of the jobs, and of these, two-thirds to three-fourths are "sworn" personnel as compared to civilian. Civilian opportunities do exist at all three levels. Over half the local police agencies employ fewer than 10 sworn officers, as summarized in Table 2-1.

Table 2-1. Estimated number and percent distribution of local police agencies sworn personnel, 1987

Sworn Personnel	Number	Percent
Total	11,989	100.0%
1,000 or more	34	0.3
500 to 999	32	0.3
250 to 499	77	0.6
100 to 249	321	2.7
50 to 99	599	5.0
29 to 49	1,446	12.1
10 to 24	3,171	26.5
5 to 9	2,872	24.0
2 to 4	2,450	20.4
1	987	8.2

Sourcebook of Criminal Justice Statistics, 1988, p.78.

Salaries

Simply put, no police officer is ever going to get rich from a government payroll. This is not to say that law enforcement personnel are destined to be destitute. On the contrary, law enforcement pay at the federal, state, county, and local levels is certainly comfortable.

When you consider the benefits associated with government work, for example retirement plans, medical coverage, sick time, and vacation time, together with job security that is usually better than in the private sector, work in law enforcement is well compensated.

In many jurisdictions, additional opportunities can be taken advantage of to make law enforcement employment even more attractive. Most jurisdictions, for example, have opportunities for some part-time work. Not only could this be overtime work (usually paying more than the 40-hour-per-week pay scale), but local businesses often hire police at good pay for security work, traffic control for special events, etc.

While it is usually something other than money that motivates the professional law enforcement officer, salary is an important consideration. Different jurisdictions pay differently, and advancement offers pay incentives.

Federal Salaries. Jobs in law enforcement at the federal level fall under the *General Schedule* or *GS* system. This salary scale has eighteen grades (GS-1 to GS-18), with salary increasing as the grade increases. Each grade has a certain number of steps:

> GS-1 to 15   10 steps
> GS-16   9 steps
> GS-17   5 steps
> GS-18   1 step

Currently, depending on experience, the starting grade levels for jobs in law enforcement at the federal level is usually between GS-5 and GS-7. The average GS rating for selected jobs in the criminal justice system is as follows (Wright, 1988, p.7):

Guard	4.6
Border Patrol Agent	8.9
Customs Inspector	9.4
IRS Agent	11.5
Criminal Investigator	12.1

Based on the January 1990 General Schedule Pay Chart, the entry level salary and the salary after five years for grades 5 through twelve are as follows:

Grade	Year 1	Year 5	Year 10
5	$16,305	$18,481	$21,201
6	$18,174	$20,598	$23,628
7	$20,195	$22,887	$26,252
8	$22,367	$25,351	$29,081
9	$24,705	$28,001	$32,121
10	$27,206	$30,824	$35,369
11	$29,891	$33,875	$38,855
12	$35,825	$40,601	$46,571

Grade 18 (one step) had a salary of $78.200 in 1990.

State, County, and Local Salaries. According to the *Sourcebook of Criminal Justice Statistics* (1988, pp. 80-83), salaries vary greatly, depending on the size of the population served. The average entry-level, senior patrol officer, and top administrative level salaries are summarized in Table 2-2.

Table 2-2 Average salaries of state, county, and local law enforcement officers, 1987--rounded to nearest thousand

Agency/Position	Entry Level	Senior Patrol	Chief or Sheriff
State	$19-24	$22-29	$51-61
County			
All Sizes	$16-17	$17-19	$29-30
Under 10,000	$14-15	$16-17	$23-24
1,000,000+	$23-28	$28-33	$62-64
Local			
All Sizes	$17-18	$20-22	$27-29
Under 2,500	$14	$15-17	$18-19
1,000,000+	$23-25	$30-33	$73-87

Promotions and Transfers

Law enforcement has definite upward salary limitations, but the main frustration for most is that promotions are limited, corresponding to the number of officers in the particular department.

The fact is, most police officers will retire at the employment level at which they were hired. While intermediate supervisory positions between patrol officer and chief exist, there are far fewer of these than there are officers. A major contributing factor to police "burn-out" is that many officers consider lack of promotion as a lack of recognition.

Many other police opportunities do exist, however, in speciality positions within a department. Traffic enforcement, accident investigations, juvenile, narcotics enforcement, K-9 handlers, and internal affairs specialists opportunities allow officers to keep from falling into a rut.

Promotions and transfers generally come from within a department. Not only would the administration know the individual, but promotions would serve as recognition. There are, however, benefits to bringing in an outsider, particularly if no one from within the department is qualified or if internal problems require someone without prior ties. Promotional opportunities outside the department for which one works are occurring more often.

Conclusion

Like anything else, getting ahead requires both time and commitment--sometimes combined with luck. People do make sergeant, lieutenant, captain, and chief. But you can't rise to the top without landing that first entry level position. From there, your job seeking skills become job advancing skills.

The following adaptation of Paul Harvey News' "What Are Policemen Made of?" sums up some of the realities faced by those who enter law enforcement. It helps keep the profession in perspective.

> Police officers are at once the most needed and the most unwanted of people.
>
> They're strangely nameless creatures who are "Sir" or "M'am" to their face and "fuzz" behind their backs.
>
> They must be such diplomats that they can settle differences between individuals so each will think they've won.
>
> But . . .
> If police officers are neat, they're conceited; if they're careless they're bums.
>
> If they're pleasant, they're flirts; if they're not, they're grouches.
>
> They must make in an instant decisions which would require months for a lawyer.
>
> But . . .
> If they hurry, they're careless; if they're deliberate, they're lazy.

They must be first to an accident and infallible with a diagnosis.

They must be able to start breathing, stop bleeding, tie splints and, above all, be sure the victim goes home without a limp.
Or expect to be sued.

Police officers must know every gun, draw on the run, and hit where it doesn't hurt.

They must be able to whip two men twice their size and half their age without damaging their uniforms and without being "brutal."

If you hit them, they're cowards; if they hit you, they're bullies.

Police officers must know everything--and not tell.

They must know where all the sin is--and not partake.

Police officers must, from a single human hair, be able to describe the crime, the weapon and the criminal--and tell you where the criminal is hiding.

But. . .
If they catch the criminal, they're lucky; if they don't, they're dunces.

If they get promoted, they have political pull. If they don't, they're dullards.

Police officers must chase bum leads to a dead end, stakeout 10 nights to tag one witness who saw it happen--but refuses to remember.

They run files and write reports until their eyes ache to build a case against some felon who'll get dealt-out by a shameless shamus or an "honorable" who isn't.

Police officers must be ministers, social workers, diplomats, tough guys, and ladies and gentlemen.

And of course they'll have to be geniuses--
For they'll have to feed a family on a police officer's salary.

Some aspects of law enforcement require careful, realistic consideration. But these fields continue to draw people to them. Ask a hundred cops why they're in it, and you'll hear a hundred different responses. And, yes, cops complain a lot --about the hours, the pay, and the administration. But there is something about it that gets in your blood.

PRIVATE SECURITY--UP CLOSE

Because private security is profit oriented, opportunities exist that are not available in the public sector. With corporate America recognizing that security and loss prevention are as critical to a successful business as management and marketing, an increasing number of very appealing job opportunities are developing.

The stereotype of the retiree sitting at a guard desk overnight is no longer an accurate portrayal of what has become a profession in every sense of the word.

While the glamor of the TV private detective's world may be going overboard, excellent opportunities exist on the private side.

Private security is, to a large extent, responsible for improving its own image. Even law enforcement officers who once may have looked down at private security as somehow being "less important" than their work, recognize the vital role played by this developing profession. The fact is, public police cannot be everywhere all the time. Police agencies are now more willing to appreciate the role of private security officers.

In addition, the continuously evolving complexity of our society is necessitating specially trained private security officers in all phases of life. Businesses need individuals who can effectively use highly technical surveillance equipment. They rely on private suppliers of search dogs and strike/civil disobedience response teams. Some need twenty-four hour surveillance. Given such needs, opportunities will continue to grow in the private sector.

It is difficult to provide an accurate listing of "average" pay in private security, primarily because the range is extreme. Entry level guard or watchman jobs may start at the minimum wage, but the upper wage is virtually unlimited. Owners of successful private security or investigation firms and upper level security directors can expect lucrative salaries, with perks like bonus plans and company cars.

When you consider that the private sector may provide more advancement potential and more overall control of your professional and personal life, it is easy to see why many law enforcement officers set eventual goals to become private security directors.

While many individuals who have enjoyed a successful career in law enforcement will enjoy a "second career" in private security, many people successfully use work in the private sector as a "stepping stone" into the public sector. The fact is, law enforcement is a popular career, and jobs as police officers are difficult to come by. Having worked as a security officer at any level says a number of things about an applicant for a police job:

* They have been successfully employed.
* They have worked in a position of trust.
* Unusual hours do not present a problem.
* The uniform does not create a power-hungry person.
* They can keep cool under stressful circumstances.

Types of Jobs Available

As the private security profession expands, so have the kinds of jobs available. Typical entry level jobs include private security guards and private patrol officers. Private security guards control access to private property, protect against loss, enforce rules, maintain order, and lower risks of all kinds. Most security guards wear uniforms and may be armed.

Private patrol officers are similar to patrol units of the public police force. They move from one location to another, on foot or in a vehicle, protecting property and preventing losses. Some patrol officers work for a single employer; others have several employers.

Mid-level jobs in private security include private investigators, detectives, armed couriers, central alarm respondents, and consultants. Private investigators and detectives may "freelance" or may work for a specific employer. Frequently the work involves background checks for employment, insurance and credit applications, civil litigation, and investigation of insurance or worker's compensation claims. Sometimes investigators are brought in to work undercover to detect employee dishonesty, shoplifting, or illegal drug use.

Top jobs in security include managing a private security company or heading up security for a private concern. Common titles include loss prevention specialist, security director, and risk manager.

According to the Hallcrest Report II (Cunningham et al, 1990, p.196) an estimated 1,493,300 individuals were employed in the security field. The largest groups was proprietary (in-house) security with 528,000 (35.4%) followed closely by contract guards with 520,000 (34,8%). An additional 120,000 (8.0%) were employed by alarm companies, 88,300 (5.9%) were employed by manufacturers and distributors of security equipment, 70,000 (4.7%) were private investigators, followed closely by locksmiths with 69,600 (5.9%) employees. Only 2,900 (0.2%) were employed as consultants/engineers.

Employment Requirements

Because private security is both recognizing itself and being recognized as a respectable profession, the field is joining the trend of others that stress the importance of maintaining certain basic professional requirements. Employers with proprietary forces usually set their own standards for security officers. Contractual security companies often are regulated by state law. Individuals who wish to provide security services on their own may need to be licensed by their state. Requirements vary, so it is important to check on your local situation.

While some states require few, if any, qualifications be met by those wishing to work in private security, some states are becoming very strict as to who may practice in this field, either as an individual or a company supplying security services. Of the three professional licenses I [J.Scott Harr] hold, my private detective license required more comprehensive qualifications and was more expensive to initially obtain than my licenses as a police officer or a lawyer. Minnesota statutes stipulate who needs to be licensed as a private investigator in Minnesota, what the application consists of, and what must accompany the application. Each application must be accompanied by:

> * A surety bond for $5,000.
>
> * Verified certificates of at least five citizens not related to the signer who have known the signer for more than five years, certifying that the signer is of "good moral character."
>
> * Two photographs and a full set of fingerprints for each signer of the application.

While Minnesota has some of the most restrictive regulations, more states are recognizing that some controls have to be in place to insure responsible involvement by those operating in these field. Table 2-3 lists the regulatory bodies charged with licensing and regulating the private security industry within each state.

Table 2-3. State Regulatory Bodies

State	Agency
Alabama	--
Alaska	State Troopers
Arizona	Department of Public Safety
Arkansas	Board of Private Investigators and Private Security Agencies
California	Department of Consumer Affairs
Colorado	--
Connecticut	Department of Public Safety
Delaware	Board of Examiners, State Police
District of Columbia	Metropolitan Police Department
Florida	Department of State
Georgia	Board of Private Investigators and Private Securities Agencies
Hawaii	Board of Private Detectives and Guards
Idaho	--
Illinois	Department of Registration
Indiana	State Police
Iowa	Department of Public Safety
Kansas	--
Kentucky	--
Louisiana	--
Maine	State Police
Maryland	State Police
Massachusetts	Department of Public Safety
Michigan	State Police
Minnesota	Board of Private Detectives and Protective Agent Services
Mississippi	--
Missouri	--
Montana	Department of Private Security, Patrol, & Private Investigators
Nebraska	--
Nevada	Private Investigators Licensing Board
New Hampshire	Department of Safety
New Jersey	State Police
New Mexico	Bureau of Private Investigators
New York	Department of State
North Carolina	Private Protective Services Board
North Dakota	Department of State
Ohio	Department of Commerce
Oklahoma	--
Oregon	--
Pennsylvania	--
Rhode Island	--
South Carolina	Law Enforcement Division
South Dakota	--
Tennessee	--

-continued-

Table 2-3. State Regulatory Bodies

State	Agency
Texas	Board of Private Investigators and Private Securities Agencies
Utah	Department of Public Safety
Vermont	Board of Private Detective Licensing
Virginia	Department of Commerce
Washington	--
West Virginia	Secretary of State
Wisconsin	Department of Regulations and Licensing
Wyoming	--

c 1984 by the American Society for Industrial Security, 2000 K St. NW, Suite 651, Washington, DC 20006. Reprinted by permission from the January 1984 issue of *Security Management* magazine.

Be sure to investigate the requirements of the state(s) in which you want to work. Some county and city governments also require certification or licensure of those working in private security positions within their jurisdiction. Because many duties of private security officers can have as critical consequences as the law enforcement officer, for example, use of firearms, K-9s, and other weapons, arresting people, rendering emergency medical assistance, and the like, it makes sense to have basic requirements in place.

Most common are regulations regarding background checks, certain minimal knowledge, and posting some sort of bond. Some states have a residency requirement. Many states have policies on autos and uniforms.

In addition, some individuals may want to be certified by the American Society for Industrial Society through their *Certified Protection Professional (CPP) program.* This program, organized in 1977, is designed to recognize individuals meeting specific criteria of professional protection knowledge and conduct. To be eligible to take the examination, candidates must have 10 years experience with no degree, 8 years experience and an Associate degree, 5 years experience and a Bachelor's degree, 4 years experience and a Master's degree, or 3 years experience and a Doctoral degree. At least half the experience must be in "responsible charge" of a security function. The examination is a full day, with the morning devoted to general security knowledge and the afternoon devoted to a choice of four speciality tests selected from a wide variety of areas.

Promotions

Both security and law enforcement careers can meet a stumbling block not as prevalent in other careers. Promotions can come few and far between--if at all. The problem in security is that jobs tend to be at one end of the spectrum or the other. At the entry level security jobs can be simply minimum wage jobs, with minimal raises. "Middle-management" positions are usually few in number. The money is in top management jobs, either for a corporation or for one's own business. At these levels there is literally no upward limit.

Conclusion

Whether you seek employment in private security as a chance to acquire valuable training to help gain future employment in law enforcement or because the security field has exceptional future potential, private security can provide satisfying work. A security officer job can serve as a stepping stone to other employment or a chance to obtain supplemental income as a second job or while attending school.

Even the lower paying, entry-level work can provide excellent opportunities. For those who want to take advantage of more advanced potential, positions involving the supervision and management of security services, whether proprietary or contractual, may appeal to you. If you want to truly be out on your own, the opportunities to provide security or private investigation services are limited only by your own creativity and willingness to work.

REFERENCES

Burden, Ordway P. "Rent-A-Cop Business Is Booming," *Law and Order,* August 1989, pp.92-94.

Bureau of Justice Statistics. *Profile of State and Local Law Enforcement Agencies, 1987.* Washington, DC: U.S. Government Printing Office, March 1989.

Creamer, J.S. *The Law of Arrest, Search, and Seizure, 3rd ed.* New York: Holt, Rinehart, and Winston, 1980.

Cunningham, William C.; Strauchs, John J.; and Van Meter, Clifford W. *Private Security Trends, 1970 to 2000: The Hallcrest Report II.* Stoneham, MA: Butterworth-Heinemann, 1990.

DeLucia, Robert C. and Doyle, Thomas J. *Career Planning in Criminal Justice.* Cincinnati, OH: Anderson Publishing Co., 1990.

Occupational Outlook Handbook. 1988-89 Edition. U.S. Department of Labor. Bureau of Labor Statistics. Washington, DC: U.S. Government Printing Office, 1988.

Occupational Projections and Training Data, 1988 Edition, U.S. Department of Labor, Bureau of Labor Statistics. Washington, DC: U.S. Government Printing Office, 1988.

Penn & Schoen Associates, Inc. *Television and Police: Attitudes and Perceptions of the Police and the Public.* A Study for the New York City Police Foundation, Inc., Final Report. May 1987.

Remesch, Kimberly A. "Shared Responsibility," *Police,* November 1989, pp.32-35, 67.

Segal, David. "Too Many Cooks?" *Police,* November 1989, pp.43-47, 70-71.

Sourcebook of Criminal Justice Statistics. Washington, DC: U.S. Government Printing Office, 1988.

Wright, John W. *The American Almanac of Jobs and Salaries.* New York: Avon Books, 1987.

Wrobleski, Henry M. and Hess, Karen M. *Introduction to Law Enforcement and Criminal Justice.* 3rd ed. St. Paul, MN: West Publishing Company, 1990.

MIND STRETCHES*******

1. Why do you think the entertainment field is so obsessed with law enforcement and private security?

2. Do you think this obsession helps or hurts the professions? Why?

3. Do you personally know any police officers? Are they like the television cops?

4. What is your favorite TV police show? Private detective show? Why?

5. Do you think TV and the movies have influenced your career choice?

6. What stereotype do you think police officers have? Why? Is it justified?

7. What stereotype do you think private security officers have? Why? Is it justified?

8. Why do you think the trend to license all professions exists? Do you think it is helpful?

9. Are police salaries more or less than you had anticipated? Does salary affect your decision as to what field of employment you will eventually pursue? Why or why not?

10. Why do you honestly want to pursue the job you are considering?

"I'm a cop, not a grammar student."

AN INSIDER'S VIEW

IT'S NOT LIKE ON TV

Dennis L. Conroy, PhD
Sergeant, St. Paul Police Department

It is crucial for anyone anticipating a career in law enforcement or private security to realize they will get a view of the world no one else has. They will do and see things that are boring, exciting, and amusing. They will also do and see things that are painful, tragic, and sometimes terrifying. Careers in law enforcement and private security can be rewarding, but the applicant must also remember there may very well be a "price to pay."

Very few, if any, people entering law enforcement know what they are getting into. *It's not like on television* in real life. The endings aren't always successful, and officers don't always get respect. Those entering law enforcement look forward to becoming a police officer and intend to wear the uniform with pride. The lessons these new officers learn are often very difficult to accept and frequently result in alcoholism, physical problems, divorce, and even suicide.

The first lesson new officers learn is that not everyone respects police officers simply because *they are police officers*. Officers soon learn that a large number of people they deal with do not even want them around most of the time. Some will call officers names like "Pig," lie to them, fight with them, and even spit on them--just because they are officers. Officers subjected to such treatment discover they are not even permitted to respond except to defend themselves from the most grievous physical harm. Even in that response, they will frequently be challenged on the level of force used and will have to justify such actions later.

The next step in the discovery process occurs when officers learn they are *expected* not to respond when spit on. Being spit on is considered "part of the job." Officers learn that everyone else in the criminal justice system demands respect and inflicts sanctions on those refusing to comply. Can you imagine a defendant spitting on a prosecutor or a judge in a courtroom with impunity? But officers are prohibited from imposing their own sanctions.

New officers are usually shocked at the amount of pain and suffering in the world. Most police officers have grown up without exposure to situations requiring police intervention. They have not seen young children, or even babies, who have been beaten or killed simply for crying. They have not had to talk with and console an elderly couple whose house has been burglarized by teenage vandals, their "world" invaded and destroyed for no apparent reason. They have probably never had to console a rape victim, and to tell her that her "hell" may only be starting because if she wants to prosecute the offender she will have to relive the experience time and again and defend her own morality each time.

As new officers learn these lessons, they respond, they change. Officers learn that to work with these problems day after day, they must build a suit of armor to protect themselves. They build this armor by (1) becoming less personally involved and (2) not believing in anyone or anything. While such armor protects officers from work-related issues, it also changes them as individuals.

Many officers find they become cynical and isolated. They lose the capacity to believe in anything or anybody because they have seen or experienced so much disappointment in performing their duties. They see humanity at its worst and the system in almost constant failure. It becomes increasingly difficult to believe in successful outcomes. This cynicism is not only an "at work" attitude, but soon pervades every aspect of the officers' lives.

As officers become more and more cynical, they believe less and less in successful outcomes and begin to invest less and less in personal relationships. This can lead to isolation and loneliness. Officers in the end may have no one but themselves, and they are not sure that they can even believe in themselves.

If applicants know they are likely to experience change, this change can be monitored and, along with the law enforcement career, have a positive outcome. Officers will find rewards in the little things they can do to help individuals they come in contact with. They can brighten a small child's life by just a smile or brief "Hello." They can make elderly couples feel a bit more secure because when they see officers driving by who take time to wave, the elderly feel better, knowing someone cares--and the officers feel better knowing that they made even the smallest difference in the lives of those they have sworn to "protect and serve."

CHAPTER 3
OTHER OPTIONS TO CONSIDER

The pessimist complains about the wind; the optimist expects it to change; the realist adjusts the sails.--Anonymous

Do You Know:

* What the field of corrections is?

* What benefits are to be found in this field?

* What the difference is between probation and parole?

* What job opportunities exist in probation and parole?

* Why animal control can be an attractive vocation?

* Where a job as a crime prevention officer could lead?

* What military service could do for you?

* What civilian jobs exist in a police organization?

* What advanced jobs exist in criminal justice?

* What international jobs are available in criminal justice?

INTRODUCTION

As you saw in Chapter Two, an incredible number of jobs are encompassed in the law enforcement career--everything from patrol officer to police surgeon assuring a niche for almost every interest. Beyond that, the criminal justice field offers even more than you may have ever consider. You may be destined for a job you have never thought of or even knew existed--until now.

Directing your career toward one of these other areas could open a whole new world of employment satisfaction. The criminal justice system is so complex it needs a tremendous number of participants. While many of these jobs may not appear as glamorous as those frequently depicted on TV, they are extremely important and provide exceptional opportunities.

CORRECTIONS/DETENTION

The corrections portion of our criminal justice system serves several purposes:

* To punish offenders.

* To rehabilitate wrongdoers.
* And to make society safer for the public.

Some of these goals can be accomplished at the same time, by the same workers. For instance, corrections officers accomplish all three goals by keeping offenders incarcerated. Specific rehabilitative services, however, require specific training. Also, different systems such as the juvenile and the adult systems emphasize different areas.

Corrections begins after the arrest and involves everything from the initial "booking" (fingerprinting, photographing, etc.) to long-term "guarding." Some positions involve counseling inmates, while others are limited to an armed position in a watchtower.

As noted by Maudlin (1989, p.38), a Colorado police sergeant: "While some detention officers are looking to go into patrol work, others are happy right where they are":

> There is a widely held belief among police officers that many of those working in detentions really only see duty in the jail as a stepping stone to "real police work." And, in fact, one detentions deputy estimated that 70 percent of her peers want to transfer to the patrol division in her agency.

Mauldin noted that while talking to a detention center deputy assigned to a duty he "wouldn't do on a bet," he came to appreciate them: "As time went on I quickly came to realize just how skilled many of these people are in dealing with individuals that have required SWAT intervention to get into custody. They deal with the people we bring out in shackles because they are so violent."

For some, work in corrections is a way to get somewhere else. It is a legitimate "stepping stone" to other jobs in law enforcement. It is also, however, an opportunity to be part of a whole other world of the criminal justice system, which many find appealing.

In 1986, over 392,000 individuals were employed in corrections, divided among federal, state, and local levels as follows (*Sourcebook,* 1988, p.28):

Federal	12,056
State	243,200
Local	136,771

As noted by the *Occupational Outlook Handbook* (1988, p.257): "Correction officers are charged with the safety and security of persons who have been arrested, are awaiting trial, or who have been tried and convicted of a crime and sentenced to serve time in a correctional institution. . . . Counseling and helping inmates with problems are increasingly important parts of the correction officer's job."

According to this handbook, earnings vary widely by level of government, with the highest salaries being paid at the local level, the lowest at the federal level. The average increase in salaries over the past ten years has been 72.3% (*Sourcebook*, 1988, p.143).

Correctional systems on all levels have been dealing with "growth in epidemic proportions" according to the Bureau of Justice Statistics, with inmate populations nearly doubling since 1980. According to the *Criminal Justice Corrections Yearbook,* 1989: "To meet current and anticipated bedspace for state and federal systems, it is estimated that five 500-bed prisons would have to be built monthly for the next two years.

Adult and Juvenile Corrections

Corrections is divided into the adult and the juvenile system. The overall goal of the adult system is often punishment; that of the juvenile system is more likely to be treatment and rehabilitation.

Typical of state statutes regarding *adult offenders* is Chapter 609 of the Minnesota Statutes which states that the purpose of the adult criminal code is:

> To protect the public safety and welfare by preventing the commission of crime through the deterring effect of the sentences authorized, the rehabilitation of those convicted, and their confinement when the public safety and interest requires.

In contrast, typical of state statutes regarding *juveniles* is Chapter 260 of the Minnesota Statutes:

> The purpose of the laws relating to juvenile courts is to secure for each child alleged or adjudicated to be delinquent is to promote the public safety and reduce juvenile delinquency by maintaining the integrity of the substantive law prohibiting certain behavior and by developing individual responsibility for lawful behavior. This purpose should be pursued through means that are fair and just, that recognize the unique characteristics and needs of children, and that give children access to opportunities for personal and social growth.

The trend of punishing adults and "treating" juveniles seems to be reversing itself to some extent. More emphasis is being placed on the *treatment* of adult offenders. At the same time more traditional penalties, for example incarceration and even manual labor, are being used more frequently as "treatment" of juvenile offenders.

Nonetheless, some people prefer working with juveniles because the system still is more treatment oriented, and our society holds the belief that youths are generally as capable as, if not more so than, adults to redirect their lives. It is particularly satisfying to see young people getting their lives straightened out.

Is it as exciting as being in on the perhaps action-packed arrest? Maybe not. But then, there are not the long-range benefits of really helping people to change. Many police officers express frustration over seeing only the misery caused by crime and not having a positive influence on people as those who work in corrections often do, particularly those who work in probation and parole.

Probation and Parole

For prospective criminal justice applicants interested in long-term personal interaction, the fields of probation and parole are worth considering.

The primary difference between probation and parole is that probation is an alternative to incarceration, while parole is supervised release from incarceration before the expiration of the sentence. Each involves considerable interaction with offenders. The probation officer oversees a correctional plan outside detention. The parole agent helps offenders prepare for eventual discharge from the system.

Forty-three states require at least a bachelor's degree for probation officers. In 1987 the average starting salary was approximately $17,700, with a low of $9,592 in Pennsylvania and a high of $26,460 in Alaska. North Dakota had the fewest probation officers, 22, while New York had the most 2,200, followed by Florida with 1,551 (*Sourcebook*, 1988, pp.139-141).

Forty-five states require at least a bachelor's degree for parole officers. In 1987 the average starting salary was approximately $19,000, with a low of $12,768 in West Virginia and a high of $31,644 in California. Nebraska had the fewest officers, 10, while Florida had the most, 3,600, followed by California with 700 (*Sourcebook*, 1988, pp.146-148).

Careers in the correctional field are quite different from those in law enforcement, but corrections officers can take defendants from the crisis point at which they enter the criminal justice system and work with them to help them alter their lives. This long-term payoff makes probation and parole work rewarding.

Electronic Monitoring and Home Detention

Because of the increasing jail population, both the adult and juvenile systems are being forced to examine the potential of *home detention* as a practical alternative to incarceration.

Electric monitoring is often used in conjunction with home detention. A typical electric monitoring system (EMS) consists of a bracelet worn on the detainee's ankle. The bracelet contains a transmitter that emits a signal which is continuously monitored. The whereabouts of the detainee is always known.

Frequent contact with people on house arrest (or home detention) combines with the more traditional supervision. The increasing use of home detention is creating new work opportunities.

According to Peck (1988, p.26):

> About 100 jurisdictions use electronic monitoring, from Florida to New York, Wisconsin to California. Earlier this year, Federal officials jumped on the band wagon and initiated a program to track some parolees by computer. The idea is spreading so fast that no one really knows just how many offenders are being watched this way. It is clear, however, that electronic monitoring will continue to grow by leaps and bounds.

> Correctional agencies see the technology as a way to ease overcrowding in jails and prisons. Probation administrators regard electronic home detention as an effective, inexpensive method of supervising probationers.

According to Putnam (1990, p.96): "In Michigan, there are more than 2,000 offenders on the state EMS. Compliance has exceeded expectations: Less than 3 percent of all offenders have escaped, and less than 2 percent of offenders have been arrested again." The program is used for three kinds of offenders: "felony probationers, inmates participating in the Community Residential Program (CRP), and parolees. Putnam (p.98) concludes: "The accelerating use of EMS clearly demonstrates that it is no longer an innovation on trial. It is effective and deserves to be solidly entrenched as a case management tool."

COMMUNITY CRIME PREVENTION AND OTHER COMMUNITY WORK

The more regular hours, the varied and interesting assignments, and the relative lack of danger are just a few factors that might motivate you to consider some exciting careers that *support* law enforcement. You can work out of a police station or sheriff's office without being subjected to some of the negatives of police work.

The last decade has seen an increasing interest in and reliance on community crime prevention. While some law enforcement agencies have sworn officers conduct such work, others assign civilian specialists to this important job. Crime prevention specialists have the luxury of working with the community in a positive effort *before* crisis occurs, with the hope of *preventing* crime. Or, they may be the contact that lends valuable assistance after a crisis.

Crime prevention specialists educate the community about such issues as locks, lighting, alarms, and personal safety. It is an excellent opportunity to be creative because much of crime prevention involves developing programs, designing brochures, presenting speeches, and even directing videos and slide presentations.

Salaries vary, but more regular schedules and an excellent opportunity to step into the private sector make this an area worth considering.

Animal Control

Animal control is one area within the realm of community service that can effectively serve as both an entry-level stepping stone to a police job or as a speciality area that many find rewarding in itself. If you have a special interest in animal welfare, this is an area where you can get paid for doing what you love.

Other Areas

Other areas traditionally done by sworn personnel are now often being done by non-sworn people. Juvenile specialists, communications directors, and dispatchers are examples of this trend. The simple reason is economic. Non-sworn personnel may be every bit as qualified and yet not need to be paid at the salary level of sworn, often unionized, personnel.

THE HELPING PROFESSIONS

The "helping" professions have a host of jobs that assist people. This area includes the entire range of rehabilitation workers from technicians in treatment centers to counselors and social workers to psychologists and psychiatrists. Employment in these areas is extremely satisfying and requires a special commitment to helping others. These alternative areas are often well suited to those who may have had problems themselves. Their insights can help guide others. If run-ins with the law have created a record that could interfere with becoming a law enforcement or private security officer, these alternative areas may still be open.

THE MILITARY

Another area to consider is the military. Even if you are not interested in the military as a career, it is a great background when job seeking. The military is particularly well suited for those who are younger and less certain as to what career direction to take. Any military experience is better than just throwing those years away aimlessly wandering from job to job. Military experience is usually directly applicable to successful employment in law enforcement and private security.

Military law enforcement assignments such as the military police provide exceptional experience. Other non-law enforcement assignments, however, also provide proof that the individual can take orders, assume responsibility, and successfully accept challenges.

ADVANCED JOBS

Criminal justice provides many opportunities in areas requiring special expertise. While these require advanced training, they also offer higher salaries. Attorneys, for example, can be intimately involved in the criminal justice process from either perspective: prosecution or defense. A law degree is an excellent education for any area of law enforcement, whether the person wants to use it in a court room or "in the trenches."

The criminal justice system needs every type of specialist, including psychologists, physicians, scientists, accountants, and engineers. The FBI, for example, specifically seeks people with very specialized training. Working in law enforcement with specialized degrees can provide attractive pay and benefits. The downside, however, is that work may not vary and travel may be a requirement . Particularly federal agencies may require a number of relocations throughout a career. Such relocations can be viewed as exciting opportunities or as extreme inconveniences.

Almost *any* specific area of interest you have can be successfully woven into a satisfying career. Police officers with law degrees, psychology degrees, or medical degrees are of great worth to their departments. In addition, the many skills that can be taken into the private sector cannot only fill important department needs, but also create attractive and lucrative speciality positions. Expertise in such areas as drawing, photography, computers, firearms, flying, or even public relations can help any professional on the move.

INTERNATIONAL JOBS

The vast majority of career areas have a new emphasis on international employment. Security and law enforcement are not exceptions. Many people are eager to travel, and if it can be part of a job, all the better. Many businesses and establishments such as hotels are opening facilities in foreign countries. Often the security director of such businesses and establishments are sent to set up the security system.

International jobs are available in law enforcement and security, but obtaining them is not easy. Most positions overseas are classified jobs, with security clearances and secrecy being requirements. Because of such factors as jurisdiction, these jobs tend to be covert, with danger being a real element. Federal agencies such as the FBI, Drug Enforcement Administration, and Secret Service, have agents around the world. Not a part of the criminal justice or law enforcement field, but also offering opportunity for excitement and travel are positions with the Central Intelligence Agency (CIA). Again, travel is a perk as well as a potential difficulty.

REFERENCES

Maudlin, Michael. "Just Doing Time?" *Police*, October 1989, pp.38-40, 68-70.

Occupational Outlook Handbook. 1988-1989 Edition. U.S. Department of Labor, Bureau of Labor Statistics, Washington, DC: U.S. Government Printing Office, 1988.

Peck, Keenen. "High-Tech House Arrest," *The Progressive*, Madison, WI: The Progressive, Inc, July 1988, pp.26-28.

Putnam, Jim. "Electronic Monitoring: From Innovation to Acceptance in Five Years," *Corrections Today,* October 1990, pp.96-98.

Sourcebook of Criminal Justice Statistics, 1988. U.S. Department of Justice. Office of Justice Program, Bureau of Justice Statistics. Washington, DC: U.S. Government Printing Office, 1988.

MIND STRETCHES*****

1. What do most people think of when they think of a "police job"? Where did you acquire the information you base your answer on?

2. What benefits would you find in a job in corrections that may not exist in a street police job?

3. Why might you *not* want to consider a job as a police officer "on the street"?

4. Do "non-sworn" law enforcement positions, such as civilian crime prevention specialists, have benefits not available to police officers?

5. What negatives would you want to be aware of in considering a job such as a community service officer?

6. Why might a military background in a candidate be appealing to a police or security agency that is hiring? Could such a background be a detriment?

7. What other vocational or avocational skills could blend well with a police career? Can you think of unique skills unique that could make a candidate for a job more attractive to a hiring agency?

8. Why might someone interested in a career in policing fail to consider other jobs in the security or criminal justice fields?

9. Is there a danger in pursuing a specific job that "really excites" you, to the point you do not believe any other job would be worthwhile?

10. What benefits could there be from jobs in probation or parole which would not be available in police or security work?

**"Actually I was hoping the job would be
a little more like Miami Vce."**

AN INSIDER'S VIEW

A WEALTH OF OPPORTUNITIES

Molly Koivamaki
Senior Crime Prevention Specialist
Eden Prairie Police Department

The job of civilian crime prevention specialist is the best, in my opinion, because it provides the excitement of working in law enforcement without getting your "hands dirty." This unique position has enjoyed increasing popularity over the past few years.

As a crime prevention specialist, I provide service to units within the police department as well as to citizens and businesses in the community. I analyze calls for service and police reports to provide the patrol division information on where certain types of crimes are likely to occur. This helps the division plan more efficient directed patrol activity.

In return patrol officers, particularly those on night shifts, leave me notes about such things as businesses with open doors or crime victims who may need special attention. I then follow up on the information and inform the officers of the outcome. This system successfully communicates because it is informal and gives officers a way to follow activities or situations that may otherwise go unchecked.

I help the investigation division by "running interference" with crime victims. This allows the detectives to spend time investigating crimes and not getting too involved with the victims' personal problems. Crime victims' needs range from simply wanting someone to talk to about the crime, to requiring assistance getting emergency housing or transportation.

Most police agencies provide standard crime prevention programs. Crime prevention specialists coordinate programs such as neighborhood watch and apartment watch groups, McGruff programs, and school-based safety programs.

The police administration relies on the crime prevention specialist to enforce the alarm ordinance, compile monthly and annual reports, and do special projects.

I also:

* Plan the review for all new construction permits submitted to the city.

* Do public speaking, addressing civic groups and organizations on a *wide* variety of topics such as personal safety, home security, and the like.

* Arrange meetings for police officers to address groups.

* Conduct business crime prevention sessions such as sessions on shoplifting awareness and prevention, bank robbery awareness, employee theft, and physical security.

Being a part of the criminal justice system is *not* limited to being a cop on the street. Of the many benefits I enjoy in my non-sworn position on our police department, I think I have better hours and less danger, while interacting with the public on a primarily positive basis.

I think many very appealing jobs are not considered because they are not the jobs TV portrays as "cop jobs." In fact, these other jobs open up a whole new world of potentially satisfying and exciting employment. Give them a look.

CHAPTER 4

ON CHOOSING A CAREER:

KNOWING THE JOB AND YOURSELF

People are always blaming their circumstances for what they are. I don't believe in circumstances. The people who get on in this world are the people who get up and look for the circumstances they want, and if they can't find them--make them.--George Bernard Shaw, Mrs. Warren's Profession

Do You Know:

* Why job satisfaction is so important?

* What behaviors unhappy workers exhibit?

* What cynicism is? What contributes to it?

* What steps to take to achieve your career goals?

* What the basic requirements of employment in law enforcement and private security are? Do you meet them?

* What factors in your background could prevent employment in these fields?

* Whether a traffic record will influence employers?

* What an Inventurer is? If you are one?

* The importance of risk taking? Why more people don't take risks?

* What factors are important to you in a career and whether law enforcement or private security can meet them?

INTRODUCTION

Chapter Two discussed some realities of the law enforcement and private security professions. As you consider these careers, understand what they are--and what they are **not.** In addition, take a serious inventory of your own abilities and interests to determine if your career goals are realistic.

In this chapter you'll combine knowledge about law enforcement and private security with an honest look at yourself, to make certain you are, indeed, on a road that will take you where you want to be. How often would you get into your car and just drive with no thought of where you want to go? Yet many people launch themselves toward a career with very limited forethought.

Carelessly pursuing a career can be costly. First, selecting a career is extremely important because the vast majority of your waking hours will be spent working. So who wants to be unhappy? Perhaps even worse is that job frustrations have a way of manifesting themselves in unpleasant, if not dangerous, ways. Police/security officers who dislike their work show it. At best, they may appear as unfeeling individuals, expressing little concern for anyone, including victims. At worst, inappropriate physical force, even brutality, could be evidence of something going on "inside." Such behavior can result in nationwide anti-police publicity as seen in the beating of Rodney King.

Career dissatisfaction and the resulting unhappiness may make a person generally negative and cynical. In *The Cynical Americans,* Kanter and Mirvas state that another symptom of unhappiness is cynicism, which they state is "growing like a cancer in the American workplace." They go on to explain that these cynics are "the ones who feel, rightly or wrongly, that they are getting less than they deserve from life." The result: "Cynical workers--whether they feel defeated or just defiant--rot the fabric of any organization, decreasing productivity and infecting morale" (p.58).

The best way to prevent career dissatisfaction is to research the field carefully before applying for employment, asking many questions of those already in the field, and carefully evaluating all the positive and negative aspects of the occupation *as they apply to your values and expectations.* There is a story about the woman who loved everything about being an engine mechanic--except getting dirty. Absolutely nothing could prevent her from leaving work each night grimy and greasy, and it was causing her to consider a career change. The simple fact was that part of this work was to get dirty. Determining whether getting dirty was worth it was an issue that had to be dealt with.

Similarly, some facts about working in law enforcement and private security must be faced. The relatively mediocre pay, the difficult hours, the odd days off, the public's perception of the job, the inherent danger, are all issues that may make the job unacceptable to some.

Take a realistic look at these issues now. Many people are trapped in jobs they dislike--even hate. How they could get trapped like this may be hard for younger job seekers to understand, especially those who are single. But the older you get, the less attractive changing jobs is. The level of benefits associated with seniority make it difficult to consider leaving. Acquired sick-time and vacation time, plus such benefits as scheduling based on seniority make leaving an "old job" more and more difficult.

Rather than jumping into a career you know little about, including how well suited to it **you** are, look objectively at the whole picture. Consider the job. Consider yourself. Is it a "match"? Or is it the frustrating pursuit of a fantasy?

This chapter presents exercises to learn about yourself and to relate this insight to the careers you are considering. Recognize that law enforcement, private security, and many related fields are like the Sirens in mythology, beckoning victims on to destruction. Take this opportunity to consider what is right for you and vice versa. It could save you and others considerable frustration and difficulties in the future.

The steps to understanding yourself and your career goals have a beginning, but never an end! Here's the beginning.

BRAINSTORMING POSSIBILITIES

Even if you are fairly certain about what you want to do with your life, it is worthwhile to consider other alternatives. These may be similar jobs, or they may be different altogether. Choices are what life is about, so start developing some.

Of all the exercises you will complete, this will be one of the easiest. Sit down with a clear mind and list the jobs that appeal to you. Don't analyze what you think you will or won't be qualified for. Simply write down the jobs that intrigue you.
****

Do any general patterns emerge? Are the jobs you listed more in the service fields? The academic fields? Are they jobs which stress physical skills? Mental ability? Both equally? Why do you think you picked these jobs?

"JUST THE FACTS"

Having generated some career choices, next determine facts about these alternatives. Areas to consider are:

> * Age requirements.
> * Physical requirements.
> * Educational requirements.
> * Background limitations.
> * Experience requirements.

Age

Some jobs are better suited for young adults; others are ideal for retired adults. Some jobs have age limitations, including certain law enforcement and security jobs. For example, in most states, you must be at least 21 years old to be a police officer. While the majority of policing jobs do not have an upward age limit for applicants, the federal system usually will not accept applicants older than 35. Some departments want very young recruits, while others may want more mature people.

Private security is even more open to a variety of ages. On the one hand, it is an exceptional field for entry-level people seeking to gather experience to help them on their way to becoming police officers. On the other hand, security work can be a great field for police officers or others after they retire.

Physical Requirements

It is likely the jobs you are interested in have physical requirements. Most agencies or companies have minimum vision and hearing requirements. One young man went through law school to be an FBI agent, only to learn too late that his vision would not allow him to even take the entrance test. Check with the agencies to find out what they require.

Most agencies want height and weight to be proportionate, even if they do not follow a specific chart. If you need to work on your weight, start an exercise program now, preferably one you can continue throughout your career. An increasing number of agencies are requiring physical "stress tests" to assess candidates' vascular health. You can prepare for this by working on a regular exercise program.

Most departments or companies will ask if you have any physical restrictions that will interfere with job performance. Be realistic with yourself and honest with the employer. While occasional back pain may not be a problem, an inability to lift probably would be.

Various medical conditions will not necessarily eliminate you either. For instance, controllable diabetes should not be a problem for most jobs. Again, be honest with yourself and the employer regarding any health problems you may have.

Education

Different states have different requirements as far as what schooling is needed. Similarly different employers have different standards. Employers in either the private or public sectors may require at least a high school diploma or GED. Some states, Minnesota for example, require at least two years of college. Some agencies, particularly in the federal system, may even require graduate credits or even a graduate degree, such as a law degree.

The more education you have, the better. This can include specialized training such as first-aid courses, first-responder courses, CPR, and the like. Knowing a foreign language, knowing how to sign to hearing impaired people, skills in photography-- any specialized knowledge is likely to be a plus as you pursue your career.

Background

Most private security companies, and certainly all law enforcement agencies, will thoroughly investigate applicants' backgrounds. Know what facts in your past will and won't affect your employment potential.

Most police departments and security agencies will not accept an applicant with felony convictions on their adult records. Depending on the nature of the crime, a misdemeanor may not automatically eliminate you. Be prepared to honestly explain the situation to the employer.

While it will be difficult to deal with any past criminal records, it is much easier to explain a petty shoplifting charge when you were eighteen than a conviction when you were twenty-eight. Unfortunately, some students made serious errors in judgment while they were studying to become police or security officers which ruined their chances. For example, one night on a drunken excursion, a student slashed forty tires, resulting in a felony conviction. It's bad to act out at any time. It's inexcusable to do so while preparing to be a police or security officer. Make responsible decisions.

Traffic records, like lesser criminal records, may or may not be a hindrance. While they generally won't be grounds for automatic elimination from the application process, they will be strikes against you. Be upfront and honest about the circumstances. Many applicants make the mistake of saying they have no traffic record when, in fact, they do. It is easier to explain why you got a ticket ten years ago than why you lied on your application. Lying is justification to eliminate an applicant. A traffic record may not be.

Other situations need to be thought out honestly. Past counseling, or even institutionalization, may not be sufficient grounds for eliminating you from the running, but lying about it would be. Some agencies may be more likely to consider applicants who helped themselves by going through Alcoholics Anonymous or other self-help programs.

Experience

Some agencies such as the U.S. Bureau of Prisons and state probation and parole agencies require previous experience in some related field. You should be aware of these requirements before applying for positions in these agencies.

WHAT DO I WANT FROM A CAREER?

A career is different from a job. A job is a short-term means to an end: money. High school and college students have jobs during the summer. People get jobs between careers to pay their bills.

A career is more long term, with more serious implications. Waitley and Witt (1985, p.ix) say: "Too many of us find our jobs dull, laborious, and repetitive, an irritating necessity of life, like death and taxes." They note that most people are afraid to make changes--to take risks, and yet this is what is needed to be happy. Their advice (p.159): "If you feel hesitant about jumping in, remember: The real risk is doing nothing."

A primary reason people find themselves in a rut is that they fell into it. The deeper the rut, the easier it is to feel trapped. Rather than allowing yourself to fall into the job rut and become trapped, plan what you want out of life and then go after it.

In *The Inventurers*, Hagberg and Leider provide a map to help people identify what is important to them and how to get there. Their "The Excursion Map" (p.6) helps people plan their own destiny rather than falling prey to a rut. They encourage readers to examine the following career issues (p.106). Take time to do so now.
****

* What are my present skills?
* What values are important to me?
* What lifestyle do I wish to lead?
* What work conditions are important to me?
* What interests do I have?

Take an introspective look at yourself and honestly apply the information learned to answer the question, "Will this job allow me to get what I want from life?" By doing so, you are being an "inventurer, one of those special breed of people who take charge and create your own challenges to get yourself moving" (Hagberg and Leider, pp.3-4). They note (pp.3-4):

> You are an inventurer if you are willing to take a long look at yourself and consider new options, venture inward, and explore. You are an inventurer if you see life as a series of changes, changes as growth experiences, and growth as positive. You are inventuring on life's *excursions* and learning about yourself as a result. You may feel lonely at times, and get discouraged for a while. But you are willing to risk some disappointments and take some knocks in your quest because you are committed to a balanced lifestyle and to more than just making a living. You are part of a unique group of people who want to make a living work. If you have these qualities, you are an inventurer.

> Inventurers are people who choose to take a fresh look in the mirror to renew and perhaps recycle their lifestyle and careers. Some inventurers, seemingly snug in life and career patterns, are exploring their "greener pasture" or "South Seas island" dreams in search of their own personal Declaration of Independence: the pursuit of happiness. Other inventurers are planning second careers or early retirements. Some are underemployed and seeking careers more integrated with their abilities and lifestyle. They are female and male, old and young, and in between.

According to Hagberg and Leider (p.6): "These inventurers prove what wise teachers have said for ages: *"The knowledge is right in us--all we have to do is clear our minds and open ourselves to see the obvious."*

In *The Right Job*, Snelling (1987, p.33) suggests you keep a "values journal" to help identify what is personally important and what is not. Write down how you spend your time. What problems do you encounter? What makes you happy, angry, sad, up, down? After keeping the journal for a while, review it, looking for patterns to such issues as the following:

* How do I, on an average day, generally spend my time?

* What are five or ten things that really interest me?

* What conflicts or problems do I have? Which ones did I create for myself, and which ones stemmed from outside factors?

* What short-range and long-range goals can I identify?

* What, ultimately, do I want to accomplish?

Snelling (p.44) also encourages you to look at "the human equation" to answer the question, "What kind of life do I want with my family?" An involved family life may not be compatible with a career that requires exceptionally long hours, a lot of traveling, and hectic scheduling. Consider also where you want to live. Is climate important to you?

At this point in your self-inquiry, look at yourself and the world around you in relatively general terms. As you develop a sense of what is important to you, apply these ideas to the specific job choices you brainstormed earlier. Ask: are my needs compatible with that particular job?

Don't fool yourself. No one is watching to make certain you are honest. You will only have yourself to blame if you kid yourself now. Begin to apply some of your answers to the previous questions to the overall requirements of the jobs listed at the start of this chapter. Can you get what you need from the jobs that interest you? Consider the following:

* Am I old enough? Too old?

* Do I have a background that will prohibit me from any certain work?

* Am I healthy enough for such work?

* Does the job coincide with my personal values?

* Do I have the skills for this work?

* Will I be able to achieve my long-term goals
  (including financial and promotional) through such work?

* Can my family goals be achieved with this
  job (considering such issues as travel and time commitments)?

Bolles (1989, pp.95-96) encourages people to pursue their dream jobs, but realistically. According to Bolles, dreams about your "ideal work" have certain "essential parts" if they are to become realities. Consider each of these "essential parts" for your "ideal work": **********

Tasks. What kinds of tasks, using what kinds of skills, do you see yourself doing? With what kind of style?

Tools or Means. What do you need by way of information, things, or other people to be doing your ideal life's work?

Outcome. What do you see your work producing, as its result? Immediately? Long-range?

Setting. In what kind of setting do you see yourself working? Setting means both physical setting and also the invisible stuff: values and the like.

Compensation. What kind of salary or other types of compensation do you want to have? What rewards do you hope your work will bring you?

You might also consider taking an occupational preference test such as "Discovery II" to see how your interests and preferences match up with different occupations. Such tests are programmed so that computers can match your answers to various questions with answers given to the same questions by representatives of different occupations. The computer compares your answers and indicates which occupational fields best match your interests.

MOVING TOWARD YOUR CAREER GOAL

Perhaps some jobs you considered in the brainstorming exercise were eliminated when you considered what you need from a career to be fulfilled in life. Perhaps you are still considering whether the career field or a specific career is right for you.

Be honest in considering a police, security, or related job because the very nature of the work is disruptive to what many consider a "normal work routine." Scheduling, days off in the middle of the week, working nights, holidays, and weekends, seeing people at their worst, having your professionalism and honesty challenged in court, are all realities of the law enforcement and security fields.

In the final equation, do your goals, needs, and desires balance with the realities of the job? Only you can make this important determination. If you were to enroll in an introductory course in law enforcement, where do you fit among the three groups of "typical" students enrolled in such classes?

* Students who have known since they were very young
  that they were destined to be police officers.

* Students who are considering the career, but have
  yet to make the commitment.

* Students who are fascinated by the subject, not the career.

If you have the chance to take an introductory course in law enforcement, private security, or criminal justice, consider doing it. It's one good way to better understand what the careers involve and they are right for you.

Acquire What You Need

As you continue to assess whether your career goals are compatible with your needs and interests, you will also learn what else is required to get into the field. If you need college, register. If you need a physical fitness regime, begin one. If you need experience, get it. Plodding along an uncharted path will get you, at best, nowhere, at worst, somewhere that you don't want to be. **NOW** is the time to develop your own realistic, exciting career map.

ALTERNATIVES

Look around and contemplate the almost infinite number of jobs people do in the world. It is truly amazing. Even if one job is not for you, another will be. Don't be afraid to change your mind, to take some risks. To many people, risk taking is more frightening than facing a gun. That lasts only an instant--a wrong career choice lasts much longer!

Our culture does not encourage risk taking. Even during the 1960s and 1970s, when a different cultural climate prevailed, a conservative work-ethic encouraged people to stay where they were and be glad they had any sort of job. This attitude has held over from the depression when people truly were lucky to have a job.

Today's culture emphasizes a satisfying career, rather than "just a job." Certainly as you grow older and family responsibilities require more security, you are not as likely to change jobs as frequently as when you were young. Still, you are living and working in an era that allows, if not encourages, people to chase their dreams.

Think about it. What is the worst thing that would happen to you if your choice of a job didn't work out? You find something else, right. People do it all the time--and grow and develop as a result.

Change *is* intimidating. But stagnation is even more frightening. The greatest hazard in life is to risk nothing. It has often been said: "Those who risk nothing, do nothing, have nothing, are nothing." Don't let it be engraved on your headstone, *Here lies John Doe, his potential fully intact.*

Over a dozen years ago I had a chance to shift careers from being a social worker to becoming a police dispatcher. I remember wondering *why* I ever said yes. It wasn't something I had trained for. It wasn't something I had planned on. But even then I knew it would be a challenge, one I could leave if it wasn't what I had wanted. It terrifies me sometimes to wonder what I would be doing today if I had not risked that step toward the unknown. As the saying goes, "Don't be afraid to go out on a limb. That's where the fruit is."

JUST DO IT!

An exercise to motivate yourself to change is the test of "on the last day of my life." Bolles (1989, p.94) suggests that you write about "'Before I die, I want to . . . .' and then list things you would like to do, before you die."

Or write on the topic: "On the last day of my life, what must I have done or been so that my life will have been satisfying to me?"

As the concluding exercise in this chapter, take time to write your feelings on one of these two topics. *********

Picking Daisies

If I had my life to live all over again, I would pick more Daisies.
If I had my life to live over, I would try to make more mistakes next time.
I would be sillier than I have been this trip.
I would relax. I would limber up.

I know very few things I would take seriously. I would be crazier,
I would be less hygienic; I would take more chances;
I would take more trips, I would climb more mountains,
Swim more rivers, and watch more sunsets.
I would burn more gasoline. I would eat more ice cream and less meals.

I would have more actual troubles, and fewer imaginary ones.
You see, I am one of those people who lives prophylactically
and sensibly and sanely, hour after hour, day after day.
Oh, I have had my mad moments, and if I had it to do all over again,
I would have more of them; in fact, I'd try to have nothing else,
just moments, one after another, instead of living so many years ahead.

I have been one of those people who never go anywhere without a thermometer,
      a hot-water bottle, a gargle, a raincoat and a parachute.
If I had it to live all over again I would go places and travel lighter than I have.
If I had my life to live over again, I would start barefoot earlier in the spring,
and stay that way later in the fall. I would play hookey more,
I would ride on more merry-go-rounds. I'd pick more Daisies.

(Reproduced from *Mindstyles/Lifestyles*, by Nathaniel Lande, published by Price Stern Sloan, Inc., Los Angeles, California. Copyright 1976 by Price Stern Sloan, Inc. Reprinted by permission.)

Decide to take some risks. Chase your dreams. Have some fun. Really learn to be.

REFERENCES

Bolles, Richard Nelson. *The 1989 What Color Is Your Parachute? A Practical Manual for Job-Hunters & Career-Changers.* Berkeley, CA: Ten Speed Press, 1989.

Hagberg, Janet and Leider, Richard. *The Inventurers: Excursions in Life and Career Renewal.* Reading, MA: Addison-Wesley Publishing Company, 1982.

Kanter, Donald L. and Mirvis, Philip H. "Conquering Cynicism: Book Summary of the Month," *Success*, October 1989, pp.58-59.

Snelling, Robert O., Sr. *The Right Job.* New York: Penguin Books, 1987.

Waitley, Denis and Witt, Reni L. *The Joy of Working: The 30 Day System to Success, Wealth, & Happiness on the Job.* New York: Dodd, Mead & Company, 1985.

MIND STRETCHES*******

1. What is your strategy for identifying a career path? Do you know anyone who just "floated along" whichever way the current carried them? Are they happy? Why or why not?

2. Do you think American workers are cynical? Why?

3. How important is job security to you? Can you see it changing in three years? Five years? Ten years?

4. How important is money to you? Will you be satisfied with an officer's pay? Can you see this need changing for you?

5. Have you ever worked nights, holidays, or weekends? What can you imagine would be good about such a schedule? Bad?

6. What prevents people from accepting change? What keeps people from taking risks? Why do you think many people stick with a less-than-satisfactory job?

7. What five jobs within the criminal justice field interest you? Why? What jobs in the field do not appeal to you? Why?

8. What elements of your personal history might be negative factors in pursuing your career goals? How can you deal with these at the interview?

9. Why do you think more people don't take an active role in their career choices?

10. What are the five most important things you will consider when selecting a job. Are these under your control?

**"Maybe I should be a cop?
I like the uniforms."**

AN INSIDER'S VIEW

THE PRIVATE SECURITY ALTERNATIVE

Bill B. Green
Manager, Security Services
Rosemount, Inc.

My exposure to the security profession started my sophomore year in college. While attending the university, I also worked full time as a sales clerk for a large retailer. My declared major was criminal justice, and I became good friends with the store's detective and its security manager. I increasingly found their daily work more interesting than what I was doing. Attending school full time and working fifty hours a week caused my classwork to suffer. Something had to give. I was persuaded to enter a company management training program and dropped out of school. The management program, however, proved unsatisfying. I was drawn back to the two mentors from my brief retail career. The store detective, who also owned a small contract security firm, offered me a job. I went to work for him, first as a night shift security officer at an industrial complex, then as an account supervisor. I also again pursued college (this time much more successfully).

Another avenue I was drawn to was the military. Both mentors were retired military, and their stories piqued my interest. A year later, I enlisted in the Army. For a young man whose world had been confined within the boundaries of Arkansas, my speciality of Military Intelligence was a real eye-opener. Those three years in Army Intelligence proved extremely illuminating, both in terms of knowledge of the world as well as a career direction. After my three years in the military, I planned to return to civilian life, probably in law enforcement or something in the criminal justice system, gain experience, and eventually return to the private sector. I began networking nine months before ending my tour of duty and was offered a parole officer position by the Department of Corrections in Arkansas. Three weeks before my release, however, an Army acquaintance called from Texas with a better alternative. I interviewed for a security consulting position in Texas, withdrew from the parole officer position, and was on my way into the field of private security.

That position opened my eyes wider, offering the chance to do in the private sector what I had just spent three years doing in the military sector--working with much senior professionals and advising clients on how to improve their security posture. While this was a dream position for a young man at such an early career stage, the financial instability of the firm led me only a year later to consider other employment opportunities. A consulting assignment with a precious metals distributor led to my next job--security director for that small company. That position provided a rare opportunity to "do it your way." The young entrepreneurial firm hired me to build a security department from the ground up. A start-up department is a tremendous, but extremely rewarding, challenge.

Two years later I found myself seeking bigger and better things. Note, however, that you cannot change jobs every few years without eventually paying a price, being labeled a *job hopper*. Few employers are interested in hiring someone who will stay only twelve to twenty-four months. Most positions take six months to a year to

absorb the company's standards, culture, products, and mode of operation. It simply does not pay employers to invest that time in you and then see you leave.
I knew my next position needed to be long term. Pursuing a local newspaper ad, I applied for a position with a high-tech manufacturing firm and found myself in the interviewing process, then in the second interview, then the third, followed by a battery of psychological exams and eventual selection as a member of their management team. Again I had the good fortune, and great challenge, to be in another start up department--the first security professional ever hired by this firm of 1,900 employees.

Today that firm has grown to 3,700 employees. Almost ten years later I have assumed a variety of responsibilities along the way while remaining in charge of the overall security effort through those years. You might sum up a career by looking at the titles held. Mine are as follows: security officer; security supervisor; intelligence analyst; parole officer (almost!); security analyst; security coordinator; director of security; security administrator; manager safety, security, and environmental; and manager security services. Today I manage a security department of fifty employees, the majority of whom are security officers, but which also includes shift supervisors, government security specialists (classified information), and office support personnel.

I'd like to offer some thoughts on developing your career, particularly if you decide on a career in corporate security:

> * Join the American Society for Industrial Security (ASIS) as soon as you qualify. There are memberships for students as well as for those already in the field.

> * All security is not the same. The same principles apply from one segment of business to another, but different facets of private security have significant, noteworthy differences--contract security services, consulting and training, financial services, manufacturing, retail, and so on.

> * Volunteer for an internship. It's good exposure for you and looks good on your resume. *Everyone you meet is a potential employer or a potential lead to an employer.* A few personal examples include the mentor who gave me direction and eventually pointed me to the military to gain further experience, the good Army friend who recommended me for the Texas job, and the client who saw my work who subsequently offered me a position. Show them all your very best--you never know which one may recommend you for your next position or promotion.

> * Plan to pay your dues. If you decide to become a police officer, you won't start with the best shift or as a sergeant or lieutenant. In private security you won't start with the best shift either or as a shift supervisor.

> * In a smaller corporation, be prepared to do it all. Security managers are responsible for physical security of the facility, protecting employees, staffing, scheduling, investigating, budgeting, and always selling, selling, selling--themselves, their department, and their security program.

* In a larger corporation, the security manager is likely to have more staff and more specialists to get the job done. In this capacity, you become more of a manager as opposed to the multitalented specialist of a smaller organization.

* Corporate security professionals are not "company cops." They are one of many specialists necessary to successfully operate a business. Their job is not to enforce laws (that's why you call the police). Instead, we protect corporate assets, which include people, property, and information.

* Be honest with yourself about your likes, dislikes, your emotional and physical makeup. Are you well suited for law enforcement work? Is your eyesight good enough? Do you have any other physical limitations that may hinder a particular career pursuit? Do you have any criminal history (including even "youthful" mistakes such as a DWI)? Talk to some police officers and security managers. Find out what they think about their work. Conduct your own surveys. Find out what the jobs are really all about.

* For law enforcement jobs in most parts of the country, a two- or four-year college degree will soon be required. While you are working on that degree, get some experience. Get a job at least related to the field you are thinking of pursuing. A stable work history as a security officer at a reputable firm will look better on that fresh graduate resume than some other totally unrelated experience.

As you settle on a career path, keep in mind that numerous opportunities will permit you to achieve the same goal--"to protect and to serve."

SECTION TWO
MEETING THE CHALLENGE: PREPARING

The normal process in seeking a job in law enforcement, security, or related areas is to find where job openings exist, apply, submit a resume, undergo various kinds of testing, be interviewed, and be hired! This book does not follow that order. Rather, it asks you to continue doing what you began in Chapter Four--looking at your own qualities, experiences, and preferences and seeing how they fit with what law enforcement agencies and security departments are looking for. It also suggests ways you might overcome any shortcomings you might find as you consider yourself in relation to what these positions require. This should be done *before* you actually begin looking for specific jobs. This section is written as though you were already actively engaged in testing and interviewing.

You'll begin by looking at physical requirements of these fields and what tests you might have to pass (Chapter Five). One of the most important attributes of successful candidates is that they are physically fit--which doesn't happen overnight. Next you'll look at educational and psychological requirements that might be considered and how they might be tested (Chapter Six).

This is followed by a discussion of the "beneficial attributes" of successful candidates in these fields, that is, who is most likely to be hired (Chapter Seven), giving you a chance to realistically assess what attributes *you* have and how you might fare. The next chapter discusses how you can assemble the information about yourself you have pulled together thus far into an all-important document for some positions-- your resume (Chapter Eight).

The section concludes with a critical part of getting ready for job hunting--being prepared for rejection (Chapter Nine). Each rejection must be seen as a learning situation, a chance to become better at presenting yourself, and as being one step closer to that job you *will* eventually get.

These chapters should be re-read at appropriate times during your actual job hunt. For example, if you are scheduled for a physical fitness text, reread Chapter Five a few days before. If you don't even make it to the testing stage, reread Chapter Nine.

Section Three will present specific job-seeking strategies to enhance your chances of getting a job in law enforcement, security, or related fields.

CHAPTER 5
PHYSICAL FITNESS AND TESTING

Good physical condition not only adds years to your life, but life to your years. Anonymous

Do You Know:

* What constitutes physical fitness?

* How physically fit you need to be to be a police or security officer?

* Why it is important for employers in these fields to hire people who are in shape?

* Why it is difficult for people in these fields to remain in shape?

* What the medical examination might consist of?

* What physical fitness tests you might have to pass?

* How you might prepare yourself to pass these tests?

* How fitness and stress interrelate?

* How personality and stress interrelate?

INTRODUCTION

One of the most critical criteria for obtaining a job in law enforcement, security, and related areas is physical fitness. The importance of having physically fit officers goes without saying. The job demands that those who pursue employment in these fields enter such work in shape and *remain* in shape. The people and property you are paid to protect will depend on your being able to do your job. If you cannot, you could even be sued. In 1988, in *Parker v. The District of Columbia*, the jury awarded $425,046 to a man shot by a police officer who was arresting him. The court noted: "Officer Hayes simply was not in adequate physical shape. This condition posed a foreseeable risk of harm to others."

Your future, in fact your very life, may depend on your level of fitness. As noted by Slahor (1990, p.55): "The FBI emphasizes that physical fitness is 'often the factor that spells the difference between success and failure--even life and death.'"

The professions of law enforcement and security, while appearing full of exciting chases and fights, actually are more likely to be extended periods of idle waiting, punctuated with demands for extreme activity. A shift, or maybe even an entire week, may have nothing exciting occur.

Suddenly, you may be called on to exercise almost super-human strength--to drag a victim from a burning car, to carry a heart-attack victim from an upper level apartment, to assist in carrying firefighting equipment up to a high-rise, to fight for your life with a physically fit, drug-crazed criminal.

What is particularly critical about physical fitness for police and security personnel is that the nature of their jobs can actually contribute to keeping them *out* of shape. Most of these jobs involve a significant amount of inactivity. For example, sitting at a desk or driving all day provides little exercise.

Combine this with the odd hours police and security personnel are expected to work, often when only the fast-food restaurants are open, and it becomes easy to understand why the stereotype of police and security employees is that of being overweight and out-of-shape. As noted by Noble (1989, p.38-39):

> Very few of us [police officers] die in shoot-outs and high-speed chases. In truth, police work takes its toll in more insidious ways. Instead of going out in a blaze of glory, the average officer dies by inches. It is the daily stresses, often compounded by poor eating, irregular sleep and a general lack of fitness, which erode our bodies and minds before helping us into early graves.

Officers who ignore physical fitness are playing with fire. It is little different than going to work with a broken gun or driving a defective squad car. It could kill you. According to Getz (1990, p.45): "As an occupation law enforcement holds the distinction of having the highest rate of heart disease, diabetes, and suicide out of 149 professions."

Employers know it is a challenge to keep their officers in shape. It is difficult for everyone to keep in shape as the years pass. This is good reason for employers to seek applicants who are physically fit.

Think about what being physically fit says about you to an employer. It says you are concerned about yourself. It also says you can project a positive image of the agency you represent. For obvious reasons, employers do not want employees who would make their agency look bad.

WHAT IS FITNESS?

Fitness refers to a person's physical well being or, to use the popular phrase, to being "in shape." Halper (1980, p.15) says:

> Fitness is related to your past medical history, family history and your life-style and personal habits--smoking, eating, drinking, physical activity. Physical fitness can be measured by levels of respiratory capacity, heart rate, muscle tone, strength, stamina, and by proper weight. Put another way, physical fitness is what too many of us have lost.

Physical fitness is often determined by meeting predetermined standards. The YMCA has administered over a million physical fitness evaluations in the past decade based on the following factors:

* Standing height
* Weight

* Resting heart rate
* Resting blood pressure
* Body composition (degree of fatness)
* Cardiovascular evaluation
* Flexibility measurement
* Muscular strength and endurance

The trend is to look at amount of body fat rather than weight as compared to height. According to YMCA standards (1984, pp.15-16): "The generally accepted normal percentage of fat for males is 14 to 16 percent of total body weight. For females. . . the normal percentage is between 23 and 26 percent of body weight."

The fallacy of using height and weight charts was illustrated by Zuti (1984, p.16), who describes what happened in a large metropolitan police department which used height and weight limitations for its officers:

> The maximum allowable weight for a six-footer was 210 pounds; anyone above this was considered overweight and subject to suspension. Indeed, two officers were suspended for being six feet tall and over 210 pounds. But both were well-conditioned bodybuilders and had only 19 percent fat in their bodies. Only after considerable explanation of the difference the amount of fat makes in a person's physical health, and that this is the true measure of a person's condition, were the officers reinstated.

Body fat standards for males ages 20 to 29 established by the internationally known Institute for Aerobics Research in Dallas, Texas and used by many police departments are: 8.3% or less, superior; 8.4 to 10.6%, excellent; 10.5 to 14.1%, good; 14.2 to 15.9%, average; 16.0 to 22.4 below average; and 22.5% or more body fat, poor (Noble, 1989, p.44).

Most police departments and agencies or businesses hiring security personnel require that job applicants have a medical examination as well as a physical test of some sort to be certain they are physically fit.

THE MEDICAL EXAMINATION

Three areas of critical importance during the medical examination are vision, hearing, and the condition of the cardiovascular-respiratory system. The vision test will include a test for color-blindness. Most police departments and security agencies will accept applicants who have *corrected* vision and hearing problems. If you think you have may problems in any of these areas, get it checked out before you apply for a position.

The cardiovascular and respiratory systems play a critical role in fitness. To a large extent endurance, the ability to continue exertion over a prolonged time, is directly related to the ability of the cardiovascular-respiratory system to deliver oxygen to the muscles.

Other medical screening tests often used are the ratio of total cholesterol to HDL cholesterol to identify cardiovascular risk factors, blood pressure, smoking status, drug use, and blood sugar level for diabetes. If a physician finds that you have a functional or organic disorder, the recommendation may be made to disqualify you.

PHYSICAL FITNESS TESTING

In addition to a medical examination, candidates will undergo some sort of physical fitness testing. This may take the form of an obstacle course to maneuver within a set time limit. The Criminal Justice Institute at Broward Community College in Florida, for example, uses the following physical agility obstacle course:

Start - climb a 6' wall.
Climb a ladder.
Clear a hurdle.
Climb a chain link fence.
Climb through a window.
Open and go through a wooden gate.
Climb a higher hurdle.
Run through a maze.
Crawl through a tunnel.
Complete a hand bar walk.
Run through a high stepper course.
Walk a log.
Complete a horizontal hand walk.
Jump up and over a short wall.
Final run around two poles.

The Institute also tests strength and endurance using the following tests:

Trigger pull (strong hand 18, weak hand 12).
10 push ups.
Standing jump.
3 pull ups (from dead hang, palms facing away).
Vehicle push (20 feet, push from rear of vehicle).
1/2 mile run (5 minutes maximum time).

Another example of physical fitness testing is that of the United States Air Force Academy (1987, pp.10-13). It has the following physical fitness requirements in their admissions test:

Test	Minimum	Maximum	Average
Pull-ups			
Males	3	22	10
Females	1	12	2
Sit-ups			
Males	39	99	73
Females	36	94	70
Push-ups			
Males	11	85	40
Females	4	50	25
Shuttle Run (in seconds)			
Males	64.7	51.4	60.2
Females	78.6	55.4	68.3

The *pull-ups* must be done with the palms facing away from the face, arms fully extended. No swinging, kicking, or stopping once the count has begun. This is an untimed test.

The *sit-ups* are done lying flat on the back, legs flexed, hands placed behind the head with fingers interlocked. Sit-ups are done touching the elbow to the opposite knee, alternating knees each sit-up. Time allowed is two-minutes, with resting prohibited.

The *push-ups* are done with the body straight from shoulders to heels, with the weight of the body resting on hands and toes. Time allowed is two-minutes, with resting prohibited.

The *shuttle run* is 300 yards long. You must run six round trip 25-yard laps (12 complete laps) between two turning lanes. Turns are made by pivoting on one foot; hands may touch the floor on the turns.

Candidates who cannot perform up to the minimum standards are disqualified. The goal of most candidates is to "max" out, giving them an edge over less physically fit candidates.

Another rigorous physical fitness test is that of the California Highway Patrol, described by Rubin (1989, p.42):

> Tests required in the Physical Performance Program include PEDOL--a minimum of 140 revolutions of the bicycle ergometer in two minutes; Side Step--13 crossings in 10 seconds; Standing Long Jump--68 inches; Trunk Strength--113 pound standard; and a grouping of three tests that measure shoulder abduction, grip strength, and dynamic arm.

Whatever tests are used, they are likely to measure your endurance, agility, flexibility, and strength.

SELF-ASSESSMENT

It is important that you know how physically fit you really are. Just because you feel good does not necessarily mean that you are "in shape." The FBI's publication *Physical Fitness for Law Enforcement Officers* (1972, pp.19-24) recommends the following:

> Feel your arms, shoulders, stomach, buttocks, and legs. Are your muscles well-toned or are you soft and flabby?

> Give yourself the pinch test. Take hold of the skin just above your belt. Are your fingers separated by more than one-half inch?

This publication describes cardiovascular condition, balance, flexibility, agility, strength, and power tests to assess your physical fitness. Their descriptions follow.

Cardiovascular Tests

Cureton's Breath-Holding Test. One simple way to test your respiratory capacity is to step onto and off a chair, bench, or stool (approximately 17 inches high) for a period of one minute and then see how long you can hold your breath. You should be able to hold it for at least 30 seconds. If you can't, it's an indication that your cardiovascular function has deteriorated below a desirable level.

Kasch Pulse Recovery Test (3 min.). This test can be performed by almost any age group. Only the infirm or the extremely unfit would find it too strenuous. You should not smoke for one hour or eat for two hours before taking the test. Also, rest for five minutes before taking the test.

EQUIPMENT

12" bench or stool
Clock or watch with a sweep second hand

PROCEDURE

a) Start stepping onto and off the bench when sweep second hand is at 11.

b) Step 24 times per minute, total 72.

c) Duration is three minutes.

d) Stop stepping when sweep second hand is again at 11, after three revolutions, and sit down.

e) Start counting the pulse rate when sweep second hand reaches 12 on the clock, using either the artery located inside the wrist or the carotid artery in the throat. Count every 10 seconds and record for one minute.

f) Total the six pulse counts for one minute and compare with the following scale:

Classification	0-1 Minute Pulse Rate After Exercise
Excellent	71-78
Very Good	79-83
Average	84-99
Below Average	100-107
Poor	108-118

Cooper's 12-Minute Walk/Run Test. NOTE: People over age 30 should not take this test until they have had a complete medical examination and have completed approximately six weeks in a "starter physical fitness program."

Find a place where you can run/walk a measured distance of up to two miles. A quarter-mile track at a local school would be ideal; however, a nearby park, field, or quiet stretch of road can be used. The test is quite simple--see how much of the two miles you can comfortably cover in 12 minutes. Try to run the entire time at a pace you can maintain without excessive strain. If your breath becomes short, walk until it returns to normal, then run again. Keep going for a full 12 minutes, then check your performance on the following scale:

Fitness Category (Under age 30)	
Very Poor	less than 1.0
Poor	1.00 - 1.24
Fair	1.25 - 1.49
Good	1.50 - 1.74
Excellent	1.75+

(distance in miles covered in 12 minutes)

Balance Test

Stand on your toes, heels together, eyes closed, and your arms stretched forward at shoulder level. Maintain this position for 20 seconds without shifting your feet or opening your eyes.

Flexibility Tests

Trunk Flexion. Keep your legs together, your knees locked, bend at the waist and touch the floor with your fingers.

Trunk Extension. Lie flat on your stomach, face down, fingers laced behind your neck and your feet anchored to the floor. Now raise your chin until it is 18 inches off the floor. (Note: Average for men students at the University of Illinois is 12.5 inches.)

Agility Test

Squat Thrusts. Standing, drop down to squatting position, palms flat against floor, arms straight. Next, with weight supported on the hands, kick backward so that your legs are extended fully. Immediately kick forward to the squatting position and stand up. You should be able to perform four in eight seconds.

Strength Tests

Pull-ups. Hang from a bar, hands slightly wider than shoulders, palms turned away, arms fully extended. Pull up until your chin is over the bar. Lower yourself until your arms are fully extended and repeat. You should be able to perform four pull-ups.

Push-ups. From the front leaning rest position, hands slightly wider than the shoulders with fingers pointed straight ahead, lower your body until your chest barely touches the floor. Push up to the front leaning rest position, keeping your body straight. Standards from Institute for Aerobics Research for push-ups done in one minute are: 60 and up, superior; 50 to 59, excellent; 35 to 49, good; 25 to 34, average; 18 to 24, below average; and 17 or less, poor.

Sit-ups. Lie on your back with your hands behind your neck, with your legs straight and free. Flex the trunk and sit up, and then return to the starting position. Standards from Institute for Aerobics Research for situps done in one minute are: 49 and up, superior; 46 to 48, excellent; 42 to 45, good; 40 to 41, average; 33 to 39, below average; and 32 or less, poor.

Power

Standing Broad Jump. From a standing position, jump as far forward as you can, landing on both feet. Do not take a running start. The length of your jump should equal your height.

Vertical Jump. Stand facing a wall, feet and chin touching the wall, arms extended over your head. Mark the height of your hands on the wall. (A piece of chalk will do.) Now jump up and touch the wall as high as you can with one hand. (Use chalk.) Note the difference between the two marks on the wall. You should be able to perform a vertical jump of 18 inches or more.

Even if you successfully pass all these tests, you want to be sure you remain in good physical shape. Your lifestyle may be such that you do not require a formal physical fitness program. Many people who are active in sports such as swimming, tennis, or who are joggers, do not need much more to keep in shape. If, however, you have a relatively sedentary lifestyle, you may want to start a basic physical fitness program.

A BASIC PHYSICAL FITNESS PROGRAM

A "basic health action plan for physical fitness" is outlined by Halper (1980, pp.27-30):

* Warm-up exercises (at least five minutes)
    Includes walking, stretching, twisting.

* Endurance exercises (at least twenty minutes)
    Includes jogging, biking, skipping rope, jumping jacks, any calisthenics.

* Cool-down (at least five minutes)

    Strength. Includes body twists, knee bends, weight raisers.

    Flexibility. Includes head rotation, arm/shoulder swings, toe touching.

* Relaxation (at least three minutes)

    Meditation, deep breathing, Yoga.

An exercise program should start gradually and then build up. You should exercise at least three times a week. As you progress into your fitness program, you can increase the number of times a week you work out.

Tips

The following tips on exercising might be considered (Halper, 1980, pp.133-134):

* Change your exercises occasionally to give yourself some variety.

* Exercise to music.

* Exercise before bed if you have trouble sleeping.

* Do not get upset with yourself if you miss your exercises once in a while.

* You have to keep some sort of record.

* Keep the program simple.

* Gradual progression is vitally important for two reasons: you will reduce your chance of injury, and you will get satisfaction from advancing to higher levels.

* Do not be discouraged if the benefits are not immediate.
   It takes regular, long-term effort.

* During your exercise routine, take a break whenever you want to. You are not in competition.

* Organize your program so that it fits easily into your daily life. It is easier to keep the habit if you exercise at the same time each day.

* Allow ten minutes after cool-down before showering. Take a warm shower. *A hot or cold shower can dangerously affect your blood pressure.*

* Wait an hour after a meal before exercising *vigorously* to avoid cramping or nausea. (A leisurely walk after eating is beneficial.)

* If you stop exercising for a while--even a week or two--start at a lower level and gradually work your way up again.

(NOTE: Never pursue an exercise program without consulting with your physician.)

FITNESS AND STRESS

Law enforcement and private security careers can be highly stressful--and so can seeking employment in these fields. An important part of being physically and mentally fit is managing stress.

Some personality types tend to be more susceptible to stress, particularly those identified as *Type A*. Hawks et al (1989, p.49) describe such people:

Individuals with a Type A personality typically speak and move rapidly, hold feelings in, have few outside interests, are precise and numbers-oriented, find it difficult to relax, are excessively time conscious, seek approval from others, are usually engaged in multiple tasks with impossible deadlines and are continually hurried and overscheduled. Due to the release of artery-damaging stress hormones associated with Type A behavior, the greatest health risk of having a Type A personality is heart disease. . .

Current research indicates that the Type A personality traits most responsible for increased heart disease risk may be hostility and anger.

If you are a Type A personality, which many people drawn to law enforcement and security are, be aware of these risks. Exercise and relaxation techniques can help reduce them.

In addition, Kobasa (1984) has identified three personality traits, called the *3 C's* that provide protection against the negative stress everyone experiences as part of living in our fast-moving, complex society: control, commitment, and challenge. *Control* means taking charge of your life, being confident in your ability to direct your own life rather than letting it be directed by outside forces. *Commitment* means being actively involved and caring about family, friends, job, hobbies, and the like. *Challenge* means you accept setbacks as something to be overcome and change as something to be adapted to.

Exercise is a powerful tool in managing stress. As noted by Zuti (1984, p.259):

A long run, a wall-banging game of squash, a weekend of hard skiing, will divert us, make us forget a stressful emotional state. It is calming, if only because the body gets tired and wants sleep. Of course, exercise does not *solve* the problem, but it is a good way to build up a conditioned, controlled response to stress.

The Up-Side of Stress

Not all stress is negative. Most people need a certain amount of stress to keep them sharp. Think of the last time you had a deadline to meet. It was the stress of the deadline that probably finally got you moving. As noted by Hanson (1985, p.xviii):

Stress can be *fantastic*. Or it can be *fatal*. It's all up to you. As well as respecting the dangers of stress, you can learn to harness its benefits.

Olympic records are not set on the quiet training tracks, but only with the stress of competition--in front of huge crowds. . . .

Serious poker players will play only if significant amounts of money are bet on each hand . . . . Many people with sedate working lives actively seek stress in the form of parachuting, cliff climbing, downhill skiing, horror movies, or simply riding a roller coaster. Such stresses bring more joy into their lives.

FITNESS AND NUTRITION

The U.S. Army's total fitness program emphasizes nutrition. Among the concepts it stresses are the following:

* Drink 6 to 8 glasses of water a day.
* Avoid too much sugar.
* Avoid too much sodium (salt).
* Include fiber in your daily diet.
* Cut down on protein and fats.

Hales and Hales (1985, p.95) say of protein: "If you're like many Americans, you're eating twice as much protein as you need. Your body treats that extra protein like any other excess of calories and stores it as fat .... A single teaspoonful of vegetable oil every day provides all the fat we need .... Most of us eat much, much more." They note that animal fats (the saturated fats) are "deadly dangers, because they greatly increase the risk of heart disease."

Obesity

According to Violanti (1985, p.58): "There are many obese police officers in the United States. Research by Grencik indicated that 56% of the nation's police personnel were overweight." Violanti further notes:

> The average age of death for officers in the United States is 59 years, as compared to 73 years for the general population. Obesity may be an important risk factor in this death rate, and may be a precursor for many diseases among police officers.

> High blood pressure, common among police officers, is an obesity related disease.

The key to losing weight is a sensible diet and exercise. Physicians and consultants at health clubs can suggest what kind of diet might be best for you if you have a weight problem.

SMOKING, ALCOHOL, AND OTHER DRUGS

These substances are harmful to your health. Enough said. Well, almost enough. Keep in mind that an increasing number of both public and private agencies are limiting candidates to those who are non-smokers. So, if you smoke, quit.

LIFESTYLE AND FITNESS

Approximately 50 percent of the deaths in the United States each year result from an unhealthy lifestyle according to the U.S. Center for Disease Control. Hawks et al (1989, p.51) suggest that the following "simple lifestyle habits can add significantly to longevity:

* Sleeping for seven to eight hours each night.
* Eating breakfast every day.
* Not eating between meals.
* Maintaining an ideal weight.

* Exercising regularly.
* Drinking only moderate amounts of alcohol (or none at all).
* Not smoking cigarettes.

Hawks et al (1989, p.48) suggest that individuals assess their lifestyle and general fitness in terms of risk factors they can control:

> The three most significant risk factors that can be controlled include hypertension (above 140/90), elevated blood cholesterol (over 220) and smoking. Additional contributing factors include obesity, lack of exercise, diet, stress, diabetes, and personality type. All of these factors are interrelated and have a multiplying effect when two or more are present.

BENEFITS OF BEING PHYSICALLY FIT

Dr. Kenneth H. Cooper (1982, p.12), from the internationally known Institute for Aerobics Research in Dallas, Texas, says:

> Here are some of the benefits of total well-being that data from our research have shown us can be yours for the asking:
>
> * More personal energy;
> * More enjoyable and active leisure time;
> * Greater ability to handle domestic and job-related stress;
> * Less depression, less hypochondria, and less "free-floating" anxiety;
> * Fewer physical complaints;
> * More efficient digestion and fewer problems with constipation;
> * A better self-image and more self-confidence;
> * A more attractive, streamlined body, including more effective personal weight control;
> * Bones of greater strength;
> * Slowing of the aging process;
> * Easier pregnancy and childbirth;
> * More restful sleep;
> * Better concentration at work, and greater perseverance in all daily tasks;
> * Fewer aches and pains, including back pains.

Several of the preceding benefits would also be advantageous to the job-seeker.

CONCLUSION

Fitness is one area you can control. You can prepare yourself to do well in this portion of the testing. At this point, however, seriously confront yourself. If you have a physical limitation that will prevent you from being hired as a police or security officer, then take time to reconsider the vocational fields you wish to pursue *before* you expend significant time, energy, and money pursuing what will remain nothing more than a dream.

REFERENCES

Cooper, Kenneth H. *The Aerobics Program for Total Well-Being.* New York: M. Evans and Company, Inc., 1982.

Getz, Ronald J. "You Can't Afford *Not* to have a Fitness Program: One Department's Cost-Effective Approach," *Law and Order,* June 1990, pp.44-50.

Hales, Dianne and Hales, Robert E. *The U.S. Army Total Fitness Program.* New York: Crown Publishers, Inc., 1985.

Halper, Marilyn Snyder. *Physical Fitness.* New York: Holt, Rinehart and Winston, 1980.

Hanson, Peter, G. *The Joy of Stress.* Kansas City, MO: Universal Press Syndicate Company, 1985.

Hawks, Steven R.; Hafen, Brent Q.; and Karren, Keith J. "How Does Your Health Rate?" *Journal of Emergency Medical Services.* March 1989, pp.46-51.

Kobasa, Suzanne Q. "How Hardy Are You?" *The American Health Magazine.* September, 1984.

Noble, Thomas R. "Let's Get Physical," *Police,* May 1989, pp.38-41, 44.

Physical Agility Testing. Broward Community College, Ft. Lauderdale, FL: Criminal Justice Institute, 1989.

Physical Fitness for Law Enforcement Officers. Washington, DC: Federal Bureau of Investigation, U.S. Department of Justice, March 1972.

Rubin, Hal. "CHP Fitness Program," *Police,* May 1989, pp.42-43.

Slahor, Stephanie. "Focus on Fitness: The FBI Way," *Law and Order,* May 1990, pp.52-55.

United States Air Force Academy. *The Air Force Academy Instructions to Applicants.* Washington, DC: U.S. Government Printing Office, 1987.

United States Center for Disease Control. "Ten Leading Causes of Death in the United States," Atlanta: CDC, July, 1980.

Violanti, John M. "Obesity: A Police Health Problem," *Law and Order.* April 1985, pp.58-60.

Zuti, William B. *The Official YMCA Fitness Program.* New York: Rawson Associates, 1984.

MIND STRETCHES*******

1. How would you judge your current level of physical fitness?

2. Are you currently working out? What is your fitness program?

3. Why do you imagine the stereotype of the fat, donut-eating cop exists?

4. How do law enforcement and security careers tend to prevent fitness?

5. Is being overweight and out of shape possibly part of the "macho" image of being a cop or security guard? If so, is this changing?

6. What does an out-of-shape officer communicate to the public by appearance alone?

7. Why do you think so few Americans exercise regularly?

8. Recognizing that perhaps working night shift would make keeping in shape difficult, what creative ways could an officer working such a shift exercise?

9. Are law enforcement and private security more stressful than other careers? Why or why not?

10. How would you define *physically fit*?

"Sure I can do the job, why do you ask?"

AN INSIDER'S VIEW

PRE-EMPLOYMENT PHYSICAL FITNESS

R.W. Stanek
Sergeant, Robbery & Homicide
Minneapolis Police Department

A well-conditioned and physically fit police applicant has an edge in today's competitive job market. You will learn through daily contacts that initial impressions are usually the first and only means of evaluating people.

The administrators who will be hiring you look for all those credentials listed on your resume, but during a tense oral interview, your physical stature and appearance also are graded. Aesthetically speaking, a grossly overweight or out-of-shape applicant is not the type officer a police department is looking for. Further, such officers are statistical liabilities in terms of coronary heart disease, stress, and injury proneness. No department wants to inherit and deal with such risks during the officer's career.

Police work involves grave physical dangers. Violent encounters are always possible, but are not the only threat to officers' safety and well being. Long hours, an occupational tendency toward poor diet and nutritional habits, inadequate exercise, insufficient sleep (often interrupted by court appearances and call-backs), can take their toll on officers' health.

Enhancing police officers' physical condition results in better crimefighting and service to the public; a sharper, more professional image; increased esprit d'corps and officer self-confidence; and a very substantial reduction in personnel costs. The benefits of a working fitness program for the employing agency includes fewer medical retirements, reduced annual sick leave, and reduced health care costs.

Increasingly, employers are setting standards for fitness levels as a condition of employment both before and during employment with their agency. A recent national study of law enforcement agencies found that over 75 departments currently have mandatory fitness standards and annual testing to insure their officers are physically fit. An even greater number of agencies require pre-employment physicals and passage of mandatory fitness tests.

Employing agencies and the citizens they have sworn to protect can reasonably expect police applicants to be in "better than average" physical shape. Nationwide research (U.S. Army standards, Cooper Institute) has determined that your fitness level should be in the top 60% of your age category. Failure to meet these standards prior to employment resulted in no job offers. In addition, failure to maintain fitness standards during employment was dealt with from progressive discipline to termination.

Physical fitness encompasses everything from strength training and cardiovascular endurance (aerobics) to smoking cessation, drug and alcohol substance abstinence, and obesity reduction. Physical conditioning helps relieve stress and keeps the mind free from worries that could compromise an officer's safety when at work.

A successful fitness program should include conditioning in strength, flexibility, cardiovascular endurance, and body composition (percent body fat).

The standard protocol agencies measure against are:

* Cardiovascular
  Timed one and one-half mile run or three-mile walk

* Strength
  Push-ups: upper body
  Sit-ups: abdominal

* Flexibility
  Sit and reach

* Body composition
  Percent body fat by skin fold caliper

* Blood pressure and cholesterol screening

* Proportionate weight and height measurements

Each fitness test has a minimum standard based on national averages and standards collected from research performed with thousands of individuals in all age categories.

You should prepare for a career in law enforcement/private security by starting and maintaining a stringent workout program while progressing through the academic requirements of licensing.

CHAPTER 6
OTHER FORMS OF TESTING

Experience is not what happens to you; it is what you do with what happens to you.--Aldous Huxley

Do You Know:

* What other kinds of tests you will be expected to take to become a police or security officer?

* What areas of knowledge you might be tested on?

* What psychological tests are used for?

* If you can prepare for psychological tests?

* What a polygraph is?

* Which states require applicants to take a lie-detector test?

* If you can "fake" lie-detector tests?

* How you can best prepare yourself for all these tests?

INTRODUCTION

The tests used in the hiring process are likely to include the following:

* Knowledge
* Psychological
* Polygraph

This chapter reviews areas frequently tested to help you understand what these tests are and what purpose they serve. You will not be given "suggested" answers or even tactical approaches. In fact for some tests, preparing for or trying to "out-psych" them can be a mistake. It's important to know what to expect and what aspects of the testing you can prepare for. Before considering the specific areas, however, take a few minutes to look at a very common phenomenon: *test anxiety*.

TEST ANXIETY

"Test anxiety," according to Brown (1984, p.412), "refers to the psychological, physiological, and behavioral responses to stimuli an individual associates with the experience of testing or evaluation":

> It is a special case of general anxiety and is characterized by feelings of heightened
> self-awareness and perceived helplessness that often result in lowered performance on
> tests or, more generally, on all types of cognitive and academic tasks.

In other words, it is the feelings of worry, concern, and stress commonly associated
with any circumstance in which individuals find themselves being evaluated.

Test anxiety is a reality for most people. Recognize its existence and take control of
it. How? First, be as prepared as possible. The fewer surprises a test-taker
encounters, the less anxiety is experienced. You probably can recall walking into a
test and being pleasantly surprised to find an essay question you knew the answer to
"cold." Conversely, you can also probably recall walking into a test and being
confronted with a question which, itself, was undecipherable.

In addition to being as prepared as possible, the following will help reduce test
anxiety:

* Get a good night's sleep before the test.
* Eat.
* Take at least two pens, two #2 pencils, and a large eraser.
* Arrive with time to spare so parking or other hassles do not make you
  anxious.

KNOWLEDGE

It is hard to imagine that only a few years ago a person could become a law
enforcement officer by merely responding to an advertisement. In fact, many fine
officers still on the road rather spontaneously applied for a police job one day and
were handed a gun and badge the next. Even today, many security jobs, some
involving immense responsibility, require little, if any, knowledge of the applicant.

As appealing as this may sound at this stage of your job seeking, it is easy to see the
many problems associated with what is quickly becoming a practice of the past. As
these fields strive to become recognized professions and respond to the increasing
demands and potential liability created by our complex society, employing agencies
are having to take their hiring practices much more seriously. Whether the job for
which you are applying requires certification or licensure or just requires applicants
to be responsible individuals, almost all employers will want to determine what the
applicant knows.

General Knowledge

Some tests are designed to assess certain basic levels of ability in areas such as math,
English, composition, and grammar. Because communication skills are so vitally
important, employers should be assured that people they are considering hiring (for
any level job) can express themselves well. Computer literacy also is becoming
more important.

While different tests can be used to examine these basic areas, they will all look at
the same basic abilities. Ask yourself if you possess the necessary reading, writing,
and math skills required of any employee. This is usually at a college freshman
level. If you are not at this level, immediately start a plan to improve your skills.

Lack of basic reading, writing, and math skill cannot be hidden from an employer for very long on the job. To avoid wasting everyone's time, many job applications include some basic questions to let the hiring agency know if you have these basic academic abilities. For example, an increasing number of application forms have a section that requires a brief essay response to test your writing, spelling, grammar, and organizational abilities.

If you need remedial help, get it *now*. Many opportunities exist to improve yourself. The only reason not to do so is often just plain being embarrassed to ask for help. The help you need may be in a review book available from a library or bookstore. You may want to consider enrolling in a class at a community college or in an adult learning program.

Specific Knowledge

Applicants may be required to know specific information for certain jobs. In states requiring certification or licensure, successful completion of requisite levels of training or education will be evidence of such knowledge.

Certainly such required knowledge will indicate the areas of specific knowledge you will be expected to know. For example, in Minnesota, which requires a minimum of two years of college to be eligible to be licensed as a police officer, areas of required knowledge include:

* Administration of Justice
* Criminal Investigation
* Criminal Procedure
* Cultural Awareness
* Defensive Tactics
* Firearms
* Human Behavior
* Juvenile Justice
* Statutes
* Patrol Functions
* Police Operations and Procedures
* Report Writing
* Testifying in Court
* Traffic Law Enforcement

Far less specific knowledge is required to be a private investigator in Minnesota, but in addition to passing a strict background investigation, a minimum of three years' experience in security work is required.

Even if specific knowledge areas are not set forth clearly, you should be able to foresee what may be asked during an oral interview. Basic statutes that apply to public or private officers would be likely questions. Frequently, such questions are intertwined with the "What would you do if . . . ?" question. Here employers test not only specific knowledge, but applications of it using problem-solving techniques and communications skills.

It's your responsibility to be prepared to the best of your ability. If you do not know what you might be tested on, it does no harm to call ahead to ask. The worst that could happen is that they won't say. But it is much more likely you will be told.

That will put you a giant step ahead of applicants who haven't a clue as to what will be asked.

Do what you can to learn and review what you think will be asked. Remember, no one can know everything. All you can be expected to do is your best. Sometimes you will be able to immediately give the exact answer, maybe even amazing yourself. Sometimes you may give a wrong answer. Sometimes you may draw a complete mental blank. You are likely to experience all these reactions at one time or another during testing.

Keep in mind the purpose of the testing process. If all employers want are accurate answers, a new computer would probably work better. Employers want someone who can think and be human. Part of being human is to *not* know it all and yet to keep functioning. In fact, tests might include an "off-the-wall" question just to see how you respond. In all probability, you will look a lot better admitting you are nervous and forgot, or don't know, but know where to find the answer, than to fake it. In short:

> * Be as prepared as you can be.
> * Seek remedial help if necessary.
> * Know as much as you can.
> * Know how to find what you don't know.
> * Don't be afraid to admit what you don't know.
> * Don't make up answers.

It's also a good idea to learn as much as possible about the department or agency you are applying to. If it is a law enforcement position, perhaps you can arrange for a ride-along. This would provide an opportunity to ask questions about the department. If it is a private security position, perhaps you can visit the facility and talk with a security officer.

PSYCHOLOGICAL TESTING

Psychological testing is an area of anxiety for applicants because so much of it is out of their control. What should I say? How should I answer? What are they looking for? Psychological testing is an absolutely immense body of complex information about which hundreds of texts have been written. So what do you need to know?

First, these tests should not and probably could not be prepared for through such traditional means as memorization. It is better to understand what these tests are meant to do, how they are administered, and what they can show.

Purposes of Psychological Testing

Although psychological testing is a relatively new practice, no doubt you have taken some form of psychological test, probably at some point in your school career. "Basically," says Anastasi (1976, p.3), "the function of psychological tests is to measure differences between individuals or between the reactions of the same individual on different occasions."

Sgt. Dennis Conroy, St. Paul Police Department, also a clinical psychologist, says about testing that is administered to police/security candidates:

To prepare for a psychological evaluation, applicants must begin to get psychologically "fit" several months before the examination. Preparation for a psychological evaluation *cannot* be rushed.

Applicants must begin preparation early enough so they can make changes to assure that they are as psychologically healthy as possible. This includes looking at relationships, mature behavior, and ways to deal with tension.

Frequently applicants take psychological evaluations just after finishing school. Their lives have been hectic. They have not taken time to relax for months. They are wound tighter than a $2.00 watch. This stress affects their entire being. It determines how they see the world. It is crucial for applicants to take time to relax before a psychological examination. This requires more than a 15-minute process the day before the evaluation. Some practical suggestions after you have taken time for yourself are as follows:

* Don't fight with your wife or husband, boyfriend or girlfriend, or parents the night before the evaluation.

* Get plenty of sleep the night before. Make sure you are at your best.

* Get up early the morning of the evaluation so you have time for yourself. Take a walk and relax.

* Leave early for the evaluation. Get there with about 15 minutes to spare. Take time to relax when you get there. Read the paper or something.

* During the exam, be honest. You have honestly worked toward entering this profession for a long time. Don't change now.

Copy from the person next to you only if you are *absolutely sure* you want his or her personality and are willing to bet your career on it.

Hargrave and Berner (1984, p.14) suggest most people would agree that law enforcement officers should be "mentally and emotionally stable," but that defining and assessing what this consists of is a complex, challenging task. Their review of the literature identified the following mental and emotional demands:

* Stress associated with constant danger.

* Many routine tasks.

* The independent exercise of discretionary power, without abuse, in an organizational context of infrequent supervision and authoritarian management.

* The frequent need to use aggression while maintaining control of temper, and while maintaining a conforming stance toward supervisors.

* Public and agency reprisals for misconduct.

* Poor promotion prospects.

Similar mental and emotional demands can be found in certain types of private security work.

Testing Methods

Methods vary greatly from test to test. As noted by Baum (1985, p.413):

> Test content can measure maximum performance or typical performance, the best one can do versus how one typically performs. For example, an ability test generally measures maximum performance, while a personality test generally measures typical performance. Maximum performance tests have correct or incorrect answers; typical performance tests generally assess stylistic differences, without specific answers being uniformly better than others.
>
> Maximum performance tests can be classified into two broad categories: ability and achievement tests. Pure ability tests measure what a person is capable of doing and generally present problems with which the person is unlikely to have had direct experience. Pure achievement tests assess the amount of information one has learned from previous experiences . . . .
>
> Personality tests tend to be of two major types, objective and projective. Objective personality tests, such as the Minnesota Multiphasic Personality Inventory (MMPI), generally ask true-false or multiple-choice questions that are objectively scored. These items frequently are grouped into scales that measure different aspects of personality . . . . Projective tests involve ambiguous stimuli that the subject must interpret, presumably by "projecting" into the interpretation aspects of his or her own personality. Classic projective tests are the Rorschach Inkblot Test and the Thematic Apperception Test (TAT).

Specific Psychological Tests

In attempting to look into the future to anticipate how an applicant might perform, evaluators look at both the past (for example, job references, grades, traffic and police records, etc.) and at the present. Psychological tests are a tool employers use to learn about the applicant's present state of mind, what is important to that person, and how that person is likely to respond to certain stimuli.

These tests' questions do not ask for "yes/no" or "black/white" answers. Rather, the answers form patterns that can be evaluated. Psychologists can compare the patterns with past studies to determine a psychological profile of the applicant. Tests frequently given include the following:

* Minnesota Multiphasic Personality Inventory (MMPI)
* California Psychological Inventory
* Myers-Briggs Type Indictors
* Wonderlic Tests
* Watson-Glaser Critical Thinking Appraisal
* Strong Interest Inventory

The *Minnesota Multiphasic Personality Inventory (MMPI)*) is a frequently used test for entry-level psychological screening. It is used primarily for emotional stability screening. This self-report questionnaire is *the* most widely used paper-and-pencil personality test being used (in all fields). Respondents are asked to indicate "true," "false," or "cannot say" to 550 statements. As noted by Tsushima (1984, p.386):

> The test items consist of a wide variety of psychological characteristics such as health, social, sexual, political, and religious values; attitudes about family, education, and occupation; emotional moods; and typical neurotic or psychotic clinical manifestations such as obsessive-compulsive behavior, phobias, delusions, and hallucinations.

According to Conroy, the MMPI is virtually impossible to study for. Its validity scales have cross-indexed questions and, in most cases, applicants who try to "fool" the test "fool" themselves out of a job instead.

The *California Psychological Inventory (CPI)* is the second most popular personality test. The test is a "multi-level self-administering questionnaire designed by the authors to 'identify and reveal the status of certain highly important factors in personality and social adjustment'" (Mitchell, p.254). According to the authors (Mitchell, p.252):

> Each scale is designed to forecast what a person will say or do under defined conditions, and to identify individuals who will be described in characteristic ways by others who know them well or who observe their behavior in particular contexts.

Gough (1988, p.45) describes the CPA as "a multi-purpose questionnaire designed to assess normal personality characteristics important to everyday life."

The *Myers-Briggs Type Indicator* [TM] is a widely used measure of people's disposition and preferences. According to Myers and Briggs (1988, p.30), over one and a half million people took the MBTI in 1987. The test describes sixteen easily understood personality types based on individuals' stated preferences on four indexes:

* Extraversion-Introversion
* Sensing-Intuition
* Thinking-Feeling
* Judgment-Perception

The *Wonderlic Personnel Test* is a timed (12 minutes), 50-item paper-and-pencil test that can be taken individually or in groups. Wonderlic (1988, p.37) suggests that his test is "highly predictive of success in learning situations" and is a "highly accurate estimate of intelligence [that] can serve as a quick assessment of cognitive skills or as a screening tool to determine the need for more detailed evaluations."

The *Watason-Glaser Critical Thinking Appraisal* has five subtests:

* Inference
* Recognition of Assumptions
* Deduction
* Interpretation
* Evaluation of Arguments

The test has 80 items and is to be completed within 40 minutes. According to Mitchell (1985, p.1692): "The exercises include problems, statements, arguments, and interpretations of data similar to those that are encountered on a daily basis at work, in the classroom, and in newspaper and magazine articles."

The *Strong Interest Inventory* has 325 items covering a wide range of occupations, occupational activities, hobbies, leisure activities, school subjects, and types of people. As noted by Strong et al (1988, p.4):

> The *Strong* compares a person's interests with the interests of people happily employed in a wide variety of occupations. It is a measure of *interests,* not of aptitude or intelligence . . . .
>
> And because the consistency of occupational interests from one culture to the next-- the likes and dislikes of engineers, art teachers, bankers, police officers--has been demonstrated, it is used in translation in similar settings abroad.

POLYGRAPH TESTING

"Historically," says Bailey (1989, p.507), "the most dramatic attempts at 'lie detection' relied upon ordeals such as placing hot irons on the tongue of suspects." Fortunately, times have changed since then. Polygraph tests are physically painless. According to field practitioners their accuracy is 90 to 95% (W. Bailey, 1989, p.509). Nonetheless, use of polygraph testing in pre-employment screening of applicants is "very controversial and, in fact, illegal in some jurisdictions." Their primary use is to substantiate the information gathered during the background investigation.

Most people are familiar with the use of the polygraph in criminal investigations, and they have a vague idea of how it works. Specifically, according to F. Bailey et al (1989, p.63):

> The polygraph is an instrument that:
>
> (A) records continuously, visually, permanently, and simultaneously changes in cardiovascular, respiratory, and electrodermal patterns as minimum instrumentation standards; and
>
> (B) is used or the results of which are used, for the purpose of rendering a diagnostic opinion regarding the honesty or dishonesty of an individual.

W. Baily (1989, p.507) describes the instrument this way:

> The modern polygraph is a briefcase-sized device that, in most field settings, records changes in skin resistance (GSR) by means of two electrodes attached to the fingertips. A standard medical blood-pressure cuff, which is partially inflated during testing, is used to record changes in relative blood pressure and pulse rate. Finally, changes in breathing activity are recorded by hollow, corrugated-rubber tubes, one placed around the abdomen and one around the upper thorax, which expand and contract with chest-cavity movement during inspiration and expiration. Activity in each of these physiological measurements is monitored by either electronic or mechanical means and is permanently recorded on a paper chart by a pen-and-ink system.

Because use of the polygraph in pre-employment is so controversial, it has become strictly regulated through the Employee Polygraph Protection Act (EPPA), signed into law by President Reagan June 27, 1988, coming into effect December 27, 1988. This law, according to F. Bailey et al (1989, p.1):

> [P]rohibits the use of all mechanical lie detector tests in the workplace, including polygraphs, psychological stress evaluators, deceptographs, and voice stress analyzers .
> . . .
>
> EPPA allows for one type of lie detector test--the polygraph--to be used by private sector employers for certain types of pre-employment screening, . . . [including] employers whose primary business is the provision of certain types of security services
> . . . .
>
> Where the particular employer is the United States government or any state or local government, EPPA does not apply. Government employers may use any lie detector test without complying with any of EPPA's procedures or restrictions.

In other words, although using the polygraph during pre-employment is prohibited in most fields, it is *not* prohibited in law enforcement or in many private security jobs. Therefore, make no objections should you be asked to take such an examination. The employer probably has the right to request this. Just be yourself. Relax. Tell the truth. You wouldn't want to live with any kind of lie during your working career, would you?

CONCLUSION

Even the word *test* is intimidating to most people, causing a certain amount of anxiety. But you should view the testing process as another opportunity to prove to a prospective employer that *you* are the one who should be hired.

Present yourself as you are. This is the purpose of testing--for a potential employer to learn who you are to attempt to predict what kind of employee you might be.

If you do not feel you would test well now, improve yourself. The most obvious areas that you can improve in right now are physical fitness as discussed in Chapter Five and knowledge. Because neither of these areas develops overnight, develop a rigorous plan to increase both your fitness level and your knowledge, starting now.

Other areas such as psychological and polygraph testing can*not* be "prepared for." In fact, as previously discussed, too much preparation or trying to "psych out" these tests can actually make you score *worse* than if you had just been yourself. Some high school and college guidance programs will administer these tests for you so you can have the experience of going through them.

You can, however, prepare for some psychological areas in advance. There may be areas of your life that could be negatively reflected in a psychological test that you *can* deal with. For example, if a traumatic experience in your life, such as the death of a loved one, is still affecting you, get some counseling so you can deal with your future with all the energy you will need.

Even some more serious problems such as prior drinking problems, earlier driving problems, or juvenile delinquency problems may not necessarily eliminate you from being considered by certain employers *if* you have seriously and adequately dealt with such problems.

Most important, seriously confront any aspects of your life that could prevent you from being a viable candidate for a job in law enforcement or private security. If you have a felony criminal record which will prohibit you from becoming a police officer in most states or a security officer in many states, do not assume they will make an exception for you, or worse, that if you lie about it, the background examination will not find out about it.

Be *realistic* about who you are and what you can be. Be honest with yourself. Because work greatly influences *all* aspects of your life, you do not want to pursue any career that will be a dead-end. View the testing phase of the application process as a positive experience for both the employer and yourself, to help both of you determine if there is a match. If not, it is best for everyone to learn this while there is time for you to find a different niche in the world of work.

REFERENCES

Anastasi, Anne. *Psychological Testing.* 4th ed. New York: Macmillan Publishing Co., Inc., 1976.

Bailey, F. Lee; Zuckerman, Roger E.; and Pierce, Kenneth R. *The Employee Polygraph Protection Act: A Manual for Polygraph Examiners and Employers.* Severna Park, MD: American Polygraph Association, 1989.

Bailey, William G. (ed.) "Polygraph," *The Encyclopedia of Police Science,* New York: Garland Publishing, Inc., 1989, pp.507-511.

Baum, A.S. "Testing Methods." *Encyclopedia of Psychology,* vol. 3. Raymond J. Corsini, Ed., New York: John Wiley and Sons, 1984.

Brown, F.G. "Test Anxiety." *Encyclopedia of Psychology,* vol. 3. Raymond J. Corsini, Ed., New York: John Wiley and Sons, 1984.

Buros, Oscar Krisen, ed. *Personality Tests and Reviews.* Highland Park, NJ: The Gryphon Press, 1988.

Gough, Harrison G. "California Psychological Inventory: Proven Measure of Normal Personality." *1988 CPP Catalog.* Palo Alto, CA: Consulting Psychologists Press, Inc., 1988, pp.45-47.

Hargrave, George E. and Berner, John G. *Post Psychological Screening Manual.* Sacramento, CA: State of California Department of Justice Commission on Peace Officer Standards and Training, 1984.

Mitchell, James V. Jr. "California Psychological Inventory." *The Ninth Mental Measurements Yearbook.* Vol. 1., Lincoln, NE: University of Nebraska Press, 1985, pp.249-254.

Mitchell, James V. Jr. "Watson-Glaser Critical Thinking Appraisal." *The Ninth Mental Measurements Yearbook.* Vol. 1., Lincoln, NE: University of Nebraska Press, 1985, pp.1691-1694.

Myers, Isabel Briggs and Briggs, Katharine C. "Myers-Briggs Type Indicator[TM]." *1988 CPP Catalog.* Palo Alto, CA: Consulting Psychologists Press, Inc., 1988, pp.30-32.

Strong, E.K., Jr., Hansen, Jo-Ida C. and Campbell, David P. "Strong Interest Inventory." *1988 CPP Catalog.* Palo Alto, CA: Consulting Psychologists Press, Inc., 1988, pp.4-11.

Tsushima, W.T. "Minnesota Multiphasic Personality Inventory." *Encyclopedia of Psychology,* vol. 2. Raymond J. Corsini, Ed., New York: John Wiley and Sons, 1984.

Wonderlic, E.F. "The Wonderlic Personnel Test." *PAR Spring, 1988 Catalog of Testing Resources for the Professional.* Odessa, FL: Psychological Assessment Resources, Inc., 1988.

MIND STRETCHES*******

1. Does your state require proof of certain levels of knowledge? How do you plan to prepare for such requirements?

2. What do you anticipate a battery of psychological tests will say about you? Are there factors in your life that need to be attended to before you pursue a career in law enforcement or private security?

3. How do you feel about taking a polygraph examination? Are there skeletons in your closet that you need to honestly confront?

4. Why do some applicants outright *lie* about aspects of their past that can easily be verified by the hiring authority?

5. As part of your job search strategy, have you taken into account what you can and cannot prepare yourself for?

6. What areas of the hiring process do you have such limited control over that it is a waste of time to even try to prepare? Is there any area of the hiring process that you have absolutely *no* control over, or is there always something you can do to give yourself an edge over the competition?

7. Is what you have done in the past a realistic indicator of how you will perform in the future?

8. Should what you have done in the past be held against you?

9. Have you ever taken a psychological test? If so, how did you feel: positive, neutral, or negative? If negative, what can you do to reduce these feelings?

10. If you suffer from test anxiety, what three things can you do to reduce it?

"I'm gonna ace this baby"

AN INSIDER'S VIEW

GETTING   SET

Dennis L. Conroy, PhD
Sergeant
St. Paul Police Department

In preparing for tests to become a police or security officer, it is crucial that applicants properly prepare for the various tests. There are likely to be tests in the areas of knowledge, physical fitness, psychological preparedness, and perhaps even a polygraph.

Applicants *can* study for knowledge tests. They must be able to not only understand the police/security function, but to articulate that function, specify ways in which that function can be fulfilled, and how the applicant will fit into the system to fulfill the function. In other words, expect more than just a multiple-choice or true/false test of knowledge. Applicants must be able to state what police/security officers do (protect and serve), how that can best be accomplished (specific methods of protecting and serving), and what role they see for themselves in that system (how they see themselves functioning as police or security officers).

Tests of physical fitness require significant prior preparation. There will often be tests of stamina (cardiovascular fitness), strength (muscle tone), and agility (mobility). Almost any fitness center can help applicants with programs to prepare for such tests. It is best that applicants find the specifics of the department(s) they are applying for and train to meet those standards.

To study for a psychological test is much like studying for a urine test. There *is* important preparation, but it cannot be done the night before the exam, or even a week before. Applicants must begin to prepare for the psychological exam *at least* several months before the actual test itself. Applicants must present themselves as psychologically fit to do police or security work, and such preparation takes time. It should be more a reaffirmation process than change for applicants. Applicants should not be afraid of psychological examinations. They should just be honest. If the assessment indicates that an applicant may not be suitable for police work or security work, it is just as often indicating that police or security work will not be good for the applicant.

CHAPTER 7
ATTRIBUTES OF
SUCCESSFUL CANDIDATES

*It's not your aptitude, it's your attitude that determines
your altitude. --Anonymous*

Do You Know:

* What a person's past says about them?

* What attributes good police and security officers have?

* What experiences reflect positively on candidates?

* What types of prior employment help get you a job
  in the criminal justice/private security fields?

* Why non-law related jobs and education may be better than law-related
  areas?

* Why military service may be desirable? Undesirable?

* What benefits volunteer experience provide?

* How important communication skills are?

* What effect education has on police and security officers?

* What role ethics plays in law enforcement and security?

INTRODUCTION

Imagine yourself as an employer responsible for selecting the best police or security
candidate from a number of applicants. What criteria would you use to make this
decision which is sure to have important consequences? What positive **attributes** or
characteristics would you, as an employer, look for? *******

What negative attributes would influence you *not* to hire a candidate? ********

Employers are not just selecting employees, they are selecting people who will
often directly influence other people's lives and who will also be representing their
department or agency.

Police officers routinely deal with the most private business of the public for whom they work. Officers bandage wounds, intervene in disputes, guard property, search homes and offices, educate children. Officers may bring victims back to life or watch them die. They uphold the law, which not only benefits the public, but also holds the guilty responsible by drawing them into the criminal justice system in a way that will alter that defendant's life forever. Being a police officer is an *awesome* responsibility.

Security officers also have great responsibility. Most security directors have complete access to every part of a company's assets--its secrets, its property, its cash, all are literally under the protection of the manager and the security officers hired. As noted by one security manager, (Remesch, 1989, p.35), it is ironic that companies: "[P]ay them $7 an hour and expose them to millions. Imagine opening a bank vault with millions and paying a guard $4 an hour to guard it."

To return to the question, what criteria is used when hiring law enforcement or security officers? This criteria ranges from how you present yourself to who you really are.

HOW DO YOU APPEAR?

Impressions are important. Initial contacts, resumes, and follow-ups are critical. But regardless of how well you look, act, and sound, you will have to rely on considerably more than such relatively superficial attributes.

Employers *will* look at both what you have done and how you have done it. If you are determined to get the job, take control of your future by establishing a solid background of knowledge and experience. Many opportunities are available to acquire those attributes employees seek in candidates.

PERSONAL ATTRIBUTES

What kind of background will help you get that entry-level job? Recognize that employers are often as interested in non-law-related experience and attributes as they are in law-related ones.

Most employers are more interested in the type of a person you are than in what you know about law enforcement or security work. A more general background helps anyone broaden their perspective of the world in which they live. A study conducted at Indiana University identified twelve characteristics separating good police officers from poor ones:

* Reliability	* Initiative
* Leadership	* Integrity
* Judgment	* Honesty
* Persuasiveness	* Ego Control
* Communication Skills	* Intelligence
* Accuracy	* Sensitivity

Another study (Gilbert *et al.*, 1988, pp.27-29) confirmed that:

... law enforcement officers are expected to do more than job-related behaviors, such as issuing traffic citations, making arrests, and taking reports, in order to facilitate overall excellence in public safety agencies. The very best officers, according to their leaders, excel in the following areas:

* Partnership with the leader.
* Technical competence.
* Motivation to do the job.
* Proper comportment [professional conduct].
* Dependability.
* Sense of humor.
* Positive working relations [a team player].
* Tendency to speak up.

These same traits are vital if you're considering a career in the private security field. These traits are not genetic. They are learned. The more general life experiences you have had, the better your chance to have acquired these traits. Broad experience also helps you better understand human behavior, a much needed attribute in officers.

Two other important attributes for officers are ego strength and anger control. Ego strength is essential and comes from having good self-esteem and a good self-valuing system. Anger control is especially important because of the nature of law enforcement and security work. An empathetic attitude toward those who come to your attention because they are violating the law or a company policy is highly desirable. True professionals do not take client behaviors personally. They try to keep emotion out of decisions that affect other's lives through a process called *intellectualization.* That is, they think before they act.

In addition to possessing the preceding characteristics, successful candidates also have performed well in the past. It is generally agreed that a good predictor of how candidates will perform in the future is how they performed in the past. Experiences that can reflect positively include the following:

* Past general employment
* Work-related experience
* Volunteer community experience
* Military service
* Education
* Communication skills/experience

Past General Employment

While some employers may be looking for specific experience, those hiring entry-level law enforcement and security personnel are usually more interested in general background. Past employment says a lot about a person.

The simple fact that a person was successfully employed says that someone wanted to hire them and that the employee was responsible enough to stay on the job. Keeping a job says that the person could operate on a schedule, complete assigned tasks, not take advantage of the basic trust placed in all employees, and get along with others.

It might also be said that the more remote past jobs were from law enforcement work, the better the experience would be viewed. Many departments would rather hire entry-level personnel and train them "from scratch." Also, more general backgrounds provide a broader view of the world and opportunities to have developed varied experiences.

Don't worry if the only work experience you have is flipping burgers or stocking shelves. It says you chose to work. The more and varied experiences you have, the better you'll look--at least on paper.

Volunteer Community Service

Having recently celebrated the Year of the Volunteer, President Bush and the First Lady officially recognized the importance that volunteering makes in all our communities. Volunteering speaks highly of the way we view our neighbors, reaching out to help when needed. Those who give of themselves make a statement--that they are willing to help. Because law enforcement and security are heavily into interacting with and helping people, any experience in doing so will reflect positively on you.

Many people looking for work, especially younger people, become frustrated that most employers want some experience. How do you get experience without a job? Volunteering in any way in your community is an exceptional opportunity to gain experience.

Work-Related Experience

While experience not directly related to your career goals has many benefits associated with it, you may be eager to become involved in the fields of law enforcement or public security. Opportunities for such experiences are abundant and provide a strong base from which to seek employment.

Explorer posts, for example, provide opportunity to combine social and learning experiences. Similar to Boy Scouts and Girl Scouts, law enforcement explorer groups have a great deal of fun while learning about the profession. Generally sponsored by a community law enforcement agency, explorers learn such skills as shooting, first aid, defensive tactics, and crime scene investigation. Good-hearted competition helps to hone these valuable skills.

Police reserve units also serve several valuable functions. Not only do such units provide backup to the paid officers in such situations as crowd control and crime scene searches, but it is yet another chance for people to gain experience in the field while serving their community. Participating in a reserve unit says that a person can work as part of a team while being associated with law enforcement and not abusing this association.

Volunteer fire departments offer another opportunity to do more than "get your feet wet (literally)." Firefighting, recognized as an extraordinarily dangerous activity, demands the same attributes required of officers. A cool head, the ability to work on a team, the ability to confront dangerous obstacles, proves that under fire, you can do it. Because officers may answer fire calls, too, it helps to know how to respond.

Other agencies have opportunities that provide valuable experience. For example, some sheriffs' departments have special rescue squads, water patrol units, and even mounted posses--all staffed by volunteers. Some departments have opportunities available for qualified individuals to provide patrol services to supplement their paid officers. In addition, some colleges have security departments staffed by students, another excellent opportunity to acquire experience in private "policing."

Military Service

Military service has many advantages for people considering work in the fields of security and law enforcement. First, military service provides an opportunity to enter an admirable field of work with absolutely no previous experience. It allows you to gain valuable experience while enhancing your reputation and developing maturity--not to mention drawing a paycheck.

Military service is a great chance to spend some time serving your country, even if you aren't sure about what your final career goals will be. Rather than wasting the time after high school or even college drifting, the service lets you demonstrate your ability to develop in a professional field.

Employers recognize that law enforcement and security are para-military and that successful military service is a very good indication of potential success in such civilian service. If you know early enough that you seek involvement in security or law enforcement, getting into a military policing unit can give you valuable experience.

On the other hand, the trend is toward a more humanistic, less authoritarian style of policing in both the public and private sectors. Because the military trains its officers to follow military law rather than the U.S. Constitution, such training may be a detriment to civilian policing. Keep a balanced, realistic view of the value of military experience.

Education

Education is more important today than ever in many fields, including law enforcement and private security. If these fields are to be considered professions, which they are striving to do, then education plays an important role.

Education says something about those who obtain it. It says the person can identify, pursue, and accomplish important goals. It shows patience, drive, and self-determination. It shows the ability to commit to both short- and long-range goals. It says those seeking education are interested in both themselves and the world in which they live.

Education *does* make you view the world differently. Education expands horizons, helping you better understand the differences that make our heterogeneous society not a threat, but a challenge.

In addition, many agencies now *require* some college. According to a survey conducted for the Police Executive Research Forum (Vanguard, 1989, p.46): "Fourteen percent of the law enforcement agencies in the nation's larger state and local jurisdictions require all newly hired sworn officers to have some level of college education." This same survey found that:

> . . . college-educated officers have better police service skills than other officers, that they are more "professionally oriented" and have fewer misconduct problems, and they are more adaptable to change.

As noted by Lynch (1987, p.274), president of the John Jay College of Criminal Justice in New York City: "For the last 20 years, every national commission on violence and crime in America has concluded that college education can improve police performance--a conclusion that may jar the thinking of many outside law enforcement." Lynch points out that physicians typically receive 11,000 hours of training, lawyers 9,000 hours, far more than police officers. He notes that over fifteen years ago the National Advisory Committee on Criminal Justice Standards and Goals warned: "There are few professions today that do not require a college degree. Police, in their quest for greater professionalism should take notice."

No longer do legal barriers stand in the way of police departments requiring college education. In *Davis v. Dallas* (1986), a U.S. Court of Appeals upheld a requirement by the City of Dallas that entry-level police recruits have completed 45 college credits with a C average.

Communication Skills

Communication skills are critical for public and private officers. They will communicate orally and in writing every day. How well they can communicate will, to a great extent, determine how far they advance.

Writing skills are especially important because once something is in writing, it is *permanent.* In 1987 Minnesota's county attorneys were surveyed about their opinions on police reports. Fifty-two of the eighty-seven attorneys (60%) responded. Of those responding, **98%** felt that police reports were either "critically important" or "very important" to the successful prosecution of criminal cases. Among their comments were the following:

* The police reports are often the first impression a judge or defense attorney has of an officer's competence, both generally and in regard to the specific elements of the offense charged.

* The decision to charge someone with a crime is based upon the police reports, usually alone.

* Good police reports help to speed up the entire system. Delays in prosecution often occur because of incomplete reports.

* A well-written report alone can settle a case.

Any experiences you can have that enhance your ability to communicate, both orally and in writing, are extremely important.

INTERNING

A great way to break into the real world of work while still learning is participating in an internship. As an intern, you get to work on the job as an educational experience. While internships are seldom paid positions, the experience itself is priceless.

Internships give you an inside look into fields that seldom open themselves to outsiders. You may be expected to merely observe, on the one hand, or to take a very active part in all aspects of the job. Be it helping to investigate a homicide at the crime scene or helping a probation officer interview a client, interning provides an excellent chance to combine experiential learning with academic learning, a true educational experience. It also provides a means to determine if this is the profession for you.

PAINTING A PICTURE

The job application process is an opportunity to present a picture of yourself to a prospective employer. The experiences you have developed for yourself are what the picture is made of. What experiences do you have that make a statement, and what do they say about you? ***********

MAKING THE BEST OF BAD SITUATIONS

How many people can honestly say that they have absolutely no blemishes on their records? If you are like most people, you learn more by making mistakes than by doing it right the first time. Did you really believe your mother when she told you the stove was hot? Honestly? Or did you just have to see for yourself?

Until it finally fell apart from age, I used to keep a poster above my desk that read: *When life gives you lemons, make lemonade.* However you say it, if you have made a mistake--which everyone has--it does not mean you have forfeited your future in security and law enforcement.

Granted, *some* mistakes will bar you from these fields. No state, for example, will permit you to be a police officer if you have a felony on your record. They may, however, allow a misdemeanor or traffic offense.

Know in advance how you will deal with past mistakes. Begin by accepting that they do not automatically make you an outcast from society or from your chosen profession. Most professions accept mistakes, but they do *not* accept people who cannot change their ways, nor do they accept dishonesty. To lie on a police or security application says nothing less than that you can't be trusted--that you are a liar. It may even be a crime. For example, *to lie on a federal job application is a felony*.

How do you deal with blemishes such as traffic citations or misdemeanor criminal charges? First, approach them up front and honestly. Since the best defense is often a good offense, you will usually want to confront these issues head on. It looks better if you bring them up rather than having the employer learn about them during the background check. If they dredge up one questionable issue from your past, it is reasonable for them to wonder what else might be hidden.

Once you have admitted you have made a mistake (or two, or three), take it one step farther. Share what you learned from the experience. If you have a less-than-perfect traffic record or a shoplifting charge from your youth, it would sound better to explain how that experience influenced you to want to become a police officer or a security officer.

Imagine how a hiring board would accept being told that you were so influenced by the professionalism exhibited by the police officers who gave you those tickets that you wanted to become a police officer and positively influence others in the same way.

What about a DWI conviction? Rather than eliminating you from the running, it could result in your taking subsequent steps to get your life together. To admit any shortcoming and prove you took advantage of an opportunity to grow and change does not make you an undesirable person. It makes you exceptional.

You can't change the past. You *can* present it so it looks positive rather than negative. Imagine, for example, that you had a questionable driving record and were in competition with one other applicant. Other than the driving record, you have identical attributes. Would the hiring board use your driving record to decide against you? Or maybe even for you? They might if you accept that you are what you are. Present yourself in the best light--honestly. While you might have made some admittedly questionable decisions in the past, you want them to fully understand that that was then and you learned from it. To do otherwise makes you look, at best, on the defensive and, at worst, a liar.

Judge for yourself which of the following sounds best in response to an interviewer's question: "How is your driving record?"

Candidate #1. Fine. (If this is true, great. But it will take about ten seconds to verify this on the computer. If you lied, you're out.)

Candidate #2. Well, I've had a few tickets. But I was only a kid, and the cops in my town had it in for me because of that. I think they just had to meet their quotas and it was easier to do picking on us kids.

Candidate #3. As a matter of fact, I got some traffic tickets when I was a teenager. I can't say I didn't deserve them because I did. I learned about obeying traffic regulations the hard way--having to work summer jobs to pay for the tickets and the increased car insurance premiums. But it taught me a valuable lesson. *I* was accountable for my actions. It wasn't the fault of the officers who gave me the tickets or my parents for not picking up the tab. It was my own fault. It worked for me. This is one reason I want to be a police officer--to help others learn.

You get the picture. Consider another situation, this time with candidates responding to an interviewer's question: "Have you ever used illegal drugs?"

Candidate #1. No. I would never do anything illegal. (Again, if this is true, great. But if the usual background investigation proves you to be a liar, you are out.)

Candidate #2. To be honest, as a teenager I did experiment a few times with marijuana. Most of my friends did pot, and I gave in to their pressure. It didn't do a thing for me, and I was forced to think about who was running my life--my friends or me. I knew it was time to stand up for myself, and it was quite a learning experience. In fact, most of my friends quit too. We each thought the others expected it of us. What an eye-opener that was!

LAW ENFORCEMENT, PRIVATE SECURITY, AND ETHICS

Ethics has become a "buzzword" of the 1990s in almost every profession. Certainly law enforcement and private security demand the highest of ethics. You can anticipate eventually having to deal with this issue. In fact, ethics is a favorite topic of interview boards, so you should thoughtfully consider your values and what you consider ethical behavior is.

To develop and maintain a professional reputation, codes of ethics have been adopted in both law enforcement and private security. The following code of ethics of the Law Enforcement/Private Security Relationship Committee is one example of such a code (*Private Security*, 1976, p.124).

Code of Ethics for Private Security Employees

In recognition of the significant contribution of private security to crime prevention and reduction, as a private security employee, I pledge:

To accept the responsibilities and fulfill the obligations of my role: protecting life and property; preventing and reducing crimes against my employer's business, or other organizations and institution to which I am assigned; upholding the law; and respecting the constitutional rights of all persons.

To conduct myself with honesty and integrity and to adhere to the highest moral principles in the performance of my security duties.

To be faithful, diligent, and dependable in discharging my duties, and to uphold at all times, the laws, policies, and procedures that protect the rights of others.

To observe the precepts of truth, accuracy and prudence, without allowing personal feelings, prejudices, animosities or friendships to influence my judgements.

To report to my superiors, without hesitation, any violation of the law or of my employer's or client's regulations.

To respect and protect the confidential and privileged information of my employer or client beyond the term of my employment, except where their interests are contrary to law or this Code of Ethics.

To cooperate with all recognized and responsible law enforcement and government agencies in matters within their jurisdiction.

To accept no compensation, commission, gratuity, or other advantage without the knowledge and consent of my employer.

To conduct myself professionally at all times, and to perform my duties in a manner that reflects credit upon myself, my employer, and private security.

To strive continually to improve my performance by seeking training and educational opportunities that will better prepare me for my private security duties.

The ethics of police and security officers play a large role in whether these fields are viewed as true professions. One area frequently called into question is that of "gratuities," alluded to in preceding private security code of ethics. The image of a uniformed officer enjoying free donuts and coffee in the corner donut shop is all too familiar. As Pennon and Skinner (1988, p.32) ask: "What are we really-- unequivocal, strong individuals or part-time moochers?"

Any questions related to ethics that arise during an interview should be answered thoughtfully and carefully. In considering your answer to questions involving ethics, remember Stephen Covey's caveat: "There is no right way to do a wrong thing."

Sherman (1982, p.109), Director of Research at the Police Foundation in Washington, DC, lists the following values often associated with police officers that should be guarded against.

* Discretion A: Decisions about whether to enforce the law, in any but the most serious cases, should be guided by both what the law says and who the suspect is.

* Discretion B: Disrespect for police authority is a serious offense that should always be punished with an arrest or the use of force.

* Force: Police officers should never hesitate to use physical or deadly force against people who "deserve it," or where it can be an effective way of solving crime.

* Due Process: Due process is only a means of protecting criminals at the expense of the law-abiding and should be ignored whenever it is safe to do so.

* Truth: Lying and deception are an essential part of the police job, and even perjury should be used if it is necessary to protect yourself or get a conviction on a "bad guy."

* Time: You cannot go fast enough to chase a car thief or traffic violator, nor slow enough to get to a "garbage" call; and when there are no calls for service, your time is your own.

* Rewards: Police do very dangerous work for low wages, so it is proper to take any extra rewards the public wants to give them, like free meals, Christmas gifts, or even regular monthly payments (in some cities) for special treatment.

* Loyalty: The paramount duty is to protect your fellow officers at all costs, as they would protect you, even though you may have to risk your own career or your own life to do it.

Although many of these values may be very apparent in popular TV shows and movies depicting public and private officers, all are totally unethical. Watch for such topics during a job interview and guard against answers that would conform with the stereotype rather than with the ethical behavior expected of a 1990's professional.

CONCLUSION

Your life is like a painting being continuously worked on. It will be developed and refined, changed and altered, bettered and improved. It is never completed. Although the canvas may occasionally be briefly set aside, the oil is never completely dried--unless you allow it to be.

At every phase of your life, you will appear to others as you have developed yourself. How will you appear to prospective employers? How can you add to your "life's painting" to be as appealing as possible? If you need more substance to your picture, get it. You have the control, the opportunity. Do you have the ambition and foresight?

REFERENCES

Gilbert, G. Ronald; Price, Robert O.; and Whiteside, Carl W. "Characteristics of the Best Officers on the Force," *The Police Chief,* Vol. LV, No. 9, September 1988, pp.27-29.

"Indiana University Develops Police Selection Procedure," *Target* 6, No.8, September 1977, p.1.

Lynch, Gerald W. "Cops and College," *America,* April 4, 1987, pp.274-275.

Pennon, Bruce L. and Skinner, Gilbert H. "Doughnut Shop Ethics: There are Answers," *The Police Chief*, December 1988, pp.32-33.

Private Security: Report of the Task Force on Private Security. National Advisory Committee on Criminal Justice Standards and Goals, Washington, DC: U.S. Government Printing Office, 1976.

Remesch, Kimberly A. "Shared Responsibility," *Police,* November 1989, pp.32-35, 67.

Sherman, Lawrence. "Learning Police Ethics," *Criminal Justice Ethics,* Winter/Spring, 1982, pp.10-19, in *Criminal Justice, 1989/90,* John J. Sullivan and Joseph L. Victor, editors. Guilford, CT: The Dushkin Publishing Group, Inc., 1989, pp.105-113.

Vanguard. "14 Percent of Agencies Require Some College," *The Minnesota Police Journal*, October 1989, p.46.

MIND STRETCHES*******

1. Do you believe your past is an accurate assessment of your employment potential?

2. Who would be a better risk as an employee: candidates who tested the system as juveniles, occasionally having run-ins with the law, or candidates who walked the "straight and narrow," never doing anything "wrong," but also never testing their own limitations?

3. What are important benefits of attending college?

4. What volunteer opportunities exist in your community?

5. What do good writing skills say about you? How can you develop them?

6. If you were an employer, name five important attributes you would seek, regardless of the job. How can you develop these attributes?

7. Why is ethics of particular importance to law enforcement and private security?

8. As you look at your past, are there facts that could hurt you as a job applicant? How will you address them to put them in the most positive light?

9. What are your personal and professional strengths?

10. Is it possible to be "over-qualified"? Why or why not?

"Man, I got job skills galore!"

AN INSIDER'S VIEW

DON'T SHOOT YOURSELF IN THE FOOT

Scott M. Knight
Sergeant
Chaska Police Department

Congratulations! You have survived a multitude of academic and technical requirements and are now eligible to be considered an officer candidate. You have invested a great deal of time and money toward a future career in law enforcement. Carefully note the phrasing _a_ career, not _your_ career. Over half of you reading this book will not get the job you have prepared so hard for. Why? For one of two reasons:

* Sheer numbers--odds.
* You.

The first reason--competition--you can do nothing about except never forget it. Everybody wants the job you want! Your degree, technical certification, and/or practical training will not guarantee you a job. Quite simply, more people seek employment in police work than there are positions.

The second reason--You--fortunately is entirely under your control. You must sell yourself if you want the prospective employer to select you. Just because you land an interview, don't rest now! Far too many people are tragically naive. They believe that once they have completed their schooling, getting hired is automatic. Remember, you are being interviewed because you meet the minimum criteria, on paper, as do all others being interviewed. So why should I hire you? I expect you to tell me why (or why not) during the interview.

At this point, you may be saying, "Tell me something I don't know." But if most people do know these things before meeting me, they forget it all when they walk in our door for their interview. What should they know?

I'd like to share with you how I evaluate officer candidates from start to finish. I have no unique magic formula, nor does anyone else. Each agency has its own system and style of candidate selection. No matter what technique is used, however, selection truly is a *process of elimination.* Remember, the first reason you won't get hired--competition--and the second reason--You. Most interviewees assist the agency by eliminating themselves in a number of ways.

Has my thrust become redundant yet? I hope so, because many people make a huge career investment and do not get past the interview. They shoot themselves in the foot at show time. The following perspectives tell you how to keep that gun holstered.

The Application

Some process--an advertisement, a professional recruiting system/service, or other means--has made you aware of a job opening. You receive a job description, a list of minimum requirements, and an application. You complete the application, return it, and anxiously await a response, an appointment for an interview.

STOP! Check to see if your gun is smoking. Do you have a hole in your foot?

Your application is the first look I get at you. I wouldn't be human if I didn't form at least a partial opinion about you based on what you submit. It's entirely up to you the opinion I form.

First I look at the overall quality. Is it prepared in pencil, pen, or typed? Can I read it? (Remember, officers spend a great deal of time writing reports others must read and understand.)

Second I look at content. Have you filled out the application completely? Answered all questions? Followed directions? Have you included any additional documentation requested? Have you met the deadline? The application is a very important step. Many people eliminate themselves from consideration immediately by not recognizing this and are never called for an interview.

Many candidates also submit resumes. They are very nice, usually professionally prepared, listings of your education, accomplishments, and goals. In my opinion, resumes are not necessary for entry-level officer positions. Your well-prepared application carries far more weight with me than a resume.

Your application is what I read first and last. The resume will fall somewhere in between. Remember the competition? Remember then, I have several applications to read and screen. Unfortunately, too many people treat the hiring agencies' application as secondary. Apparently, they believe a dazzling resume will "knock their socks off." Somehow their resume, more than our carefully designed application, will create a great desire on my part to meet this candidate and forgive a poor job on the application. This is a major mistake. Hopefully, you will provide a living resume during the interview.

The Interview

If you apply with our department, you potentially face two interviews. During the first you will meet with me and two officers from the patrol division. Remember the competition? This interview, intentionally short (30 minutes), is a screening interview. It is entirely up to you to convince us to invite you back.

If you make the first cut, you are invited to a second interview. This time you meet with the chief of police, our chief investigator, and me. This interview is longer and more in depth. Four absolutes:

 * Arrive early.
 * Be well groomed.
 * Talk.
 * Be honest.

Arrive Early. At minimum, arrive at least 15 minutes ahead of your scheduled appointment. It is very important we be considerate to all applicants and afford everyone the same amount of time. We maintain a tight schedule, and rarely do we keep an applicant waiting. I consider your time to be very valuable. I appreciate your interest in our department, and I sincerely want your interview to be enjoyable. Don't keep the interviewers waiting for you.

Be Well Groomed. How you present yourself speaks volumes. It tells me how you feel about yourself, your career pursuit, and our position. Look clean, neat, and professional. That is how we will expect you to look when you represent our department.

Talk. Interview formats differ. No matter what format is used, however, you are expected to talk. In fact, you are responsible for most all conversation. I am amazed at the number of candidates who simply sit and say nothing. If you suddenly realize you are responding with yes/no answers, or there are long pauses, or the interviewer is doing most of the talking, you are in trouble.

Be Honest. Unlike any other job you have ever applied for, you will be interviewed by professional, experienced police officers. Relax and be yourself! Don't try to guess what type of person we are looking for. You can have no idea and make a reckless gamble if you try.

Don't lie. Cops hone in on a lie almost faster than any other reflex. If you are perceived as untruthful, you have not just shot yourself in the foot; check for the hole in your head.

If you are selected as the top candidate, an extensive background investigation will be conducted before you are hired. So, address during the interview any possible issues or problems in your past. Have the first word! If you raise these points and offer understandable, acceptable explanations, you can minimize the damage. In fact, you can make a problem work to your advantage at times and generate respect and credibility.

Don't gamble. Anything out there *will* be discovered during the background investigation.

After the Interview

"Don't call us. We'll call you." Please. After your interview has come and gone, so has your opportunity to "give it your best shot." Unless you are told to or invited to call back, don't. This may sound pompous and ostentatious, but this position has valid reasons behind it. When you leave the interview, your work is done. We, on the other hand, have to evaluate your performance independently and collectively. We may have 30 to 50 other people to interview and as many comparisons to make.

Rest assured, most departments strive to make timely, responsible notifications. As we give all candidates equal interviewing opportunities, we maintain this posture through our entire process.

Attributes and Characteristics of the Ideal Candidate

An exact listing of the particular attributes and characteristics I personally look for in officer candidates is difficult. The practice of licensing peace officers has caused dynamic advancements in the quality of Minnesota law enforcement. It is also a great equalizer for entry-level officers. All have met the same academic and technical standard. Thus, selection is based on the science/art of choosing the person whose personality best melds with our department's approach and philosophy.

When I look at candidates, I consider all factors previously discussed. Beyond these factors, I look at how the person responds to specific questions. Certain common questions are asked in every interview, regardless of the format or interview style.

Typically, "Why do you want to be a police officer?" is one such question. The answer varies in substance with each person. Anything from a vomited rehearsed speech to a vague, gray mumbling is offered. Either extreme usually boils down to, "Because I want to help people."

Okay. Why do you want to help people? How do you think you will be able to help people? All kinds of vocations are built around helping people. What you must tell me is:

--Why do you want to help people?

--How do you feel police officers help people?

-*And,* how do you envision incorporating the first two answers into your performance as a police officer?

If you can do this in a sincere and *concise* answer, you will have captured my attention.

Overall, I look at each candidate from this standpoint:

Is this person someone I would want to respond to an emergency or crisis at my home?

Best of luck in your job search! Keep that gun holstered and your feet intact.

CHAPTER 8

THE RESUME:

SELLING YOURSELF ON PAPER

Writing a Resume: Spend time on self-assessment first. Identify all the achievements of your past that illustrate skills. Describe them in active verbs and look for consistencies. That's the clue as to what you should emphasize. A resume is scanned, not read. It's a sales tool that should give someone a sampling, not details in full.--Jean Clarkson

Do You Know:.

* What a resume is?

* What purpose it serves?

* What should be included?

* What is best left out?

* How it should appear?

* What types of formats you can use?

* What type best suits your situation?

* What your resume says about you?

* How to strengthen your resume?

* How your resume should be delivered?

INTRODUCTION

You've spent a lot of time thinking about your goals and yourself, your fitness, education, attributes. Now it's time to pull all this information together into one of your most important job-seeking tools--the resume.

You probably know what a resume is. But that's a little like saying you know what surgery is. A vast amount of territory exists between recognizing a concept and grasping its true meaning. To have a working understanding of such a concept is even more involved.

This chapter gives a working knowledge of the resume. *Resume* is a French word pronounced *REZ-oo-may* and means "summary." In French, the two "e's" have accents over them, but since you're writing in English, it's all right to omit them.

What is a resume? Webster's defines *resume* as: "A short account of one's career and qualifications prepared typically by an applicant for a position." Weinstein (1982, p.26) expands on Webster's definition, explaining that: "A resume is simply a brief, well-documented account of your career qualifications. . . . a capsulized account that *highlights* and describes *significant* aspects of your background and qualifications for a given job. . . . It is a statement of purpose, a summation. Realistically, it is a sales promotion tool designed to sell you."

According to Jean Reed (1986, p.3): "For the job applicant, a resume has become an indispensable tool. A good resume can be the most important factor in determining whether a prospective employer decides to call you in for an interview. In short, a well-prepared resume may literally get you a 'foot in the door.'"

Corwen (1988, p.1) reiterates this idea when he says of the resume:

> It is your autobiography, condensed to fit a #10 envelope. . . . Your resume is like a snapshot which, once developed, becomes a permanent reflection of you. And, since it will probably precede you in all of your dealings with prospective employers, it must be the best image you can project. Otherwise, you will be among the thousands of eager, qualified job applicants who walk the streets or sit at home or at the office waiting for the mail that never comes, the phone that never rings, and the job that never materializes. . . .
>
> The competition to attract an employer's attention is keen, bitter, and brutal. You need every tool you can get, and at the outset your resume is the only one you have.

Besides knowing what a resume is, it also is important to know what it is *not*. As noted by Weinstein (1982, p.26), a resume is not:

* Your life story typed neatly on two pieces of letter-size paper.
* A chronological listing of dates and places
* A boring recount of your life to the present.
* An exercise in tedium.
* A compilation of self-congratulatory adjectives.

Your resume may be your first contact with a potential employer. It may also be the last. The choice is yours. The resume is important for the employer *and* for you.

In some instances, however, particularly larger law enforcement agencies, resumes are not used because they go through a civil service commission. Applicants fill in only the civil service commission's paperwork and can add nothing to it. A resume can backfire if you include it and it is *not* asked for or wanted.

THE PURPOSES OF THE RESUME

The resume is important to the *employer* because it helps *weed out* unqualified candidates. This is its most important function to most employers. They will use any flaw in a resume to cut down the number of individuals to be interviewed. Resumes also serve positive purposes for employers. They help employers cut through a lot of preliminary questioning about applicants' qualifications. They also help employers to structure their interviews.

The resume is important to *you* because it can help get you in the door for an interview. It serves other purposes as well. Preparing your resume will force you to take a good hard look at your skills and qualifications, at your past experiences and accomplishments. It will force you to recall (or look up) dates and addresses. It will force you to organize your past in a clear, concise way. This will help you present yourself in an organized manner during the interview as well. In addition, you can approach the interview confident that you have the qualities and background the employer is looking for, or why would you be called in?

During the interview, it will save time because you will have a common ground to start from. Further, the resume will keep you honest. The temptation to exaggerate your past experience or accomplishments will be removed when you know the employer has seen your resume. Now that you know how important your resume is, look at the specific steps in creating one.

STEPS IN CREATING A RESUME

Creating a resume is like painting a picture of yourself. From the conception of the idea to the completion of the masterpiece, you need to take seven specific steps.

1. Compile all relevant information in a worksheet.
2. Select the most appropriate type of resume.
3. Decide on a format.
4. Write a first draft.
5. Polish your draft.
6. Evaluate the resume. Revise if needed.
7. Have it printed.

Creating an effective resume is *hard work*, but the results will be well worth it. Without an effective resume, you are wasting your time applying for most jobs. You won't get to first base--the interview. Even if an agency does not require a resume, they will expect you to be a "living resume" at the interview. Get yourself organized before that. Make up your mind to devote several hours to this important document.

COMPILE INFORMATION

Gather all the information that could possibly be included in your resume. Some will be used; some won't. But painters gather all their brushes and paints before they begin to work so they aren't interrupted during the creative process. Likewise, you want at your fingertips all the information you *might* decide to include. You don't want to interrupt the creative flow of writing by having to look up a phone number or address.

Use the worksheets in Appendix A to organize your resume information. Don't cut corners during this first step. Your background makes a great deal of difference, especially in the fields of law enforcement and private security. As you compile information, you may be amazed at how much data an employer will need to even consider you.

Don't guess at dates. Verify them. Don't guess at addresses. Check them out if it has been several years since you last worked or lived there.

You'll look at three kinds of information: (1) data you must include, (2) data you might include, and (3) data you should probably not include but should be prepared to discuss. Look first at what *MUST* be included.

Personal Identifying Information

Name. Obvious? Yes. Believe it or not, some people actually forget to include their name. In addition, think carefully about how you want your name to appear. Do you want to include your middle name? An initial? A nickname?

If you include a nickname, put it following your first name with quotation marks around it like this: *Robert "Bob" T. Jones.* This lets the employer know what you prefer to be called. Avoid extreme or inappropriate nicknames like "Killer." How do you want your name to appear in your resume? *******

Address. It is usually best to give only your home address. Put the street address on one line. Do not abbreviate. Put a comma between a street address and an apartment number. Put the city and state on the next line with a comma between the city and state. Use the two letter state abbreviation--both letters capitalized and NO period. Include your zip code. Do *not* put a comma between state and zip code.

Example: 123 Third Avenue South, #401
                      My Town, MN 55437

If you move frequently, you may want to include a permanent address in addition to your present address. *******

Phone Number. *Always* include a phone number. Busy employers often prefer to call rather than write. Make it easy for them. Put the area code in parentheses, followed by your phone number. Indicate if it is a home phone or a work phone number. Some people give both. Many people prefer to *not* include a work phone to avoid being called at work. Would getting job-seeking-related calls at work cause you any problems? If so, do *not* include your work number.

Some people also include the hours they can be reached at a given number. Others put this information in their cover letter.

Example: Home Phone (612) 888-8818 (6 to 10 pm)
                      Work Phone (612) 999-9929 (9 to 5)
****

Did you know there was so much to think about in simply giving your name, address, and phone number?

Education

College. List each college attended, city and state, number of years completed, major/minor, unique areas of study, and degree(s) earned. Start with the most recent and work backwards. Include any honors, awards, or positions of leadership. Include grade point average *if* outstanding. *******

Professional Schools. Include the same information as for colleges. Include police academies here also. *******

Certificates Held. Relevant certificates would include first-aid, CPR, and the like. Give the year the certificates were awarded and expiration date if relevant. *******

Other Educational Experiences. Include here any relevant seminars, workshops, correspondence courses, and the like. *******

High School. Include name, city and state, year of graduation, grade point average if it is outstanding. Include your high school *only* if you graduated within the last ten years or if you have no other education to include. *******

Work Experience

Begin with your present job, or your most recent job if you are not currently employed. Work back in time. Use the worksheet in Appendix A. Make as many copies of this worksheet as you have had jobs. Of special importance are the qualifications and skills you bring to the job. According to McNally and Schiff (1986, p.243-244): "[W]hatever the job, your resume should stress achievements more than education and experience. After all, education and experience do not guarantee performance." They suggest that managers like to see the following qualifications and skills in candidates:

* Ability to complete a project.
* Energy and willingness to work hard.
* Motivation; ability to work without close supervision.
* Communication skills.
* Enthusiasm.
* Cooperation; ability to get along with others.
* Integrity and reliability.
* Leadership skills.
* Loyalty; the desire to be a team player.
* Organizational ability and planning skills.
* Professional commitment.

Wherever and however you can in your work experience section, demonstrate these qualities and skills. In fact, if applicable, you might also demonstrate these qualities and skills in the education portion of your resume as well. *******

In summary, the three basic areas you *must* include in your resume are personal identifying information, your educational background, and your work experience. Several other areas might be included also, depending on your specific background.

Even if you do decide *not* to include much or most of this information, it is important for you to think about and have clear in your mind because the information could come up during the interview.

Position Desired or Employment Objective. What specific job do you have in mind? Are you open to any position in law enforcement, security, or related work? This information can be very helpful to busy employers as they skim through stacks of resumes. An example might be: *Position desired: Entry-level officer with opportunity for rapid advancement.* *******

Other Information. Other information that may be put in your resume includes the following: birthdate, height, weight, health, travel (if willing to travel), location (if willing to relocate), military experience, professional memberships, foreign language(s) ability, foreign travel, awards, publications, community service or involvement, interests and hobbies.

You might also want to include your availability, that is, can you start immediately or do you need a certain amount of time to give notice to your present employer? Can your present employer be contacted?

Your resume should also include a statement that "References are available on request." Be sure they are. Choose them *now* and fill in that portion of the worksheet in Appendix A. Try to have business/professional/academic references and personal references. Choose your references carefully. *Always* ask your references if they are willing to provide you with a *positive* reference. Most people do *not* include the references in their resumes. You can simply state: "References available on request." *******

Photograph. Some books on resumes suggest that a photograph should never be included on or with a resume. Other books highly recommend it. Those who would not include a photograph suggest that it violates anti-discrimination laws, providing information an employer cannot legally ask about. For example race, sex, and approximate age are revealed in a photograph. If you feel these factors may work in your favor, you may decide to include a photograph.

One advantage of including a photograph is that it will probably make your resume stand out from the rest--always a primary goal. However, unless the photo represents you in a way the employer will appreciate, it could detract from the comfortable black-and-white print approach a resume affords. If you do include a photograph, be certain it is recent, professional, and puts you in a favorable light. You should be neatly groomed and the reproduction should be clear and crisp.

WHAT NOT TO INCLUDE

What not to include is a matter of opinion. You obviously want to present yourself as positively as possible. While you will *never* lie on a resume, you will want to present yourself so that even negative occurrences look good for you. If you have to explain them in depth during an interview, that's fine, as long as you *get* to the interview. What *not* to include depends to a great extent on your particular circumstances.

Including too much data is the *number one* fault on resumes. Not only does it present a document that won't get read, but you can harm yourself by saying too much. You will usually have no need to state in a resume why you left past jobs. If the reason was somewhat spectacular, for example a series of promotions, put it in. The presumption will be that you moved upward and onward to better positions.

Exceptionally personal data can also detract from the emphasis that should be on *you*. If you want to state your family status, fine. But don't give names and ages of everyone in your family. Does the employer really care? Could it work against you? What if you have very young children and the employer thinks you should be at home with them? What if the employer sees your children are all grown and concludes you are too old for the position?

The resume is not the place to deal with difficulties you may have experienced. It is a chance to provide a *brief* overview of yourself which will be expanded on once it has served as a ticket to get you into the interview. Make certain everything you include is relevant and cannot in any way detract.

Avoid Including. Items that should *not* be included in your resume:

> * Reasons for leaving your current or previous job.
> * Salary (previous or desired).
> * Religion or church affiliations.
> * Race, ethnic background, nationality, color.
> * Political affiliations/preferences.
> * Anything that negatively dates your resume, such as your age or
>   ages of your children.

SELECT THE TYPE OF RESUME

When you go fishing you select the bait that will best serve your purpose based on the specific conditions that exist at that particular time and the fish you're after. You should have all the bait you need to land an interview in the form of the data about yourself you have just put together. Now decide how to present it. Three basic types of resumes are appropriate for positions in law enforcement, private security, and related fields:

> * Historical or Chronological
> * Functional
> * Analytical

Each type has a specific format, specific content, and serves a specific purpose.

Historical/Chronological Approach

The historical/chronological resume is the most traditional and is often considered the most effective approach. As implied by the name, this style presents information in the order in which it occurred, but goes backward in time. The educational and employment information worksheets in the appendix are organized this way. Both education and employment lend themselves to this style. Always include dates. Explain any gaps in the chronology.

The historical/chronological resume is easy to read and gives busy employers a familiar, quick-reading form. According to Corwen (1988, p.24) you should use a chronological resume if:

> * You have spent three or more years with previous employers and have not changed jobs frequently.
>
> * You are seeking a position in the same field in which you have been employed during the course of your career.
>
> * You have worked for prestigious companies that are well known.
>
> * You can show steady growth in responsibilities and salary.
>
> * Your references are impeccable.

The chronological resume is best when staying in the same field. It is not the best format if you have little related experience. See Appendix B for a sample chronological resume.

Functional Resume

The functional resume emphasizes your qualifications and abilities as they relate to the job you are applying for. After each job you briefly describe your duties and expertise. Dates do not receive as much attention.

This style is most applicable if you have had only a few jobs or have been with a particular company or department for a long time. Such a resume stresses experiences and abilities rather than a chronological listing of jobs.

The functional resume minimizes irrelevant jobs, employment gaps, reversals, and maximizes scant work experience. Corwen (1988, p.24) suggests you use a functional resume if:

* You are seeking a job in a new field not related to your present career.

* You are re-entering the job market after a long absence.

* You have been unemployed for more than three months.

* Your present salary is below average for your age and experience.

* Your duties and responsibilities are complicated and require explanation.

* You can point to specific accomplishments while on your last two jobs.

* You have an age problem, having to compete with younger applicants for the same level position.

See Appendix B for a sample functional resume.

Analytical Resume

The analytical resume stresses an order of your particular skills. This style is good for changing career goals. It lets you stress *skills* and *talents* instead of past jobs. Dates are usually omitted, but past jobs and experiences are referred to at some point. Again, you must determine if this approach can best reflect your particular abilities.

The analytical resume is especially helpful if you are changing career goals but you have obtained necessary skills and qualifications from your present and past jobs. See Appendix B for a sample analytical resume.

You may be wondering if these three styles are rather boring. You may want to be somewhat more creative. Think carefully about it. An imaginative or creative approach may be of great benefit, or it may burn you. The positive side of such an approach is that it may set your resume apart from the dozens, hundreds, even thousands of others, thus receiving the attention it deserves.

The negative side of an imaginative or creative resume is that it might be the reason the employer is looking for to jettison your resume, along with any others that do not appear "normal." Remember that your potential employer is probably **conservative.**

Lewis (1983, p.9) cautions: "It is dangerous to be too gimmicky or too cute. Overly creative resumes might catch the eye. Nevertheless, they often fail to sustain interest, and become completely ineffectual. Most resume readers feel that a resume is a business matter and should be presented in a businesslike manner."

If you decide to use an imaginative/creative resume, be sure to include all the information any other style would present. If you can do so, you just might be on to something. For example, what could possibly catch a police department's eye quicker than a resume that takes on the appearance of a "Wanted" poster? It might work, but give very serious consideration to such an idea at an entry-level job position in either law enforcement or private security.

FORMAT THE RESUME

The format is the layout of the information. Decide what to put first, second, and third. *Block* your material and use *headings* to guide the reader. If you have recently graduated, your educational background is probably of most importance and should come first. If you decide to include hobbies and personal information about yourself, this is usually "tucked" in at the end.

Plan for margins around the resume, that is, top and bottom as well as both sides. Use white space freely. The format you design should be attractive, businesslike, and professional. Actually *design* your format on a sheet of paper. Will you center your identifying information? Have it flush left? Will you use one or two columns for the bulk of the information? Try to format it so all the information goes on *one* page.

WRITE THE RESUME

If possible, use a word-processor to write your resume. This will make editing it much easier and will also make updating less painful. The key to writing an effective resume is to use short, action-packed *phrases.*

Short. Omit all unnecessary words. This includes:

> * Personal pronouns: *I, me*, and *my.*
> * Articles: a, an, and *the.*

Action Packed. Write with *verbs* not with *nouns.* For example, don't say *conducted an investigation*, say instead, *investigated.* Writing with verbs also is shorter than writing with nouns. Look at the following:

> I conducted an analysis of all the in-coming calls to the dispatcher,
> and I compiled detailed analytical reports based on my analysis.

Twenty-two words. Eliminate the pronouns (*I, my*) and articles (*an, the*) and use verbs instead of nouns. What you'll get is something like the following:

> Analyzed all in-coming calls and wrote up results.

Which of the two statements would you rather read? Which conveys an image of the writer as forceful and authoritative?

Phrases. Phrase your writing. Watch where lines end. Avoid hyphenating words at the end of the line. For example, read the following:

> It was a difficult job because my boss was a rat-
> her rigid person.

Get the idea? Pay attention to effective ads on television and in print and see how the words are strung together for maximum effect. You can do the same in your resume if you concentrate. Try using short "bullet" phrases that begin with active verbs. Strive for variety in the verbs you use. Here are some that might fit your experience:

achieved	decided	investigated	represented
adapted	delegated	invented	researched
administered	designed	led	reviewed
analyzed	developed	managed	revised
applied	edited	modified	scheduled
approved	educated	monitored	selected
arranged	encouraged	operated	served
assessed	established	organized	set up
assisted	evaluated	planned	solved
built	examined	presented	spoke
chaired	guided	produced	supervised
completed	hired	proved	surveyed
conducted	identified	provided	taught
consulted	improved	published	trained
controlled	increased	recorded	updated
coordinated	inspected	re-designed	wrote

Once the draft is written, let it sit, at least overnight.

EDIT AND POLISH YOUR FIRST DRAFT

First drafts simply don't cut it. Continue to work with it until it has the punch you want. Because employers are busy, say as much as you can with as few words as possible. Spend time refining each phrase. Work at developing brief statements that explain clearly and strongly what your education and experience are, what opportunities you've taken advantage of, and what qualifications and skills you would bring to the job.

You might consider hiring a professional editor or even a professional resume writer at this point. It will be much less expensive if you have completed all the background research, designed a format, and written the first draft.

Proofread your draft. Check the spelling of every word. Check every capital letter, every punctuation mark. Then check it again. Better yet, have a friend whose writing skills you respect check it for you. It is very hard to see your own writing errors. Some people find it helpful to proofread by going from right to left in each line, looking at each word.

EVALUATE AND REVISE

Use the form in Appendix A to evaluate your resume. Consider both appearance and content. Grade each category as Excellent, Average, or Poor. If a category is poor, decide how to improve it. *******

PRINTING YOUR RESUME

You are at the final step. Don't blow it now. Have your resume professionally printed. Consider the following:

* Use 8 1\2 by 11 inch, white, bond paper.

* Buy a quantity of blank paper and matching envelopes for the cover letter.

* Have it printed using black ink.

* If necessary, have it slightly reduced in size to assure adequate margins.

* Do NOT use all capital letters, script, bold, or italic print. Use such graphics sparingly.

* Most people prefer a *serif* typestyle. "Serifs" are the little curves added to the edges of letters to make them more readable. This book uses a serif typestyle. *Sans serif* typestyles do give a crisp, clean appearance, but are much harder to read.

MAKING IT A 10

Your resume is a direct reflection of you on paper. Make certain it depicts you as you want--a professional for a professional job. Everything about your resume will say something about *you*. Because employers have to start cutting back the number of finalists, they look for reasons *not* to pursue you as a candidate. For example, secretarial applicants with typos on their resumes can count on being eliminated. This would, and frequently has, served as a legitimate reason for disregarding that application for any number of other positions.

Sometimes, when there are a lot of very good applicants, reasons for getting rid of one resume and keeping another become, at best, arbitrary. What will top off an otherwise excellent resume? It may boil down to the final presentation. Just like a fine meal is made all the better in how it is served, so is a good resume.

Take time to put your resume in an attractive binder or enclose it in an attractive envelope with the name and address of the prospective employer typed. This may say that this particular applicant put that extra effort into the process and should, therefore, be given consideration--an interview. Think about it. Do not, however, use anything slippery or difficult to file. You do not want your resume to stand out from the rest because it is hard to handle.

THE COVER LETTER

Never send a resume without a cover letter, even if the employer has asked you to send a resume. Cover letters should be individually typed, addressed to a specific person and company or department, and signed. Anything less will be ineffective.

Keep your cover letter short and to the point. It is a brief personal introduction of the "you" embodied in your resume. Don't repeat resume information. Entice the reader to want to find out more about you. Make clear in your opening paragraph which type of resume submission yours is:

> * Unsolicited.

> * Written as a referral or from personal contact,
>   for example, "My mechanic told me your department
>   was looking for qualified security officers."

> * Written in response to a job advertisement.

If your letter is unsolicited, give a reason for selecting this particular employer.

Whenever possible send the letter to a specific person. Use that individual's title. It is usually a simple matter to get this information. Just call the company or department and ask who is in charge of hiring and ask for the spelling of that person's name and official title. The little time this takes can pay big dividends. As noted by Reed (1986, p.13): "Employers are people, and people tend to be complimented when you know their names and titles." Reed also suggests that you "Let your letter reflect your individuality, but avoid appearing familiar, overbearing, humorous, or cute."

An effective format for a cover-letter is the full-block style--everything begins at the left margin. The parts of the letter should be as follows:

Your Address (Street number and name, #)
Your City, State and Zip
The date you are writing

The name of the person you are writing to
That person's title
The name of the company/department
The address of the employer

Salutation (Dear . . .):

Opening paragraph--why you are writing.

Second paragraph--provide some intriguing fact about
yourself as a lead into your resume.

Concluding paragraph--suggest that you will be
calling to arrange an interview.

Complimentary closing (Sincerely, or Yours truly),

(Skip four lines--sign in this space)

Typed name

Encl: Resume

Notice the spacing between the various sections. Notice the capitalization and the colon following the salutation and the comma following the complimentary closing.

Avoid starting every sentence with "I." *Never* start with: "I am writing this letter to apply for the position I saw advertised in the paper." BORING! Focus on the reader. More effective would be something like this: "Your opening for a police officer advertised in the *Gazette* is of great interest to me." Kaplan (1987, p.82) suggests twelve steps to writing an effective cover letter:

* Type each letter individually.

* Address the employing person by name, and, if possible, by title.

* Catch the employer's attention by opening with a strong statement.

* Keep your letter short. It should be one page . . .

* Use the center of your letter to arouse the employer's curiosity by stating brief facts about your experience and accomplishments.

* Include clues that hiring you will lead to higher production, greater efficiency . . .

* Try to include a challenging thought that will cause

the employer to feel that meeting with you would be worthwhile even if there are no present openings.

* Be direct in requesting an interview.

* Sign and date your cover letter.

* Plan on mailing a group of letters at the same time.

* Prepare one for yourself and mail it with the others. (This will give you an idea of when they arrive.)

* Mail your letter so that it will arrive in employers' offices on a Tuesday, Wednesday, or Thursday.

One final suggestion--consider using certified mail, with a return receipt requested. Not only will you eliminate those nagging doubts about if it got delivered, but again, it says something to the employer about the kind of person you are. Here is a candidate concerned enough to make *sure* it arrived. That's the kind of a detail a lot of employers are looking for. See Appendix C for a sample cover letter.

HAND DELIVERING YOUR RESUME

It's always a good idea to hand deliver a resume if possible because it is a chance to present yourself so the employer associates a name with a face. Dress well and look professional when you deliver your resume. Even if you don't get to the boss, you will make a good impression on the staff person accepting it. These people can have a great deal of influence on their bosses. Don't let your guard down because you aren't dealing directly with upper management. When you drop your material off, it is another opportunity for you to emphasize that you really want the job.

Be sure to follow up. The follow up is another opportunity to prove what kind of person you are--the kind they should hire! A day or two after you have delivered your resume, write a brief letter to the employer. Recognize that the employer will be busy, and only a short letter stands a chance of being read.

Confirm that you delivered your resume and thank the employer for the chance to participate in the hiring process. Even if this merely gets stapled to your resume without getting read initially by the employer, or gets forgotten by the employer who might read it, it is something just that much different for the interview committee to see when your resume surfaces. If they are looking for reasons to keep some and get rid of others, this could be the reason yours stays in the running. See Appendix C for a sample follow-up letter.

FOR MORE HELP

Bookstores and libraries have dozens of texts on resume writing, each with its own particular advice. The references at the end of this chapter provide a start if you want to go into this topic in more detail or from other perspectives.
Your resume is critical. As noted by Weinstein (1982, p.28):

A resume is not going to get you a job. But it will propel you in the right direction . . . . If your resume is good, you will have the equivalent of a well-placed ball into center field, putting you on first base . . . . And if it's excellent or superior, you might find yourself on second base.

Suffice it to say, a good resume puts you securely in the game. The rest is up to you. Once you're on the playing field, you have to maneuver yourself accordingly so you move strategically from base to base, finally leaping to home plate and the job you worked so hard for. Understand from the start that you're never going to feel first base under your feet unless you have a winning resume.

REFERENCES

Brennan, Lawrence D., Strand, Stanley, and Gruber, Edward C. *Resumes for Better Jobs*. New York: Arco, 1987.

Corwen, Leonard. *Your Resume: Key to a Better Job*. New York: Arco, 1988.

Dickhut, Harold W. *The Professional Resume & Job Search Guide*. New York: Prentice Hall Press, 1981.

Kaplan, Robbie Miller. *Resumes: The Write Stuff. A Quick Guide to Presenting Your Qualifications Effectively*. Garrett Park, MD: Garrett Park Press, 1987.

Lewis, Adele. *How to Write Better Resumes*. 2nd ed. New York: Barron's Educational Series, Inc., 1983.

McNally, Terry and Schiff, Peter. *Contemporary Business Writing: A Problem-Solving Approach*. Belmont, CA: Wadsworth Publishing Company, 1986.

Reed, Jean. Ed. *Resumes that Get Jobs*. New York: Prentice Hall Press, 1986.

Weinstein, Bob. *Resumes for Hard Times. How to Make Yourself a Hot Property in a Cold Market*. New York: Simon and Schuster, 1982.

MIND STRETCHES******

1. Imagine you have been assigned the task of reducing an extremely large pile of resumes to a more workable number. Regardless of the position, what are five reasons you can think of to get rid of applications right away?

2. After eliminating many applications, what are three things you might look for that would make a resume stand out as being worth taking time to look at further?

3. Paint with words the picture you want your resume to make. Use three words. Use six words.

4. How can you liven up your resume?

5. What might be dangerous about preparing a resume that is too creative? What benefits might result?

6. What attributes do you have that will impress an employer?

7. What concerns do you have about your qualifications that you will need to consider in preparing your resume?

8. What are five power verbs you associate with yourself?

9. Which resume style could work best for you? Why?

10. What unique ways can you present your resume?

**"I hope they accept a resume
written on an apron."**

AN INSIDER'S VIEW

THREE KEY OPPORTUNITIES

Jim Clark
Chief
Eden Prairie Police Department

The hiring process generally affords you a minimum of three opportunities to "catch the eye" of those responsible for hiring:

* The resume and application
* The written test
* The interview

The Resume and Application

The resume and application provide the first, and most lasting, opportunity to present information about yourself. In some cases applicants are eliminated through a resume-screening process. Consequently, take great care in preparing your resume and completing the application.

The best resumes are short, truthful, and powerful. Carefully consider the qualifications before beginning to prepare your resume. Most applicants tend to "under inform" or to "over inform." For instance, if the position requires you to be licensed by the state, document your license. Generally you need not provide details of your schooling related to that license.

If, however, the hiring does not specifically require a certain qualification but you are aware that, after employment, the agency will train you in a specific skill you already have expertise in, make that known. For example, a police department may require only first aid training meeting the state requirement, but provides Emergency Medical Technician training for all officers after employment. If you are already trained to that level, make it known in your resume.

Make certain the information you provide is pertinent to the position. This demonstrates that you investigated the job requirements.

A cover letter lets you show interest also. It should be short (one page), but powerful. It gives you a chance to share something you know about the position that someone else who didn't do their "homework" would not know.

When submitting a resume or application, avoid distractions, for example, letterhead with personal graphics. Another common mistake is including pictures. Often applicants who submit pictures do more harm than good. I once reviewed an application that had a picture attached of the applicant holding a gun.

Simply stated, resumes should be clear, professional in appearance, show a strong interest, be short, and focus on the position you are applying for.

The Written Test

The second chance to "catch the eye" of those responsible for hiring is the written test. Unfortunately, being noticed in this environment without being perceived as a "pest" requires some creativity and common sense.

In the police written test setting, it is common to test hundreds of applicants at the same time. The written test is most often used as a screening device. Consequently most applicants do not try to "put their best foot forward," believing the only important part is their test score.

That belief is only partially true. In fact, in most departments, police officers and supervisors attend solely to spot and track good applicants. Even though the testing environment appears very hectic, opportunities exist to impress people. The most common mistake I have observed at a written test relates to dress. Apparently most applicants do not believe it is important to look "sharp." Remember, you may not get to talk to someone; consequently, our only memory of you may be what we see.

I have memories of people attending a written test without shoes, or wearing torn pants and T-shirts. To me this is unacceptable and demonstrates lack of concern which may spill over to work habits.

My most vivid memory of an applicant goes back approximately eight years when a young man appeared for the testing and was the only applicant in the room with a suit and tie. Needless to say, he was watched. When he was finished testing and was handing in the test, he made a point to thank our staff at the table for the opportunity to test, and on the way out the door he again thanked the chief of police. His choice of clothing and a simple thank-you on the way out left a very positive impression. It showed his common sense and a very positive personality.

Although he did not test extremely high, he tested high enough to be granted an interview and was later hired. The decision to hire him began in earnest when he took that written test.

The Interview

The third and most important opportunity you will have to "catch our eye" is at the interview. If you are among the small group of applicants fortunate enough to earn an interview, approach it like you may never have another chance.

The interview process is very difficult for the *interviewers* as well as those being interviewed. The interviewers are subjected to listening to responses to the same questions asked over and over. Consequently, how you look and present yourself may be as important as your answers.

Again, dress is very important. However, applicants sometimes make serious mistakes when selecting appropriate clothing. If it is not normal for you to "dress up," consult with someone who knows what it takes to look "sharp."

Consultants are available who will work with you, or you may consider a friend employed in a position requiring a professional appearance to help you. Either way, spend some time and money preparing for this very important interview.

Be personally comfortable with your appearance. Try some "dry runs" if time allows. Applicants often spend a lot of time tugging at a tie or simply looking uncomfortable. Also be certain to get several "opinions" from friends or associates regarding your choice of clothing. Tell them to be honest. Your career may depend on it.

Avoid bright colors and unnecessary jewelry that may distract the panel. In a male-dominated profession, women applicants tend to wear more masculine clothing in an attempt to gain an advantage. It is much more appropriate to be yourself.

As you prepare for the interview, learn as much as possible about the city and agency. Visit city hall, the school district offices, the chamber of commerce. Visit with people who live in the city or are clients. Locate and read any books, annual reports, or other documents. Talk to current employees. Talk to the personnel department about benefits and salary.

The police officer who wore a suit to his written test and did an outstanding job did the same at the interview. Even though his raw interview skills would not have carried him through, he had outstanding answers. He clearly had researched the city. His answer to why he wanted to work here was that he had a strong interest in working with children and knew our department had a commitment in that area. In fact, he told us, "I talked with several people who were very impressed with your program that allows police officers to go on camping trips with school groups." Clearly, he had done his homework and discovered this little-known fact. Today he is one of our school-liaison officers and accompanies children on these trips.

I later learned his research was not an accident. It was well planned and required commitment. He actually walked through neighborhoods on a Sunday afternoon and visited with anyone willing to talk to him.

On the other hand, applicants arrive at the interview totally unprepared. One recent applicant, when asked if he knew anything about our city, responded that he knew the population was 29,000. The actual population is nearly 40,000. He obviously got the 29,000 figure from the outdated sign displayed as you enter the city on the interstate freeway. He clearly had made no commitment.

Arrive for the interview at least 15 minutes early if possible, but never arrive late. As you wait your turn, employees may pass in the lobby. I would strongly suggest a simple smile and hello. They may be on the interview panel, and this may give you an edge.

Opinions differ on what time slot you should pick--near the beginning, the middle, or end. I am not certain there is a perfect time; however, avoid being first or in the first third. If you can select, pick a time in the early morning. Most panels are more alert and, consequently, better listeners then.

As you are introduced to the panel, try to remember names and greet each with a handshake. A simple handshake generally tells something about you. I would suggest a firm, but not overpowering handshake.

Remember, we expect you to be nervous, but control your nerves so you don't lose control. Most questions are simple, designed to help us learn about you, the "person." Most interviews do not get into your education or experience. Most of that is on your resume. You may, however, be asked questions to judge the accuracy of your resume.

Some thoughtfulness, without long delay, is very appropriate. Asking to have a question repeated is also appropriate. If you ask for repetition very often, however, your listening skills may be questioned.

Avoid asking inappropriate questions. In one case an applicant asked before the interview began what type of guns we carried. I can honestly say, I did not listen to the remainder of that interview.

The panel wants to know about the real you--a challenge to accomplish in one-half hour. Take advantage of questions and "feed" us more information without being overly obvious. Most questions are not designed with a right or wrong answer.

Also, do not bring any materials with you unless requested. All too often a notebook becomes something to fidget with and, thus, a distraction.

Remember during an interview, time is generally a premium; consequently, use it well. Applicants, given the opportunity, ask questions about pay, benefits, uniforms, and the like that could best be asked at another time or before the interview by calling the personnel department.

As you leave the interview, a parting handshake and thank-you can be very important memories for the panel.

In Conclusion

Employment in this job market takes work. You must do research, spend some money, and invest some time. Be powerful, but to the point, short, and truthful. Most important, learn everything you can about the position, the hiring agency, and the clients served. It is not always what you learn, but the fact that you are willing to make an investment in your career that demonstrates character.

CHAPTER 9

ON NOT GETTING THE JOB:

PREPARING FOR REJECTION

Forget your personal tragedy. We are all bitched from the start and you especially have to be hurt like hell before you can write seriously. But when you get the damned hurt use it--don't cheat with it.--Ernest Hemingway in a letter to F. Scott Fitzgerald

Do You Know:

* How you will feel if you don't get hired?

* How to develop a support system?

* What the sequential reaction to loss and change is?

* How to draw strength from rejection?

* The importance of maintaining a positive attitude?

* Why most people will make multiple applications?

* What applicants who fail to get a job may do to hurt future attempts?

* Why some job applicants just give up?

* Why it is so important to seek help if the process gets you down?

INTRODUCTION

While the majority of this book deals with how to get a job, this brief chapter deals with *not* getting a job because that is a reality of the game. You need to know how to deal with failure in order to continue on. You may want to re-read this chapter when you get that first almost inevitable rejection. It should assure you that your feelings are normal.

It's hard to get a job in these fields! It is most unusual for a person to get the first job they apply for. You should gain comfort in knowing that the vast majority of successful applicants were eventually successful because they had a lot of experience in the application process. Many people, in any negative situation, fail to take advantage of a great opportunity to gain from it. Energy *is* present, albeit uncomfortable. This energy can be re-channeled in a positive direction.

HANDLING REJECTION

Consider the following adages:

Failure is not falling down; it is remaining there when you have fallen.

The only time you mustn't fall is the last time you try.--Charles F. Kettering

You will hear similar sentiments following a less-than-successful interview:

There must be something better around the corner.
They didn't deserve you anyway.
You can do better than that place.
They must be jerks anyway.

These statements may be true, and you will no doubt hear them from your friends and family. After all, they want to support you. You will agree, of course, but inside you may be saying things like:

I knew I could never get that job.
I'm no good.
Everyone else is better than me.
I'll never get a job.
I should never have gone into this profession.
Etc., etc., etc., etc.

If you are not careful, this negative "self-talk" can become overwhelming, acting as a self-fulfilling prophecy. If you get to the point that you don't believe in yourself, why should a potential employer believe in you?

No one ever said job hunting was easy. For all practical purposes, job hunting will have to be a full-time job itself, at least for a while. If it isn't full-time time-wise, it will be energy-wise. But, in the beginning, you probably believe rejection could never happen to you.

It is similar to the "It Can Never Happen to Me" syndrome frequently heard during discussions of officer safety. The idea is that life would be too difficult if officers thought that lurking around every corner was the possibility of harm, perhaps death. Officers instinctively develop the attitude that "It Can Never Happen to Me" to be able to continue on with their day-to-day lives. To a certain degree it helps prevent them from becoming hopelessly paranoid.

Problems arise, however, when all caution is thrown to the wind. Police and security officers must accept the natural risks associated with their jobs, but they must be prepared. They must be realistic.

Similarly, job applicants have to balance the risks. If you knew you were going to be rejected, why even try? This is what happens to some job-seekers who started out feeling they could never be rejected. Two or three rejections turn them into defeatists who simply go through the motions.

Part of life is competing for what you want. No one can always be number one. The top doesn't have that much room. Accept this and decide that doing your best is what it's all about. Eventually this will pay off. You will get where you want to be.

Accepting the facts of job seeking from the start will keep you from becoming overwhelmed when rejections are received.

Consider the applicant who had become so defeated after several "thanks but no thanks" letters that when he woke up on the morning of an interview and found that it was raining, the weather became the last straw. He decided to stay in bed. This would-be police officer made it easy for the employer to weed out one more applicant. Who does this applicant really have to blame for this failure?

Success is getting up one more time than you fall down. Make up your mind right now to accept the facts of job seeking.

> Fact #1: Law enforcement and security are *very* popular, sought-after, competitive jobs.

> Fact #2: You're up against many, many applicants.

> Fact #3: Eventually you will get hired IF you're right for the job.

The benefit of having to keep applying is you will improve each time. The downside of having to keep applying is you can let it get you down. The choice is *yours.*

REMAINING POSITIVE

You can and, in fact, must turn the negative energy from rejection into positive momentum. Rather than giving up, become determined to strive that much harder, knowing you are stronger and more polished. It's what makes a boxer or any other professional athlete more determined--what's often referred to as "having the heart of a champion."

No one likes to be turned down, especially for a desperately wanted job. It is bound to happen, and it is going to sting. It does not get any easier the second, third, or sixth time. In fact, the more you are turned down, the heavier it may weigh on you.

Maintain a positive attitude. To deal most effectively with that most common part of job hunting--the rejection--keep the following basics in mind:

> * Go into the process understanding you probably will have to try for several jobs. With so many applicants, odds are against you.

> * Not getting this job does not mean you deserve to be banished from planet Earth. It simply means you did not get this one job.

> * Another job is just around the corner (trite, but true). Avoid the temptation to believe that a particular job is your one-and-only dream job.

> * If you need help, *ask for it!* No law says you must go it alone. If you are not confident about your job-seeking skills, seek help. If you get depressed, seek help. Just ask--not always easy for officer-types!

> * Most important--keep trying. You've come this far. It is no time to give up. *Listen* when everyone tells you that you can get a job. You can. Just give yourself time.

Take advantage of everyone else's understanding of rejection and build a support system from the start. It really helps to talk, and there *is* strength in numbers.

Do not be afraid to get support and help if you need it--professional or otherwise. To get frustrated, disheartened, and down is normal. Do not let it get the best of you. Negative feelings can become overwhelming. Besides not feeling good, they can sap so much of your energy that your interview skills become less than adequate, and you will not perform as you need to. In short, if you do not deal with the uncomfortable feelings, you will eventually come to believe that you do not deserve to be hired, and it will show. Pick up and press on.

NORMAL REACTION TO LOSS

The fear of the unknown is always the worst. Since it helps to know what to expect, here's a brief explanation of what people usually experience when they loose something (like a death in the family, a ruined love relationship, or a lost job opportunity). It is called the *Sequential Reaction to Loss and Change.* That is how people *normally* act when they lose something important. If you get a rejection, you will probably feel the following, in roughly this order:

> Denial
> Anger
> Sadness
> Hopelessness
> Disorganization
> Withdrawal
> Reorganization

Denial. This is the "It can never happen to me" phase. It hasn't quite sunk in yet that you didn't get the job. Denial helps because it keeps you from getting too hurt from rejection(s). It can be harmful, however, if you deny that a shot at one particular job is over and don't move on or get too hung up on that rejection (possibly thinking that this is the only job in the world for you).

Anger. Once you have accepted the rejection, the understandable response is anger. "I wanted that job. I deserved that job. They aren't going to get away with this. The process was unfair." Maybe these things are true. So? The fact is you did not get the job. Permitting yourself to remain angry too long will, at best, depress you. At worst, it will drive you to do something you will later regret, like writing a nasty letter, making a nasty phone call, or paying a hostile visit to the employer.

Sadness. After the anger subsides, you may feel sad. Sadness can run from a mild case of the blues to a bout with deep depression. It depends on many factors and reflects the absolute need of a strong support system as you seek work. Don't beat up on yourself too much if you feel down. Who doesn't after rejection? Rather than fight it, accept it, draw some energy from it, and move on. If it becomes overwhelming to the point of your being unable to continue the job search, or if it begins to seriously affect other areas of your life, get help.

Hopelessness. Hopelessness may occur as the feelings of anger and depression subside. The hopelessness may seem overwhelming, but it is a normal part of adapting to rejection. The natural assumption after one or more employers reject you is that you are unemployable. No one wants you. This is not true. It simply means those jobs did not work out. You have to keep going. But this isn't always easy because of the natural progression of feelings.

Disorganization. At this point you may want to continue on, but nothing seems to fit anymore. You find it difficult to organize your time or your thoughts. You spend time haphazardly reading help-wanted ads and making futile attempts to schedule a productive day. Frustration may set in and you may simply give up.

Withdrawal. Wanting to give up or withdraw is also natural. It is understandable that you are frustrated, uncomfortable, and may want to simply quit. This is how your psyche lets you rest, regroup, and get ready to jump into the battle again.

Rather than fight this desire to withdraw, help it along. Get away from job hunting for a while. Go to the zoo, to a movie, for a long walk, or even on a vacation. Retreat and regroup. Do not, however, withdraw by skipping scheduled interviews or by showing up and not putting forth your best effort. If you need a break, take it.

Reorganization. At last! You have worked through the normal feelings associated with being rejected (work in itself). You're now ready to get back out there and get that job.

How long it takes you to work through the negative feelings associated with rejection depends on how serious the rejection is. The first rejection is not as bad as the second. The more rejections, or the more important a job is to you, the more extreme your reactions may be. Remember: Accept the inevitable and understand that this is how it is going to feel. There is strength in self-awareness. As George Bernard Shaw says: "Better keep yourself clean and bright; you are the window through which you must see the world.

CONCLUSION

The knowledgeable, prepared applicant understands and accepts that *everybody* experiences these negative feelings when they lose something they want. It may sound a bit extreme, but one of the hardest things about the job-hunting process, particularly if it goes on longer than anticipated, is that it can sap your strength. If you find yourself dealing with rejection, be prepared to deal with the "negative" feelings.

> *You may be disappointed if you fail, but you are doomed*
> *if you don't try.--Beverly Sills*

MIND STRETCHES*******

1. What benefits can come from *not* getting a job?

2. Why is it helpful to understand the "sequential reaction to a loss"?

3. Why is it harmful to ignore negative feelings arising from a rejection to an application?

4. Why would someone ignore these feelings?

5. Do you think applicants for police or security jobs are less likely to deal with their feelings? Why?

6. Why do you think unsuccessful candidates might lash out at an employer who didn't hire them? Could this ever be successful?

7. Do you think there is ever one perfect job?

8. Is there danger in believing there *is* one perfect job?

9. Who is included in your support system? How can you best use them?

10. Can you think of "failures" or "losses" in your life that actually benefitted you?

"This rejection thing has got to me."

AN INSIDER'S VIEW

EACH FAILURE IS ONE STEP

CLOSER TO SUCCESS

Timothy J. Thompson
Director of Human Resources and Corporate Relations
Minnesota Timberwolves

Accomplishing your employment objective is often not in your control. Any decision to hire involves many factors. Since you're looking at the situation of *not* getting the job offer, let's analyze the hiring process to understand why you sometimes don't have control.

As discussed in previous chapters, the hiring process involves three main areas:

> Education--what you've been taught.
> Work history--what you've done.
> The interview--how you appear.

Additionally, one other component of the hiring process is a vital factor in the employment selection: *who* is doing the hiring. If you know someone involved in the hiring process or are related to the president of the company, your chances of getting the job are obviously many times better than those without such connections.

How the hiring is done and by whom often differs greatly from agency to agency and firm to firm, making it difficult for applicants. You must research the hiring process as well as the position to be properly prepared. The hiring system may involve a simple application to a company president or personnel manager or may be much more complex, involving panels and boards.

Because the process is not uniform, the people doing the hiring are not always proficient at employee selection. Many do not have practical experience to adequately evaluate the ability and qualifications of applicants. Police commissions and selection boards are good examples of such lack of practical experience. All too often the groups doing the hiring are made up largely of community lay people, lacking professional credentials in the field for which applicants are applying. Even city managers and personnel directors have not always had enough experience in hiring to make good choices.

So where does this leave you? Well, when the candidates appear on paper to be equally qualified, that is, their educational credentials and work history are very similar, the selection comes down to an interview and personalities. With so many variables operating, no one can pick a favorite.

I have discovered that my ability to conduct interviews and effectively examine applicants' backgrounds to determine job suitability has dramatically increased with experience. Unfortunately, many management people, selection boards, firms, and the like lack adequate experience to hire effectively. It is no wonder many people are performing jobs for which they are unsuited. It is also no wonder that perhaps you and your talent are being overlooked.

Even when you have done all your homework, researched each position, individualized your application and resume for the job, looked for inside people to help, and prepared for each interview separately, you still may not get the position.

It is easy to become frustrated, bitter, and resentful when you have worked so hard to prepare and you feel so confident in your ability to perform the job--given the chance. Remember, you are seeking employment in an extremely popular field, and you have plenty of competition. You do not have to give up, however. You *will* get a job that is right for you. And it may come when you least expect it.

I know how frustrating it is to receive rejection letters. I have a file full of them. I would like to share with you from my experience, some do's and don'ts related to the feelings of frustration and hopelessness involved in being rejected for a job.

DO

* Do develop a support system. It is important to have an avenue to vent your feelings. Find an understanding friend who will listen while you express these feelings.

* Keep networking. The more people you know, the better your chances of learning about job openings. Often when you least expect it, a job will appear. Just ask some friends and acquaintances how they got their jobs.

* Look for alternatives. Often people get tunnel vision when looking for jobs, limiting themselves to one particular area when in fact they have abilities in many areas. You may want to be a police officer, but what about other possibilities such as being a U.S. Marshal, a state fraud enforcement officer, a postal inspector, an FAA enforcement officer, an FBI secret service agent, and on and on.

DON'T

* Don't spend every hour of your day worrying about your job situation. Take time for other things as well, especially recreation. Remember, jobs often appear when you least expect.

* Don't give up. Talk with friends. Acquaint yourself with other people in your chosen field. Join associations.

* Don't make compulsive decisions. This is no time to make major changes in either your employment situation or your lifestyle. Do not, for example, pack up and move to Florida because you believe more job opportunities exist there, unless you really want to live in Florida. Nor should you buy a house or new car because you think it will make you feel better.

Hang in there. Press on. You *can* and *will* land that job.

SECTION THREE
JOB-SEEKING STRATEGIES

You've decided law enforcement, private security, or a related field offers what you're looking for in a career. You've also closely examined your personal characteristics and have found a fit. You've created an impressive resume to demonstrate that fit to potential employers. And you're prepared to handle rejection if it occurs. You're ready. Where to find jobs and how to get them is the focus of this section.

Chapter Ten looks at the application process. It takes you through various strategies for locating job openings and making your availability and interest known. It discusses the importance of the application form itself and the role of your resume and reviews the testing process you might be involved in.

If all goes well to this point, you will be invited for a personal interview. The basics of presenting yourself for an interview are the focus of Chapter Eleven--how to dress, communicate, and following up. Chapter Twelve takes a closer look at the all-important interview process and what to expect from it.

CHAPTER 10

THE APPLICATION PROCESS:
FINDING AND APPLYING FOR JOBS

(1) Regard job hunting as a real job - and expect that it, like any other job, demands time, persistence, and discipline. (2) Recognize that while you can get a good job through ads or employment agencies, competition for jobs that are advertised tends to be fierce. (3) Apply directly to an employer even without any hint there is a job opening. Positions constantly become available and it's wise to be on a good list. (4) Try to get as many job interviews as you can and concentrate on smaller firms. (5) If you can see a layoff coming, start looking for a job while you are still working. (6) Expect to be discouraged. Guard against anger, apathy, or feeling defeated.--Sylvia Porter

Do You Know:

* How many jobs you can plan to just hear about?

* How many jobs are never advertised for or are filled before being advertised for?

* Where to look for ads in the classified section of the paper?

* What specialized periodicals to review?

* The importance of looking and acting your best during any contact with a potential employer?

* What networking is?

* The importance of follow up?

* The different ways to make preliminary contacts with potential employers?

* Why it is important to never "burn your bridges"?

* What your strategy is to look for job openings?

* What the application form usually asks about?

* What Equal Employment Opportunity (EEO) guidelines employers must follow?

* What the entire application process usually involves?

INTRODUCTION

Although waiting to hear about a job opening may work once in a great while, you usually must look for work. More accurately, you have to *work at finding work*. Serious job-searchers find that pursuing employment requires as much, if not more, effort than a full-time job and that a thought-out strategy is essential.

A well-developed search demands action. No one who creeps or shuffles along a career path can expect success in this competitive world. They will be trampled over by people who really want to work and to advance. Unmotivated, unenthusiastic, undirected individuals are easily identified and weeded out by employers. *You've got to be a tiger!*

Employers are looking for that *special* applicant who exudes drive, energy, and genuine enthusiasm. Develop your strategy so you not only maintain the energy necessary to pursue your career goals, but so your energy *shines brightly* to employers.

Don't just plan to look for work. Chase it! Hustle! Scramble! Be creative! Have fun! Turn what can be a frustrating experience into a personal challenge. Each disappointment, each new challenge, is part of the training that will let you succeed. *Get what you want!* Let the process feed you, not defeat you.

If this all sounds a bit too "rah! rah!"--the opposite of the stoic, macho attitude police officers and security personnel are "supposed" to exhibit--think again. Employers are looking for *real* people who truly want the job and will, in turn, do a great job for them. Job hunting is frustrating at times, so you *need* to keep yourself charged up for the process.

DEVELOPING YOUR JOB SEARCH STRATEGY

To keep on track, physically, emotionally, and intellectually, you have to develop a strategy. The first step is to determine *what* you are looking for. Even the smaller newspapers have an incredible number of employment want ads. The unemployed are frequently asked, "How can you not have a job? Hundreds (thousands) are advertised for!" True, but take a closer look. You are not going to apply for every job advertised. Somewhere between *actuarial* and *zookeeper* are the jobs you will consider.

Begin with the questions: "What do I want? How do I get it?" If nothing short of police officer will satisfy you, do not apply for private security positions. On the other hand, might a position as an armored truck driver, for instance, be a good stepping stone to lead to your end goal of work as a police officer?

Unless you are desperate for money, taking a full-time position of no interest or value to your career goals could result in several problems. For example, say you start applying randomly and get a job in an unrelated field and eventually quit for a job you probably should have waited for in the first place. This could make you look like a "job jumper," create hard feelings with that employer when you leave, and maybe result in a negative reference.

Do not confuse this idea with that of sitting at home unemployed until you get your "dream" job. For a variety of reasons, including financial and emotional, it is frequently much easier to get a job when you have a job. What is important is to identify what you want before going after it.

WHERE TO LOOK

Begin with the most obvious place to look for employment--newspaper want ads. After watching the local papers daily for several weeks, you will identify the generally accepted procedure employers in various fields use to advertise for employees. Ads for law enforcement positions, for instance, are usually placed in the Sunday paper, under "police." Private security positions generally appear under the heading of "security." Is this how it is always done? Of course not.

Think creatively. Ads for police officers could appear under such headings as "law enforcement," "public safety," or "officer." Security jobs may appear under the title of "risk management" or "loss control." Take time to familiarize yourself with all the possible headings your job could fall under and continue to scan the entire listings.

Perhaps a clerk or a secretary placed the ad without knowing anything about the actual job and thought "safety officer" or even "city employee" would be the best spot. Maybe the ad will appear, accidentally or purposely, on a Tuesday only. Do not let yourself get lazy just because such ads are usually in the Sunday paper under a specific section.

Under what other headings might a police position appear? *******
Under what other headings might a private security position appear? *******

Law enforcement and private security job openings usually are placed in the classified ads that appear in columns, row after row. Take time, however, to also check the display (box) ads used most frequently by corporations. These bigger ads are more expensive, but occasionally a city or private employer that wants to state specific needs or is particularly in need of people will use this approach. Scan ALL the newspaper ads.

Also consider the possibility of ads appearing in papers other than those published in your own particular city. A Minneapolis job seeker, for instance, should check the St. Paul newspaper. The Los Angeles job seeker should check a San Francisco paper. The Seattle job seeker should be looking in a Tacoma paper. Read the local and neighborhood papers as well as those of surrounding cities.

SPECIALITY PERIODICALS

Every field has trade publications. Law enforcement and private security are not exceptions. They have many magazines, frequently with ads appearing in them. Such periodicals as *The Police Chief, Law and Order*, and *Security Management* may not only contain position openings at the higher levels, they also contain very current information that individuals applying in these fields would benefit from knowing.

Other publications deal with more general topics and could contain an ad for your job. For example, magazines that deal with municipal government could contain such ads. Become familiar with a variety of specialty periodicals.

Also become familiar with any periodicals that list only jobs. One such publication of particular interest to those seeking employment in law enforcement and private security is the *National Employment Listing Service*, which contains only related employment opportunities. Other specific publications deal with only federal jobs, state jobs, county jobs, or city jobs. If not contained in such specialized publications, they will usually be posted. If you are interested in a federal job, the *Federal Jobs Register* is a valuable resource. Another source for federal positions or for positions out of the country is the U.S. Civil Service Commission, 1900 East St. NW, Washington, DC 20006.

The serious job hunter routinely stops at the federal, state, county, and municipal offices every week or two to check job postings and to ask what is available or anticipated. For law enforcement employment, one of the best sources of information at the local level is the city or county personnel office.

You may be able to subscribe to job listing mailers used by government agencies, as well as the privately published services. These are often quite expensive, so become familiar with what your local libraries have. Regularly review these sources.

Placement officers of educational institutions that offer programs in law enforcement, criminal justice, or private security often post job notices and have excellent employment listing services. Know where to look, what to look for, and regularly watch postings and other resources. Appendix D includes a list of such resources.

MANY JOBS AREN'T ADVERTISED

It is essential to know that many jobs are either not advertised or are actually filled before an ad is placed. How could that be? Probably because an aggressive job seeker with an effective strategy found a way in long before you ever became aware of that opening, either by having established a relationship with the employer, perhaps as an intern, or by making the employer aware of their interest before the employer knew that they would have an opening. Frequently, in such cases, an ad is run because of department policy or to meet a legal obligation. Your strategy, then, is to learn about these jobs before these probabilities occur. Just because an employer doesn't yet know a job will open up doesn't mean you should not be trying for it.

Take steps to become aware of position vacancies before they are announced if possible. Prompt application for such jobs can result in employment offers in some cases.

TELEPHONE INQUIRIES

Active job seekers put considerably more effort into their pursuit than just browsing through newspaper ads. You've got to get out there and investigate.

An easy, quick, relatively nonthreatening way is to telephone and ask if a certain department, agency, or company has, or expects, any openings. Ask if they send out a mailer for job openings or if you could get on a specific list to be notified for a particular job. With a little polite interaction, you may be able to get an individual notice from the contact person you impressed (hopefully) while inquiring. Even if the contact you made proves fruitless, never hang up without asking if they know of anyone *else* who is hiring.

When making such calls, begin by asking whoever answers who you should talk with about possible job openings. Then ask that person if you should contact anyone else, at that particular place or elsewhere. Your goal is to develop an ever-expanding list of resources and contacts.

PERSONAL INQUIRIES

Another approach to inquire about a position is to stop in. This can be risky. First, most employers are extremely busy and do not usually have or take time to visit with someone who has no appointment. This could result in closed doors or even in aggravating a potential employer.

On the other hand, it shows real interest on your part, as well as a willingness to take risks. You will also have the chance to let them see you as a person they would want on their team. If you use this approach, don't take up too much time of those willing to see you. Get in, deliver your message, and get out in a few minutes.

Never go empty handed. Have a resume to leave even if you are not able to see anyone. Follow up with a letter, especially if someone took time to talk with you.

ON BEING YOUR BEST

An absolutely essential part of your strategy is to be your best at *every* phase of the job search process. Because of the natural frustrations of the process, this is sometimes difficult.

Even when making phone inquiries, consider dressing as you would for a personal interview. If you look sharp, you will feel sharp, and will then act sharp, making a better impression than if you were calling while lounging in your bathrobe at 11 o'clock in the morning. If you are making phone inquiries, be away from crying babies, barking dogs, and other distractions for both you and the person you're calling.

When making personal contacts, coming across well is equally important. Applicants who drop off resumes while wearing cut-off shorts, extremely casual attire, or something bizarre, take a possibly fatal risk. There is always a chance you could meet with someone, even if you meant to only leave your resume and ask about possible openings. Perhaps the person responsible for hiring will walk by or has told the person at the front desk to send any applicants to see him/her. Maybe a new receptionist or a temporary employee will mistakenly send you into the employer's office. If you are wearing cut-up jeans and lizard skin cowboy boots, you have ruined what should have been a spectacular opportunity. The prepared job seeker is always ready for the unexpected.

Finally, be courteous to every person you have contact with. You may not think the receptionist, secretary, or person who casually strolls up and asks if they can help you is important. They are. You never know who you are talking with. The boss may be covering the phone or sitting up front while that person is taking a break. It happens.

As is more likely, the first contact person delivers your message or resume *with* an editorial comment. It had better be something like:

> * This applicant sure was polite.
> * This person dressed well.
> * This one seemed like she would fit in.
> * This is the one who called and was so courteous.

You don't want something like:

> * Wait till you see this slob.
> * This guy was really rude just now.
> * This is the gal who hung up on me last week.

Not only does niceness go a long way, you will probably be talked about after you leave, so make sure the discussion is positive. You may also get something more from being nice. The person taking your call or greeting you at the front desk may be willing to give you advice, a tip on future openings, and perhaps even a little encouragement. It is also possible that they may go back and tell the boss, "There is someone here you may just want to meet," or even contact you with information about a new opening. Because you never know, always be prepared. Even if you feel frustrated, frazzled, and tired, look like this is *the* most important contact you are making.

CONTACTS BY MAIL

The importance of appearance in making a good impression also applies to providing written material. Such material is a direct reflection of you. While you may not personally see the person doing the hiring, if you supply a resume, chances are it will at least get looked at. Provide that person with something that interests them, not something that gives them a reason to throw it away.

Contacting prospective employers by mail is perfectly acceptable. Like telephoning, it is quick, easy, and even more nonthreatening. It may, however, be less effective. While it may be hard to say "no" to someone in person, it is easier over the phone, and easiest with a letter (usually by promptly depositing it in the circular file). But letter writing is a viable strategy.

Note here the recommendation is *not* "resume mailing," but "letter writing." It makes little sense to send an agency or company only a resume. The receiver will have little idea why it was sent, and even if a position is open, a bare resume shows lack of common sense by the applicant. A cover letter makes the process more personal and sincere.

Whether responding to an ad or merely inquiring about what might be available, include both a cover letter *and* resume. The cover letter, recall, introduces you and tells why you are writing. It tells about you not only through words, but also by showing a command of English and that you are neat, succinct, and courteous. Writing skills are exceptionally important, and here is a chance to shine.

To make a favorable impression when you write, avoid the following:

*Don't provide a letter without a resume or a resume without a letter.

*Don't submit anything in pencil (and write neatly in ink only if you are absolutely unable to locate anyone within the Continental United States who can type it for you).

*Don't fold your material into strange shapes. A neatly folded packet in a business-size envelope is fine, as is a large folder.

*Don't use sheets torn out of a spiral notebook.

*Don't use lined, three-hole notebook paper.

*Don't use the back of a used piece of paper or an old invoice or receipt.

*Don't cram a letter or resume material on a 1" x 1" post-it.

*Don't send form letters, especially when they were designed for another job area.

*Don't send copies of letters or resumes that have been copied so many times even the copy has become faded and hard to read.

As difficult as it may be to believe, all of the preceding have been submitted, and all have been thrown away without ever allowing the applicant to recover from the negative impression made.

Employers are busy, especially if they are shorthanded and have to be hiring. They will not have time to go through all the applications, so they will look for reasons to throw out most of them. Foolish applicants provide plenty of justifiable reasons to jettison their letters and resumes. When providing a prospective employer with *anything* in writing:

* Make sure it is neat.

* Make sure it is typed.

* Make sure it is personalized for *that* contact. (Call ahead to find out who to address it to and the proper spelling.)

* Proofread it; proofread it again; proofread it again. Have another person proofread it. Then proofread it one last time. Improper grammar and typos provide an excellent reason for a resume to be thrown away.

If this sounds like plain common sense, it is.

FAX

You may make yourself stand out from the crowd of applicants by faxing a letter and resume. Even if you don't own a FAX, you can usually purchase this service from major hotels or from large secretarial services. According to Fowler (1989, p.lJ): "Some job seekers find fax works where phones and resumes don't." She cites the experience of a placement service executive: "Some of our candidates do have good luck. One of them who is very aggressive at marketing herself got interviews with three very important people using fax."

NETWORKING

Because the vast majority of job applicants make several applications, you will want to constantly seek new contacts and new possibilities. Since once hired, you may eventually change jobs (probably several times), continue to expand your contacts. This process, called *networking*, is being encouraged more and more. According to Krannich (p.174):

> Networking is the process of purposefully developing relations with others.
> Networking in the job search involves connecting and interacting with the individuals who can be helpful to you. Your network consists of you interacting with these other individuals. The more you develop, maintain, and expand your networks, the more successful should be your job search.

Salespeople have effectively used this networking concept for years, only they call it "developing leads." You are a salesperson, selling yourself. The process involves setting up your network of resources who you will not forget and who will not forget you. It begins with making whatever contacts you already have and taking every opportunity to add to this list. You then use each contact to make more contacts, and more contacts, etc., etc., etc.

For instance, you make a contact at a particular company or city. Ask if you should check with anyone or anywhere else. Imagine if each contact gave you two or three other employers' names. You could quickly develop literally hundreds of possible contacts.

What becomes difficult and complex is *how* you develop your networking strategy and to what extreme you should take it. Because networking can, and in fact should, mushroom into many contacts, proceed in an orderly way. This is best done in writing, with a plan in mind. Here's how:

1. Make an initial contact.
2. Document that step.
3. Acquire additional contacts.
4. Document them.
5. Take action.
6. Follow up.

It's easy until you start to develop more than about five such contacts. Then you will want to record your efforts on something more workable than scraps of paper or old grocery lists. You can buy networking workbooks, but it may benefit you to make up your own networking book. You can design it for your own particular needs, and you will feel like you are really working at developing your own strategy. It will make the entire process more personal, not to mention more gratifying by accomplishing something concrete.

Simply list the important information you need to keep track of and organize it so it is workable. Data to be maintained should include:

* Company, agency, department name, address, phone.
* Names and titles of contacts (spelled correctly).
* What you did.
* What you will do.

Also have a separate calendar to set up dates you will contact or recontact sources. A week or two is a good period to recontact, perhaps followed by monthly contacts, or even longer if you determine that such a period is appropriate. How you feel is important. Make a plan and follow through. Recognize the fine line between an assertive applicant sure to be remembered and a pest they want to forget. Strive for a balance.

Unlike the process of actually applying for specific jobs, the networking process should have no limits. You have no way to know where job information is lurking. Effective networking includes not only professional contacts (both individuals and agencies or companies), but also your acquaintances, friends, and family. Someone may know someone who knows someone who knows someone in the field who may be looking for someone just like you. This is how you get a jump on your competition--by finding out about job openings before they are advertised or even before they become openings. The thing is, you never know who has this information, so let the world know that you are available.

A study conducted by the Los Angeles Police Department (Slater and Reiser, 1988, pp.168-176) compared how people learned about job openings with their department in 1988 as compared to in 1966. This study found that 50 percent of the job applicants for their department learned of openings from other police officers in 1988, compared to 37 percent in 1966. Forty-two percent learned of openings from friends or relatives in 1988, compared to 38 percent in 1966. Only 8 percent learned of the openings through the newspaper in 1988, compared to 43 percent in 1966. Networking appears to be *the* best approach in the Los Angeles area.
Pursue your job search positively and energetically. Develop every opportunity to show yourself off in your best light. Be creative and learn from each experience. Even the contacts that appear to be unproductive give you a chance to learn more about the market and yourself. If nothing else, you come away from the experience knowing you are tough enough to accept a setback and survive. As noted by Bolles (1987, p.48): "You only need one YES--and the more NOs you get out of the way, the closer you are to that YES."

ON BURNING BRIDGES

No matter what approach to contacting prospective employers you take, be it responding to an ad, phoning, writing a letter with resume, sending a fax, stopping in, or for that matter, sending smoke signals, *never* leave a door permanently closed behind you. In other words, don't burn any bridges that may eventually lead to a great job.

You will find that people can be terribly insensitive, unfeeling, and downright rude. You are bound to get tense yourself because job seeking is difficult. But never let any negative feelings show to anyone who may affect your future professional life. Don't be rude or vent your frustrations on anyone where you are applying for work, no matter how they treat you. If it's bad, it is in all probability not you they are upset with. They are probably having a bad day. You may well return, if you have kept the door open.

If you have sworn at someone, had a temper tantrum, or otherwise behaved in an unprofessional, unacceptable way, you might as well cross that resource out of your networking notebook.

Two personal experiences illustrate that bridges must never be ignited. While attending law school, I replied to an ad for a police investigator with a local public safety department. Although I was a finalist, both the employer and I determined this was not a good time for me to consider the job. I let the sergeant I was dealing with know I appreciated the opportunity, and then I called the chief. I had not had contact with him, but I thanked him and let him know his sergeant was great to deal with and that everyone involved was the type of person I would love to work with. I certainly did not have to call the chief. The likelihood of me ever coming into contact with him again was almost zero.

Years later I did have contact with him. Not only did he remember me, he said he was impressed that I had bothered to call him and that no one had ever done that before. He also offered me a job--which I accepted. It was one of the best jobs I ever had. We have since become friends. I am sure none of the subsequent benefits would have come to me had I just "blown off" that job.

Similarly, my present job could easily have never been. It turned out that my former boss and I were the two finalists for the public safety director position in Chanhassen. As the result of a number of factors, some of which I perceived as being unfair, Jim got the job. I was devastated and still classify that day as one of the biggest disappointments I have ever had. I *really* wanted that job and couldn't figure out why I didn't get it. In fact, I am embarrassed to say that on several occasions I actually started driving out to tell the city manager, the mayor, and Jim just what I thought of them and how they had "ruined" my entire life. Fortunately, I always came to my senses and retreated.

When Jim and I finally did meet, we hit it off so well, he offered me a job as his assistant. That gave me the chance to learn from him, an unanticipated opportunity that I could have ruined. He was hired away to head up security at Walt Disney Pictures and Television, and I got his job. It turned out perfectly, although I never would have believed it at the time.

The moral: accept reality as it presents itself and make the best of apparently bad situations, even if you don't yet know what "the best" is going to be. Things do have a way of working out for the best.

REMEMBER THE MAGIC WORDS--THANK YOU

One absolute: *never* leave a contact without following up with a thank you. Not only is such a thank you good manners in a world sorely lacking in this area, but it also is another chance to show both your name and you positively. The more you can get your name in front of employers, the more they will remember you at hiring time.

You can phone or write your thank you for the opportunity to interview or to submit your resume. If you can't decide which way is better, do both. Don't drop a note or call just the chief of police or the president of the security company who took time to see you. Also thank the secretary who took time to set up the meeting or greeted you for your appointment. Show them you are thoughtful and courteous, the kind of person they would like working with them.

WARNING

If you think job hunting sounds like a lot of work, you are absolutely correct. Every aspect of the process is emotionally taxing, time consuming, and physically tiring. You will be approaching other people trying to sell yourself, knowing the chances of immediate success are slim.

None of us likes to hear the word, *no*. It becomes increasingly difficult to dial the phone, knock on the door, or send the next letter. It is risk taking at the most critical level. You are setting yourself up for a certain number of rejections. It is difficult, if not impossible, to keep from taking the entire process too personally.

Take care of yourself. If the whole thing starts to get the best of you, treat it like you would any other job. Set hours, including breaks. Plan your days. Take an occasional vacation. Finally, recognize the very real need for a support system. Plan into your schedule time with people who accept you. You can do this informally with family or friends, or more formally by organizing a support group with others in the same position. Such groups work extremely well for sharing support, ideas, and helpful hints. Most important, be sure your strategy allows you to keep at it. The next contact could have your job for you.

YOU'VE FOUND AN OPENING AND THEY'VE ASKED YOU TO APPLY

Once you've found an opening and have been asked to apply for the position, you can expect to do the following:

> * Complete an application form.
> * Take a series of written tests.
> * Have a preliminary interview.
> * Undergo a thorough background check.
> * Have a final interview.
> * Take a medical examination.

The order in which these steps occur may vary, but in almost all instances, the first step will be to complete an application form.

THE APPLICATION

Some application forms are very simple. Others are extremely complex. If you have done a thorough job on your resume and have a copy of it along, you should have all the information you need at your fingertips. If they will allow you to take the application home to type it, do so. If not, take time to complete it neatly. Use your best printing. Think before you write so you do not have to erase or cross out information. Be complete. If you do not understand something on the form, ask.

Many forms have optional sections to complete. Such sections contain information that is not legal for employers to insist on because of Equal Employment Opportunity (EEO) guidelines, for example, ethnic background, religious preference, and marital status. It is usually in your best interest to complete these sections. One job candidate who knew employers were interested in this information but could not legally ask it filled in his job application and then attached a second sheet, titling it: "Everything my Equal Opportunity Employer would like to know about me, but cannot ask."

Appendix E contains sample application forms. Appendix F contains Equal Employment Opportunity guidelines.

You've already looked at the types of tests you may be asked to take and how you can prepare for them. The next two chapters focus on the all-important personal interview.

REFERENCES

Bolles, Richard Nelson. *What Color Is Your Parachute?* Berkely, CA: Ten Speed Press, 1987, p.48.

Fowler, Elizabeth. "Some Job Seekers Find Fax Works Where Phones, Resumes Don't, *Star Tribune,* April 9, 1989, p.1J.

Johnston, William B. *Civil Service 2000.* Washington, DC: U.S. Government Printing Office, June 1988.

Krannich. *Careering and Re-Careering*, p.174.

Slater, Harold and Reiser, Martin. "Los Angeles Police," *Journal of Police Science and Administration,* September 1988, pp.168-176.

MIND STRETCHES*******

1. List as many sources as you can in which employment ads might appear.

2. Why are many jobs filled without being advertising or filled before the ad appears?

3. List ten contacts you have available right now through which you could begin networking.

4. If you could approach a potential employer in only two ways to sell yourself, which would you choose? Why?

5. If you were an employer deluged with applications in response to an ad you placed, how would you eliminate 50 percent of the applications right away?

6. What errors could applicants make when contacting a prospective employer by mail?

7. When visiting a potential employer, invited or otherwise, what things would you consider to make the best personal statement?

8. Whether you contact an employer by phone, mail, or in person, what three things would you want that person to remember about you?

9. What creative things can you do to get the attention of an employer? What possible benefits and detriments can you think of for each?

10. What strategies will you use to locate employment opportunities?

"Believe it, I'm looking for a job."

AN INSIDER'S VIEW

FROM BOTH SIDES OF THE PROCESS

Brain Beniek
Police Officer
Plymouth Police Department

Way back in 1982 I made a very important decision. That decision--I wanted to be a police officer. So already one year into my college education, I checked out how to do it and how fast I could complete the courses. If you can believe it, one and a half years later I was pounding the pavement looking for a cop job.

I always could interview for a job and get it. I never had been turned down for a job in my life. . . . until I entered the world of law enforcement. No one ever told me it was going to be so hard. Let me tell you, it was a rude awakening.

After some rejections I decided to enroll in a few job-seeking classes, and then I would *for sure* get a job. Unfortunately, they never taught me how to get a cop job. So now you're asking yourself, how did I get a job as a police officer?

The first thing I did was set a goal and made the goal happen. It took a lot of hard work and trial and error, and most of all determination. But the day came five years later when I got the call: "We would like to offer you a job as a police officer with the City of Plymouth." I will never forget those words.

Following are a few tips, tricks, and ideas that helped me land that job. As a person who has sat (on the edge of my chair) not only in interviews, but who has also had the chance to interview candidates for police officer jobs, I have some valuable experience to pass on. These things worked for me. They should work for you.

YOUR BACKGROUND

Besides the interview, you will find your background can make or break you. Once you have decided law enforcement is what you want to do, stop all activities that can get you in trouble. Remember, a background check is standard on any applicant. An investigator's job is to do nothing but dig up any dirt on you. Now don't think these guys are that closed-minded. They realize we all have some skeletons in our closets. They're just trying to weed out those who have a whole cemetery!

Your *education* is very important. A four-year degree can make a big difference. Try to take additional law enforcement-related classes. Grades are important. Make sure yours are solid and consistent. English and math are just as important as your law enforcement classes. (You should remember that from your parents.)

Probably your *current and past jobs* will speak the loudest about you. Try to get a job where you deal with conflict and make decisions. Remember, cops deal with conflict daily. Probably one of the best jobs I had that must show what a cop does on the street was working hotel security. This job dealt with some of the exact things I deal with out on the street. So if you can find a job in hotel security, take it.

(Thank you, Radisson South.) If you can become active in a police reserve program, do it. Your foot will be in the door with that department.

The other things you have to consider are what your friends, family (remember sisters and brothers count too), neighbors, teachers, employers, and "drinking buddies" are going to say about you. A good background investigator will look further than just those people listed on your application. Now is not the time to start burning bridges.

Just as a side note, when you *first* fill out that background form, usually no less than 27 pages, *make a copy* of it. You will probably need it again. Be sure you are thorough and do not try to hide anything. Honesty goes a long way.

APPLICATIONS

As you enter the world of law enforcement, you may have to look a little to find out who is hiring. Not every department advertises in the Sunday paper. Make some friends in the law enforcement field. Believe me, cops know what's happening and who is hiring and when. It's always a topic of discussion at coffee. Look in newspapers, watch job postings. And it doesn't hurt to call a few departments.

Never, never, turn in a hand-written resume or application. All correspondence with a department should be typed. Always enclose a cover letter. You want to sell yourself and bring out some of your major points. Keep it to one page. Make it sound like their department is the only one you are applying to.

THE RESUME

The resume is what can really bring out your strong points. Make it neat and include all those standard items resumes have plus one exception. Add extra-curricular activities. Don't be afraid to get involved in such activities and to list them. Employers like to see involvement.

THE ALL-IMPORTANT INTERVIEW

The interview separates the men and women from the boys and girls! This is where you make your lasting and most critical impression. Besides all those things you have been taught about interviews, a few tips from my personal list are important. Remember, I have seen both sides of the process.

Some Do's and Don't's

Do:
* Be on time.
* Be honest. The background check will reveal a lot.
* Conduct some research on the department and city. (Maybe even arrange for a ride-along.)
* Look sharp. Wear a suit. Shine your shoes.
* Shake hands firmly.
* Make good eye contact with all board members.
* Show interest and initiative.

    * Be friendly. SMILE.
    * Show compassion.
    * Use common sense.

Don't:

    * Come unprepared--expect the unexpected.
    * Pass yourself off as a know-it-all or be cocky.
      Remember, board members have experience too.
    * Try to hide how nervous you are. They understand that you're under a lot
      of pressure.
    * Mumble.

The Situation Questions

Be prepared for situation questions. Practice with a friend or an officer. Know your deadly force statute. I guarantee you'll be asked about it. When you are asked about a situation, most people are looking for common sense and compassion, not just right or wrong responses. You do not have to know every policy to get through these questions, but hopefully *common sense* will prevail. Be flexible and have a good reason to back up your statement.

If you do give an answer, don't change your mind. You don't want to be shown as someone who changes position just because someone questions your decision. Even if you're not correct, you will have a better chance with the board members if you can explain your decision and show common sense. It's from the old school, but it still applies.

THE FINAL TOUCH

This last hint will help you throughout every step. It's called a *thank you*. We sometimes forget these two little words, but it shows you care. I always (no exceptions) sent a thank-you letter (typed) after the test and interviews. Send it to the chief. He makes the final decision. You want him to remember your name. Don't send letters to every oral board member. By this time they have already made their decision. Even if you don't get the job, follow up with a thank- you letter. Remember, don't burn those bridges.

IN CONCLUSION

Hopefully these tips will give you an added advantage over the competition. Some day you will look back and say, "I'm glad I listened to those who have been through the process. They had some good ideas."

Believe me, all this will be worth it when you have applied, interviewed, gotten the job, and completed your field training program. Your greatest day will come the first time you are on your own and you make your first traffic stop, write your first ticket, or make your first red light and siren run. Good luck. I'll see you on the streets. And remember, be careful out there!

CHAPTER 11
PRESENTING YOURSELF AS
<u>THE</u> ONE TO HIRE!

You never get a second chance to make a good first impression.--Will Rogers.

Do You Know:

* What the job seeking uniform is?

* What the investment of the employer is in this process?

* What the elements of an interview are?

* What the four-minute barrier is?

* How important knowledge really is in an interview?

* How to make yourself remembered?

* How to avoid making yourself a pest?

* The importance of how your written material looks?

* What your strategy will be for presenting yourself?

* The importance of follow up?

INTRODUCTION

One important aspect of how you present yourself is in the written material you submit. The importance of written materials was discussed in Chapter Eight. It is emphasized again here because it is a vital part of how you will be viewed. Whatever you do, do it well. Don't send in insufficient, incomplete material. Don't submit anything that doesn't look perfect. Just as "you are what you wear," so you are what you write.

Typos, misspellings, poor grammar, erasures, messy cross-outs, tell an employer a lot. You cannot afford to look inept, uneducated, careless, or sloppy. According to Bolles (1987, pp.12-13): "[O]nly one job offer is tendered and accepted in the whole world of work for every 1,470 resumes that are floating around out there." The weeding out process becomes arbitrary at times, particularly with a number of equally qualified applicants. You may find yourself out of the running for something as simple as one misspelled word in your resume. This is not necessarily fair, but it is a fact.

How you present yourself begins with your written materials. If you do an effective job there, you are likely to get an interview. How should you appear at such an interview?

Barney Miller's Wojo may exemplify what the public has come to expect an officer not in uniform to look like. A mismatched outfit, a too-short tie held in place by miniature handcuffs, accented by a basketweave belt, all brought together with a pair of spit-shined jump boots. Plainclothed officers are often like unmarked squad cars. There's just no mistaking what they really are. Now you understand the importance of the uniform to many officers.

Perhaps such an appearance is part of an officer's identity, or maybe it's just the most comfortable way to dress between shifts. Probably it's the image being sought. In a sense, we *all* wear uniforms, whether they have badges, patches, and whistles, and whether we are actually on the job.

A uniform is apparel that makes a statement. The police or security officer duty uniform is designed to make a specific statement: *I am in charge!* Clothing worn by undercover officers also makes a statement, although quieter: I fit in (hopefully unobserved). Similarly, nurses have uniforms that meet their professional needs, as do bus drivers, waitresses, letter carriers, custodians, delivery people, orderlies, flight attendants, pilots, and military personnel.

Once you are hired, you will discover that wearing a uniform in law enforcement or private security is easy. In fact, most of us who no longer work in uniform miss the days when we had clothing supplied by our department and had no decision as to what to wear.

When matching clothing to a day's work, consider: What image do I want to project? What encounters will I have today? What does this sportscoat say about me? This dress? This tie?

YOUR JOB SEEKING UNIFORM

How you present yourself during an interview is an important aspect of the overall getting-a-job process. Your strategy for presenting yourself must encompass the entire spectrum of how the prospective employer views you.

Many factors come into play here. Employers will tell you that while someone may appear spectacular on paper, the interview provides an opportunity to eliminate many such candidates. Unwary applicants fall prey to this phase of the process for one of two basic reasons. First, they don't consider the importance of the various aspects of presenting themselves. Second, importance is placed on the wrong factors. Going into an interview having misunderstandings is something like going into an exam only to find you have studied all the wrong materials.

THE EMPLOYER'S INVESTMENT

Before getting into specifics of *how* to present yourself, look first at the situation from the employer's perspective. When hiring, employers are making an extremely important organizational decision. Employers are hiring someone to represent them to the public. In both law enforcement and private security, public perception is critical.

Employers can find themselves in serious trouble if they hire the wrong people for police and security jobs. In fact, employers may face civil lawsuits called "negligent hiring" (holding the employer responsible for hiring unsuitable employees who cause some sort of harm). Combine this with the fact that it is increasingly difficult to fire people, particularly in the public sector, and you can see the importance employers must place on the entire process.

THE ELEMENTS OF APPEARANCE

Appearance consists of the "whole person." The physical self, the emotional self, and the spiritual/ethical self combine to create the balance that makes up "you." If one aspect outweighs the rest or is significantly lacking, you are out of balance. Something appears wrong.

For instance, police officers may work odd schedules and perhaps compound things by attending school on the side. They may not have sufficient time to exercise regularly. Weight gain or a poor nutritional program could affect their health, making them rundown, irritable, and out of sorts. They will want to re-examine their lifestyles to restore balance.

Similarly, employers will try to view the "whole" applicant during the hiring process. The obvious difficulty is that what employers get to see represents a small portion of your overall identity. After all, how long does it take for you to get to know another person, even yourself, before acquiring an accurate perception? Certainly more than the thirty minutes spent during the average interview.

Employers will look for high self-esteem, alertness, intelligence, critical thinking abilities, and humanistic traits. They will also consciously watch for indications of sadistic, brutal, obsessive-compulsive personalities as well as those who will become victims of "groupthink" and "deindividualization" in the face of peer pressure, as in the case of the Los Angeles police incident involving the beating of Rodney King.

Most employers will look specifically at such elements as the following to "get a feel" for the "whole" applicant. The basic *elements of appearance* examined during the hiring process are:

*Initial contact	*Personality
*Clothing/grooming	*Enthusiasm
*Physical condition	*Knowledge
*Grammar and speech	*Follow up
*Manners	

This is a lot of data to an employer, particularly in the short time you have. You have to develop a strategy to take advantage of the opportunities to sell yourself in each area. Properly pursued, you will have more than enough time to provide employers with an accurate picture of you. To best understand this, consider the dynamics of the interview process, that is, the mechanics of the system and the importance of the first few minutes.

THE PRIMACY EFFECT AND THE FOUR-MINUTE BARRIER

In *Effective Human Relations in Organizations*, Reece and Brandt (1987, p.268) discuss the criticality of the first moments of any interaction among people: "When two people meet, their potential for building a relationship can be affected by many factors. Within a few moments, one person or the other may feel threatened, offended, or bored." This tendency to form impressions quickly is called the *primacy effect*. According to Reece and Brandt (p.267): "The general principle is that first impressions establish the mental framework within which a person is viewed, and later evidence is either ignored or reinterpreted."

How long does it take for the primacy affect to occur? Leonard and Natalie Zunin give their opinion in the title of their book, *Contact-The First Four Minutes*. The Zunins introduce the concept of the **four-minute barrier** and suggest that within this short time, people in social settings will decide whether to continue the interaction. If you get through those first four minutes successfully, your interaction is likely to continue, and on a positive note.

Reece and Brandt also suggest (p.268): "The way you are treated in this world depends largely on the way you present yourself--the way you look, the way you speak, the way you behave. Although human contact is a challenge, you can learn to control the first impressions you make on others. The key is to become fully aware of the impression you communicate to other people." You can test the primacy effect theory by asking yourself some questions:

> Have you ever sat next to someone on a bus, train, or plane and almost immediately wanted to talk with them? Or--decided to quickly get your nose into your book or magazine? Why?

> Have you ever had someone come to your door seeking contributions for some worthy cause and known almost immediately that you'd probably contribute? Or cut them short? Why?

> Have you ever had a teacher you just knew was not approachable to discuss a grade you received? Why?

> Have you ever gone into a job interview and known within minutes that you were a strong candidate? Why?

It is natural to like some people and not others. How do you get to feel that way? How long does it usually take? How do you come across to others? Have you ever considered asking someone how you came across to them when you first met?

DIFFICULT INQUIRIES

It is important to understand *how* you come across to others because you can seldom judge this for yourself. How could you know how others perceive you? Do you dare ask? Most people seldom think of this. It is just too risky. But it may be necessary, particularly if you are experiencing repeated rejections. We can all take constructive criticism. If that is what is needed to identify your weak points, take that risk.

For example, after leaving my initial law enforcement career path to go to law school, I returned to seek employment in the police field. Armed with experience, training, and extensive education, I finished number two on almost every interview in which I participated. Why? I had to know. Finally I simply asked. I called several individuals I had applied to and explained my motives for inquiring. Not to criticize them, not to come back for another try at that job, but to understand how I could improve. I was stunned to learn I had not convinced them I did not want to practice law. They were all sure I would stay with them only until a "real" lawyer job was offered to me.

Was this *their* fault? Of course not. It was mine for failing to anticipate this reaction and making false assumptions. My only regret was not taking this step earlier. In this case it worked. I got the next job I applied for.

GETTING TO KNOW YOU

The goal of the preliminary process is really the same for both the prospective employer and for you: *getting to know you.* It would be considerably more fair and accurate if time was unlimited. But it is not. For better or worse, you must deal with the brevity of the process and acknowledge the reality of the four-minute barrier. This is not all bad, however. If you recognize the elements of the interview, this is actually an ideal amount of time.

KNOW WHAT'S IMPORTANT

The biggest error most applicants make when presenting themselves to employers is misunderstanding what the prospective employer is looking for. In the hiring process, this can be fatal. The purpose of the hiring process is for applicants to present themselves to prospective employers. The only thing the employer is interested in learning about is *you.* But most applicants go into the process thinking the employer wants to learn how much the applicant knows. If you concentrate entirely on memorizing facts, data, laws, rules, and procedures, you have missed the point. They want to get to know *you,* not your capacity for memorizing.

In fact, this is why the application process is so frightening for most applicants. They worry that they do not know enough. This is *not* what employers are looking for. This is not the police licensing exam. This is not the Certified Protection Professional licensing exam. **The interview is a chance for the employer to get to know you**.

In reviewing the *elements of the interview,* you can see where a misunderstanding and overemphasis on what you *know* could effectively prevent you from concentrating on the important factors. The incorrect assumption is that you will be hired for what you know instead of for who you are. If you get "hung up" thinking knowledge is all important, you will waste an incredible amount of time before the interview trying to memorize reams of data that, for this particular purpose, is irrelevant. Concentrate on presenting yourself in the most positive way possible.

Knowledge *is* important. That is why it is included in the elements of the interview. Part of what the employer must know about you is what you know, but it is only one part, and a fairly small one. Depending on what field and position you are being interviewed for, you need to know, should know, could find out, or could figure out certain things.

For example, in Minnesota a person applying for any level law enforcement position must know such elementary laws as the use of deadly force applicable and some very basic Fourth Amendment search and seizure concepts. Such an applicant should know some basic procedures that might be asked about, for instance, situations dealing with Miranda, citizen safety, or officer safety. You might want to take some criminal justice classes.

Things you should be able to find out involve more complex legal issues. For example, if asked about fifth degree assault, be able to tell the interviewer where you would go for that information. Or, given a hypothetical situation and asked how you would respond, be able to explain the process you would use to analyze the situation rather than just saying what you would do.

If you were applying for a position as a brain surgeon or scientist, *what* you knew might, in fact, be of primary importance. But for law enforcement and security jobs, particularly at an entry-level position or at the initial promotional stages, employers recognize that the right kind of person will be able to learn and grow with the job. Keep things in perspective, trying always to remember the interviewer's goal. Now take a more detailed look at each element of the interview, including what comes before and after.

Before the Interview

One critical event before the interview might be a *phone call* to arrange the interview--or even a preliminary telephone interview. Yate (1987, pp.63-67) discusses this important aspect of job seeking:

> Whatever circumstance creates this telephone interview, you must be prepared to handle the questioning and use every means at your disposal to win the real thing--the *face-to-face* meeting. The telephone interview is the trial run for the face-to-face, and is an opportunity not to be bumbled; your happiness and prosperity may hinge on it .
> . . .

Here are some tips:

> *Take a surprise call in stride.*
>
> *Beware of over-familiarity.*
>
> *Allow the company representative to do most of the talking, to ask the questions.*
>
> *Beware of giving yes/no answers.*
>
> *Be factual in your answers.*
>
> *Keep up your end of the conversation.*

Speak directly into the telephone.

Take notes.

The telephone interview has come to an end when you are asked whether you have any questions. Ask any more questions that will improve your understanding of the job requirements. If you haven't asked before, now is the time to establish what projects you would be working on in the first six months. By discovering them now, you will have time before the face-to-face meeting to package your skills to the needs at hand . . . .

And if you have not already asked or been invited to meet the interviewer, now is the time. Take the initiative.
"It sounds like a very interesting opportunity, Ms./Mr. Smith, and a situation where I could definitely make a contribution. The most pressing question I have now is, when can we get together?"

The interview itself is the brass ring you strive to get.

CLOTHING AND GROOMING

Clothes make the person--and get (or lose) the job. Like so many other things, the "experts" have made a science of dressing for success. John T. Malloy, who coined the term *wardrobe engineering* was among the first to stress publicly the link between professional accomplishments and wardrobe in his well-known *Dress for Success.* His research indicates that your credibility and likability are immediately established by what you are wearing.

Likewise, William Thourlby, author of *You are What You Wear--The Key to Business Success,* says (1978, p.1):

When you step into a room, even though no one in that room knows you or has seen you before, they make ten decisions about you based solely on your appearance. They may make more, but you can be assured that they will make these:

1. Your economic level
2. Your educational level
3. Your trustworthiness
4. Your social position
5. Your level of sophistication
6. Your economic heritage
7. Your social heritage
8. Your educational heritage
9. Your success
10. Your moral character

To be successful in almost any endeavor, you must be sure that these decisions about you are favorable, because in that first impression you make--you are what you wear.

The same message is voiced by Wallach in *Looks that Work* (1986, pp.21-22):

> Clothes talk. They say volumes about how we feel, how we want to be perceived, how we see others. We communicate through our appearance. The way we package ourselves sends out a particular message.
>
> The major marketing corporations spend millions of dollars annually deciding how to package their products. The difference between a product that has been packaged well and one that hasn't may be the difference between success and failure. No one will know if the cookies taste good if they never buy the box . . . .
>
> The same applies to people. You may have more talent than anyone else in your field, but unless you present the right kind of package, no one will bother to find out about you.

Wallach (p.20) explains that the wrong kind of clothing can make you feel awkward and out of place. Conversely, the right kind of clothing can make you feel confident and competent: "Most of us have also had the pleasure of wearing something that we feel makes us look attractive. That gives us confidence, and the confidence helps us to do a good job. All of these positive feelings become self-fulfilling. The better we feel about ourselves, the better the job we do."

Few would argue with the research that tells us that people's appearance has a direct impact on how they come across to others and how they will be treated.

Since clothing is extremely important, how should you dress for a job interview to make a favorable impression? You have dressed effectively if your interviewers do not even remember what you were wearing. You want them paying attention to you, not your clothing.

In planning an "appearance strategy," begin by identifying exactly what job is being interviewed for. An applicant for an executive position would dress differently than an applicant for a manual labor position. An interview for an officer position falls somewhere in between. Start with several givens:

> * The jobs themselves are conservative.
>
> *"Extremists" generally are not well accepted.
>
> *The fields are viewed as important.
>
> *They are seeking to be viewed as professions.
>
> *You've got to look the part.

Begin by deciding on clothes that fall between the extremes, that is, *conservative*. A spangled three-piece suit and lots of gold jewelry is obviously inappropriate. So is a hopsack loincloth. Most agree that a smart looking, fresh, low-key appearance is called for.

Is a suit the way to go (for a man or woman)? Here *comfort* is a factor. You will not perform up to your potential if you are dressed uncomfortably. If you do not feel good, it will show. Therefore, pick clothing you feel comfortable wearing. You can build on your interview outfit from this point.

A suit is traditional for an interview for men and women. A suit conveys a statement: the person wearing it is business-like, is capable of creating a positive image, and is taking the interview and the interviewers seriously. The same can be said for a sharp sportcoat with a nice pair of slacks, or a good- looking skirt with a neat appearing blouse or sweater. The final decision is yours, but consider the following:

* Is your outfit conservative?

* Is your outfit comfortable?

* Could a suit work to your advantage or disadvantage? (Might a rural jurisdiction view a suit as "too much"? Might another jurisdiction view a tweed sportcoat as "too little"?)

* What do you own now? Chances are you feel comfortable in clothing you own. Can you afford new clothes for your interviews? Can you afford *not* to buy new clothes for your interviews?

*How do you think you look?

Be aware that a dirty, stained, or frayed item of clothing draws attention to it and away from you. A new shirt does not cost that much, particularly considering that a worn collar looks just plain terrible.

The bottom line is: you are selling something--*you!* You need the tools to make that sale. If you do not have the proper clothing to make a good impression, buy some. Do so even if it means borrowing money or throwing yourself on the mercy of your family. You *must* appear like someone the interviewers would want representing their city/county/ department/company.

A frequently overlooked area is that of accessories: socks, belt, tie, jewelry, shoes, etc. In addition to the previously discussed term conservative, *common sense* comes into play. To review a few basics you probably already know:

*White socks? No way.

*Socks that are too short, or droop, or have runs or holes in them? Ridiculous.

*An old, cracked, mismatched leather belt? Absurd.

*Too much jewelry? Leave it home.

*Still using your father's old clip-on tie? Spend a few dollars for a new one.

*And don't forget to shine your shoes.

Avoid wearing pins or other jewelry identified with a particular fraternal, religious, athletic, or other group or club. You risk offending someone participating in the interview. Even if such would not be the case, a lapel pin depicting a particular organization gives the interviewers something other than your face to focus on. Do not give them excuses to avoid eye contact. This reasoning also suggests that loud colors, wild patterns, or any unusual apparel should be avoided.

A final consideration is personal grooming. Plan ahead to get a haircut so you are not panicking at the last minute or, worse, ending up looking like Shaggy, the wonder mutt. Maybe the interviewer won't notice. The real danger is that you will be uncomfortable and waste valuable energy worrying about something that should have been taken care of. Some applicants plan far enough in advance of an interview so as to get a haircut a week or so before to avoid that "freshly cropped" look that makes some people feel self-conscious and uncomfortable.

Your perception of yourself is too subjective. Solicit feedback from someone you trust. Ask them how you look. Hear the answer--good or bad. Listen and make any necessary improvements.

Consider other resources when setting up your strategy for dressing. Many books and magazines deal with how to dress. Some go into great detail about what certain types of clothing and color mean. These sources provide interesting reading. Such an approach may give you a slight advantage. Whatever works.

Colors and styles come and go. It is not a good idea to wear an obviously outdated style into an interview, no matter how well preserved that old lime-green leisure suit is. Seek help from clothing store clerks. Usually these people are fashion conscious. If you explain the purpose of the clothing you need, they can often offer very good suggestions. And remember the advice from an unknown source:

> *In clothes as well as speech, the man of sense will*
> *shun all the extremes that give offense, dress*
> *unaffectedly, and without haste, follow the*
> *changes in the current taste.*

A final word about appearances--smile. A friendly smile can be key to the impression you make during those critical first four minutes. Make them feel good when they look at you.

PHYSICAL CONDITION

Closely related to clothing and grooming is your physical condition. A survey conducted by *Glamour* magazine (1982, p.33), asked: "Have you ever felt people wanted to get to know you or rejected you because of the way you look?" Ninety-two percent said "yes." One respondent lamented: "I've been rejected and even ostracized because of my physical appearance. It seems that being overweight cancels five years of college and fluency in four languages."

Chapter Five was devoted entirely to physical fitness and its importance. The fact is simple. Few other professions require you to be more physically fit than those of law enforcement and private security. You are not expected to be at your peak for only a few seasons or to compete in a once-in-a-lifetime event like the Olympics.

You want to be in top physical condition every day you report for duty. The public depends on it. Your partners depend on it. **Your** life may depend on it. The very nature of the job is stressful. Many officers die, not only at the hands of criminals, but as victims of their own clogged arteries and unhealthy hearts.

Employers in these fields *will* notice your physical condition. Every police and security administrator knows it is hard to keep their officers in peak shape as the years tick by. They certainly do not want to start out with officers who are out of shape. It's not good for the employee, and it's not good for the department, practically or for appearance's sake.

Health factors aside, every organization is concerned about how the public perceives it. So much of law enforcement and security work is accomplished by easily identified officers. They are often uniformed and drive marked cars. No department wants fat, out-of-shape officers representing them.

Your job search strategy should include being in good physical shape, not only because employers expect it, but because you will feel more confident about yourself. And confidence shows.

Finally, don't smoke. If you do--quit. An increasing number of police departments and private employers are including "nonsmoker" in their initial requirements. Public buildings are also quickly becoming totally smoke free.

Besides the obvious health-related problems, smokers today look out of place, and many feel smokers present a bad image. Further, most smokers don't realize just how obvious the odor they have clinging to them is. An interview panel of nonsmokers will almost certainly be overwhelmed by the offensive odor of an applicant who smokes. It sends a message you don't want. In addition, regardless of whether you smoke, be concerned about your breath and oral hygiene. Nothing turns another off more than *bad breath.*

GRAMMAR AND SPEECH

Individuals employed in law enforcement and security are expected to present themselves like any other professional. As educational requirements for applicants increase, so do expectations about communication skills. Use of slang, obviously mispronounced words, or limited vocabulary can embarrass an applicant.

Like physical fitness, communication skills take time to develop. Some people are better than others, and some simply need to brush up in this area. If you need to improve the way you speak, take some speech classes. Join Toastmasters. Volunteer in ways that require you to interact with the public. Feeling confident in how you sound will make you feel better because you will know you will be perceived better.

Be yourself. To try to come off too intellectually or too much like a seasoned professional, or anything else you are not will be perceived as phony. Don't address your interview panel as though you were giving a grand performance at Radio City Music Hall. Present yourself as you want to be perceived.

MANNERS

Good manners make a great impression. They start with being on time for your appointment. If circumstances you cannot control dictate that you will be late, call to explain your delay.

Shake hands with people at the beginning and end of each contact. Make your handshake an extension of yourself. It can communicate warmth, strength, and confidence. Use a firm, full, deep grip and maintain eye contact. You might want to ask some friends how they feel about your handshake and, if need be, work to improve it.

Reece and Brandt (1987, pp.281-282) offer seven "rules of etiquette" important in a business setting:

1. *When establishing new relationships, avoid calling people by their first names too soon . . . .* Informality should develop by invitation [call me Bob] rather than by presumption.

2. *Avoid obscenities and offensive comments or stories . . . .* Never assume that another person's value system is the same as your own.

3. *Do not express strong personal views regarding issues that may be quite controversial . . . .* There is seldom a "safe" position to take in the area of politics or religion.

4. *Never smoke in the presence of a fellow employee, customer, or client unless you are sure he or she will not be offended.*

5. *Avoid making business or professional visits unless you have an appointment . . . .* A good rule of thumb is always make an appointment in advance and arrive promptly.

6. *Express appreciation at appropriate times.* A simple thank you can mean a lot. Failure to express appreciation can be a serious human relations blunder.

7. *Be aware of personal habits that may be offensive to others . . . .* Chewing gum is a habit that bothers many people, particularly if you chew gum vigorously or "crack" it. Biting fingernails, cracking knuckles, scratching your head, and combing your hair in public are additional habits to be avoided.

Never let any contact with a prospective employer end without thanking the individual(s). Good manners go a long way toward impressing people.

PERSONALITY

Let the real you shine through! The stress associated with the job search process makes it hard to appear as well as you need to. Stress and anxiety can intimidate you to the point that you sit rigidly upright during the interview, responding with short, one-word responses--the only goal being to live through the interview.

Relax. Let them see you. You wouldn't buy a car or house based solely on how it looked from the outside. The same goes for hiring someone. Employers want to see who it is they are hiring, so let them.

ENTHUSIASM

Do you want the job, or do you WANT the job? Employers are not interested in hiring someone who will pursue their work halfheartedly. They want people who greet each day as a unique challenge, make the most of every opportunity, and do a *great job.* If you meander into the interview and respond to questions casually, why should they hire you? *You have to show them.* Make it clear that you don't just want a job. You want *this job.* You want to work for this organization. Let them know why. If you don't, someone else will.

KNOWLEDGE

Recall that what is of most importance in a job interview is how you present yourself, *not* how much you know. Knowledge does play a role. Think about what basic knowledge a person applying for that position should have. Ask people who have applied for similar jobs what questions they were asked. Keep things in perspective. Knowledge is usually a small part of the total picture.

FOLLOW UP

Follow up refers to the extra steps taken after the interview, the time when most applicants sit and wait to hear from the employer. Just as you must never leave a contact with an employer without saying "thank you," you must not walk out of an interview never to be heard from again. A single follow-up thank you letter can review several elements of the interview, giving you another chance to show off such elements as:

* Grammar
* Manners
* Personality
* Enthusiasm
* Ability to follow up
* Knowledge

Six of the nine elements of the interview can be reinforced *after the interview.* You can also demonstrate again your proficiency with written material, and you provide the employer with one more reason to remember your name positively. Imagine the employer sitting with half a dozen or fewer resumes that all look good, pondering a decision. Suddenly you call to say thank you for the interview. This simple thank you can tip the scales in your favor.

How you follow up is up to you. Some employers prefer not to be called while they are making a decision. While a phone call may not be a bad idea, it should not replace a letter. A letter is a necessity. Write to everyone who participated in your interview. Get their names, proper spellings, and titles from the secretary on your way out or call the secretary later to get this information. Remember a thank you for the secretary too.

Too much of a good thing is never good. Recognize the fine line between being remembered positively and becoming nothing more than a pest. Where that line is depends on your specific situation. You have to decide. Remember, however, that no one likes to be smothered, even by kindness.

Keep up appearances whatever you do.--Charles Dickens

REFERENCES

Bolles, Richard Nelson. *What Color Is Your Parachute?* Berkeley, CA: Ten Speed Press, 1989.

Reece, Barry L. and Brandt, Rhonda. *Effective Human Relations in Organizations.* 3rd ed. Boston, MA: Houghton Mifflin Company, 1987.

Stallings, James O. and Powell, Marcia. *The Look of Success: How to Make a First Impression that Counts!* New York: Frederick Fell Publishers, Inc., 1982.

"This Is What You Thought About . . . The Impact of Beauty," *Glamour,* April 1982, p.33.

Thourlby, William. *You Are What You Wear: The Key to Business Success.* Kansas City: Sheed, Adnreus, and McMeel, 1978.

Wallach, Janet. *Looks that Work.* New York: Viking Penguin, Inc., 1986.

Yate, Martin John. *Knock 'em Dead with Great Answers to Tough Interview Questions.* Boston: Bob Adams, 1987.

MIND STRETCHES*****

1. If you were doing the hiring, what would you consider the five most important elements of an interview?

2. What three things have made you feel very accepted by another person while you attempt to break the four-minute barrier?

3. What three things have made you feel very **un**accepted by another person while you attempt to break the four-minute barrier?

4. How would you work your responses to Questions #2 and #3 into the job application process?

5. List opportunities you could create to sell yourself in addition to the traditional resume and interview.

6. Why is it important to approach the elements of the interview as a whole rather than looking at the pieces separately?

7. What is the importance of developing a **strategy** rather than just jumping into the interview process?

8. Who could you ask for constructive feedback on how you come across to others by your clothing? Your handshake? Your cover letter and resume? Their initial reaction to you?

9. Which elements of the interview do you think you need to work on? How will you do so for each?

10. How might videotaping yourself be beneficial in preparing for an interview?

**"Don't worry about the oral,
just tell them what they want to hear"**

BE PREPARED

Bob Meyerson
Minnesota State Trooper

Most law enforcement departments look at many applicants before filling an available position. Successful candidates find a way to distinguish themselves. Working at each step of the job application process is vitally important. Successful candidates will impress the potential employer both with the substance of their abilities and background, *and* with their candidates' style that shows that they care enough to try a little harder than the rest of the field. If you follow the steps outlined below, you will land the job you want.

An initial job interview may last only 20 or 30 minutes. Successful candidates make every minute of the interview count. This requires preparation well before the interview takes place.

Before you ever get an interview, you will undoubtedly submit an application and a resume. Make a good first impression. If possible, have the application typed. If you submit a resume, make it look as professional as possible. It is money well spent to have your resume professionally type set or prepared on a word processor. Emphasize those matters on your resume that will impress your potential employer. Obviously, law enforcement-related activity is important (both past employment and education).

But also remember other activities which show that you are a dependable team player who will work well in the department: community activities, participation in athletics, and volunteer work are just some examples of activities you should include in your resume. Caution: include all important information, but limit your resume to one or two pages. No one wants to read your autobiography.

If you are asked to appear for an interview, *get prepared*. Find out everything you can about the department that will interview you. How large is it? How is it organized? What are special projects or cases that have received attention within the department, in the community and the like? What will your starting pay be if you are hired? What will the job requirements be? What benefits are offered? What kind of person is this department looking for? Who will conduct the interview? What kind of person is he or she?

These questions are all important to you, but why waste your valuable 20- or 30-minute interview getting the answers? You can learn much of this information by checking local newspapers, getting any community or departmental information pamphlets which describe the department, information given with the job posting, and talking with people who are familiar with the agency.

If you know someone with connections in the department, do not be shy about letting that person know about your interest in the job. These contacts can be an invaluable source of information, and you never know when they may communicate a favorable impression of you to the department.

When you get to the interview, look your best. Wear a professional-looking suit. If you do not own one, now is a good time to buy one. Be well-groomed. Remember: an interviewer will see many candidates. Everything you do to rise above the competition increases your chances of success.

During the interview, be *confident*. You should be. You have already put your best foot forward with a well-prepared application and resume. You have learned everything you can about the department and the interviewer who is interviewing you. Now be a salesperson. Let the interviewer know that you have done your homework by asking intelligent questions. (Example: "I know that the department has an active accident prevention program. How would a new officer have an opportunity to participate?")

Let the interviewer know that you truly believe you can contribute to the department by giving examples of how your experience has prepared you for the job. (Example: "I was a referee in Pop Warner football; I learned to maintain my authority when others lost their cool.") Be confident, but do not be cocky or full of hot air. A good interviewer or officer will spot B.S. immediately.

Remember that a department has many candidates applying for the same job. If you work at each step of the process to be a little better than the rest of the crowd, you *will* get the job you want.

CHAPTER 12
THE INTERVIEW:
A CLOSER LOOK

Whenever you are asked if you can do a job, tell 'em, "Certainly I can"--and get busy and find out how to do it.--Theodore Roosevelt

Do You Know:

> * What the definition of *interview* is?
>
> * What a stress interview is?
>
> * What a courtesy interview is?
>
> * What the purposes of interviews are?
>
> * What two critical aspects of getting a job are?
>
> * What six factors employers observe during interviews?
>
> * What to do if you freeze up during an interview?
>
> * What *your* interview strategy should be?
>
> * What the importance of follow up is?

INTRODUCTION

The interview. It even sounds ominous. Fear of the unknown can be debilitating. So take a good look at what you might expect because the interview *is* what it's all about in the job-hunting game.

Webster's defines *interview* as: "A formal consultation usually to evaluate qualifications (as of a prospective student or employee). A meeting at which information is obtained." Here are some facts about job interviews:

> * Interviews are anxiety provoking.
> * Interviews are necessary.
> * Everyone has to have them.
> * Everyone working has had them.

TYPES OF INTERVIEWS

Interviews provide employers with a chance to observe you from a variety of perspectives. The majority of interviews can be classified as one of the following:

* Informational
* Mass
* Stress
* Unnecessary
* Courtesy

Informational. This is the "classical" interview. You are asked in to provide employers a chance to check you out in the areas just outlined. These interviews are straight-forward. Presumably you enter this interview in a relatively equal position with the other applicants. You have no say about what format your interview will take, so "go with the flow." You can expect the interview to be formal, relaxed, or somewhere in between.

The formal interview is rather rigid, with questions being asked one after another, with the interviewers giving little or no response to tip you as to how you are doing. They purposely do not want you to have any advantage over other applicants by picking up on how the interviewers respond. This can be rather disconcerting since everyone likes feedback, but just continue on.

On the other extreme, you may find yourself caught off guard by the informality of your interview. Your interviewers may be so laid back, it may seem they don't even care. While possible, don't let a group that likes to have fun throw you off.

In either case, or wherever you find yourself in between, provide your interviewer with as accurate a picture of yourself as you can. Just because you find yourself in a formal setting doesn't mean you must perform as rigidly as a stick, nor should informality lull you into a false sense of security and make you lose your edge.

Mass Interviews. The number of individuals that employers like to interview varies. One or two applicants may be invited to be interviewed if they are exceptionally strong candidates, or many people may be asked in.

"Assembly line" interviews are hard on everyone, including those conducting the interviews. The applicants seem to melt together, making it difficult to remember who was who. This is when it is critical to not only provide a very strong interview, but also to pay particular attention to your follow-up.

Stress Interviews. Here you have good news/bad news. The good news first. True "stress interviews" are seldom conducted. The bad news is that law enforcement and private security do lend themselves to this type of interview. These jobs involve a great deal of stress, so the approach is justified to see how applicants respond under stress. Don't expect these to be comfortable. They are designed not to be. You cannot do anything about it. Go into the interview with the commitment that, regardless of the type of interview you are confronted with, you will do your best.

During stress interviews rapid fire questions give you little time to think about your answers or to regroup before the next question. The interviewer may seem harsh, if not downright mean. Furniture may be placed in unusual configurations, for instance putting your seat in a corner, or maybe you won't even have a chair.

Recognize what the game is here--to get you uptight. You *should* feel tension. In fact, you have much more reason to be concerned if you *don't* respond nervously to this setup. Draw energy from a stress interview and maintain your cool. Use the strength that brought you this far. When you get the job, you'll find yourself confronted with similar stress. The interviewers want to be sure you won't become overly defensive, hostile, or panic.

While many interviewees would tell you that *every* interview is a stress interview, in fact, few are set up to purposely get you uptight.

Unnecessary Interviews. Many jobs are filled before they are even advertised. Letting this fact influence you too greatly is similar to not trying to get a job because the world is eventually bound to end. There is always a chance you'll survive.

What if the job is promised to someone else? Who's to say that person will accept it? If they do, who's to say it will work out? What if someone even higher up at that agency doesn't like that person? Most important, what if they like *you* better?

No interview is unnecessary. It's just that some seem more necessary than others. At the very least, it is a chance to practice your interview skills and find out you can survive rejection. Both opportunities are valuable.

Because you are unique, you may be the perfect candidate. Never let an opportunity pass by. You have no way of knowing if this job will be the one. It says a lot about a person who tries, even in the face of adversity.

Courtesy Interviews. *Never* say, "Ah, I only got this interview because the chief knows my dad. He did it as a favor to him." So what? It doesn't matter *how* you got into an interview, just that you did. Once you're there, it's all up to you. Some opportunities to interview do result because the applicant knew someone or was related to someone in the agency. So what? All that matters is that *now* you have the opportunity to impress the interview panel. Worrying about how you got there takes away valuable energy. Go for it!

PURPOSES OF THE JOB INTERVIEW

For you, the purposes of the interview are to show the panel the "real" you and to find out who the "real" employer is. Ask any employer, and they will have stories of applicants who looked nothing short of spectacular on their resumes, but were absolutely unacceptable in person.

A good resume, in addition to the other preparatory material and contacts, is just your ticket *into* the interview. You have an advantage during the preliminary phases of the process in that you can get help from friends, for example, proofreading your written material. But once you are led into the interview room, you are on your own. It is completely up to you--as it should be.

For employers, the purpose of an interview is to get to know you. Simple? Your entire future based on a brief interview? Simple?!

Bolles (1987, p.182) likens the interview to the "dating game." He notes: "*Both* of you have to like the other, before you can get on to the question of 'going steady.'" According to Bolles, employers' four key questions are:

* Why are you here? (Why did you pick us?)
* What can you do for me?
* What kind of person are you?
* How much are you going to cost me?

The main thrust of any interview is to see how you interact on a personal level. This is extremely important. The process of getting a job and developing a strategy to meet this challenge boils down to two critical aspects:

* Having a resume that can withstand the "weeding out" process.

* Developing a strategy to not only withstand the interview process, but to emerge victoriously.

The primary purposes of the personal interview are the following--and the employer usually has a specific number which are of greatest interest:

* Looking at you.
* Listening to you.
* Seeing how you perform under stress.
* Observing how you analyze problems.
* Testing your knowledge.
* Testing your people skills.

Looking at You. Employers would no more hire an unknown person than they would purchase a home or a car they had never seen. They want to see what they are getting. Particularly for a job in law enforcement or private security, you do not want to make a negative impression by the extreme way you appear.

If hired, you will represent the agency. To most future clients you will *be* the agency. Think about it! The interviewers will be thinking about it, rest assured.

Remember the importance of grooming. Find the restrooms on your way into the building to make that final check: comb your hair, straighten your tie, adjust your slip, zip up your zipper. *Look sharp. Be sharp.* Also get a drink of water.

Listening to You. No matter how great your resume looks or how sharp you look, employers want to know that you also speak good English. There will probably never be a better test of this than during the job interview. In addition to testing your general grammatical ability, employers want to hear how you sound. They want their employees to sound *normal.* If you get uptight during an interview (and understand that everyone does), just be yourself. Do not try to cover up your anxiety by being cute, funny, smart alec, or a host of other facades you no doubt have seen people try when uptight.

What if you *sound* nervous? You may succumb to the pressure and have your voice crack, or say something you did not intend to, or just plain forget where you were or what the question was. Don't panic. It is reassuring to employers to see you as capable of recognizing a mistake and being able to reorganize and continue. Do not fake it. If a major goof occurs, simply proceed as follows:

* Grip the side of your chair.

* Take a deep breath.

* Admit to the interviewer(s): "This job is really important to me, and I guess I'm more nervous than I thought."

* Continue with your answer.

There is nothing wrong with being honest. If you are really nervous, admit it; 99.99999% of the time interviewers are sympathetic. Your honesty will make a positive impression. Also, they just may be easier on you.

Take a moment or two before you answer questions, especially if the question is *not* one you "practiced." What may seem like an eternity will probably be only a matter of seconds. Never answer without thinking through your response.

Seeing How You Perform Under Stress. As noted at the beginning of this chapter, some employers use a "stress interview." The rationale is that the job you are seeking is stressful, so they want to see what you do under stress. Such interviews often involve "rapid fire" questions during which you have little or no time to think about your response. The interviewers may appear hostile or demanding to you. They may ask questions you just can't answer--either because you lack the expertise or because there *is* no answer.

Because the purpose of stress interviews is to see how you will act, do your best to keep your wits about you. Brainstorm all the possible weird things that could be set up in an interview. Ask others what they have undergone in interviews, and you will be as well prepared as you can be for this experience. Fortunately, these interviews are not too common.

Observing How You Analyze Problems. You may be asked to solve problems presented to you. Particularly at an entry-level position, you are *not* expected to know every exact answer. For example, an interview for police dispatcher might well include questions in which you are asked, "What would you do if . . . twenty-five 747's crashed in various parts of the city at once?" Or a potential security officer might be asked, "What if you were accosted by seventeen chapters of Hell's Angels demanding a solution to world hunger?" Remember that, even if there is an answer, in all probability you are not expected to know it.

They want to know if and how you think. A good strategy is to begin your answers with your own variation of the "policy/will learn" statement. That is, say that you understand that every company/department is likely to have its own policy on how to handle most situations as well as to state that you are eager to learn.

For example, if asked, "How would you handle a situation in which you find an open door to an office after hours, and the boss is inside with his partner's wife?" A reasonable answer could be: "Because I have had no previous security experience, that situation is certainly a difficult one. Based on the information you have given me, I would follow the applicable company policy; for instance, filling out an incident report if required, as well as immediately advising my supervisor. In addition, I would anticipate learning how the company would want me to handle such sensitive situations during my training period. If it is not brought up, I will bring it up now that you've asked me about it."

During such analytical interviews, rather than looking for a right answer, the interviewers are interested in the *process* you use in coming to some conclusions.

Testing Your Knowledge. You may also be asked questions to check your knowledge in specific areas, depending on the state in which you are applying. For police officers, you could be asked about very basic statutes, for example, the deadly force law. You should be as prepared to answer as many of these questions as possible, but do not panic if you cannot. In such a situation admit that you do not know, but that you would look it up in the state statute book, or the traffic code, or wherever it is likely to be found. **Do NOT guess.**

If you draw a blank, admit it. In such a case, you may want to follow up with a letter providing the answer to show you can find needed information.

Testing Your People Skills. Your resume may look spectacular, but if you cannot come across as friendly, sincere, and at least somewhat appealing, you will not get the job. No matter how nervous you get, no matter how frustrating the interview is, do not forget your manners. Let the interview board know that you appreciate their time and that you appreciate the challenging questions raised. Shake hands with each, smile, say, "yes," not "ya," and use *common sense.*

This is all more easily said than done. Whether the interview is specifically intended to create stress, it will! The "little things" are so easily forgotten. Well before the interview, make a list of what you want to do. For example:

> * Shake hands with everyone when introduced.
> * Look at everyone personally during your responses.
> * Thank the group at the end of the interview.

Thinking about it all ahead of time will put it in your head. It is then easier to remember during the pressure of the interview.

Most of the important purposes of an interview can be addressed during one question posed by the panel. A common question for police officer applicants is: "What would you do if you stopped an off-duty officer for drunk driving?" Try the "policy/will learn" approach to come up with an answer.

For example, "If the department had a policy, I would follow it. I would certainly advise my supervisor. Recognizing that DWI is a serious offense and that police officers are not above the law, I would . . . . " You get the idea. Such a question gives you a great chance to appear at your best--or worst.

Imagine you are an employer seeking to fill the position of either police officer or security officer. An applicant has just walked into the room. List five things that would turn you off immediately. *******

Next list five things that would strike you positively. *******

A San Francisco financial recruiting firm surveyed 100 large corporations to find out how some job applicants performed during the interview. Included among the responses were the following:

> * Said he was so well qualified, if he didn't get the job it would prove that the company's management was incompetent.

* Asked to see the *interviewer's* resume to see if the personnel executive was qualified to judge the candidate.

* Announced she hadn't had lunch and proceeded to eat a hamburger and french fries in the interviewer's office.

* Wore a Walkman and said she could listen to me and the music at the same time.

* Dozed off and started snoring during the interview.

Unbelievable, but true. What should you do during the interview? Bolles (1987, p.184) suggests:

> Beyond the issue of *what* to say, is the issue of *how* to say it. Studies have revealed that generally speaking the people who get hired are those who speak half the time in the interview, and let the employer speak the other half of the time. Fifty-fifty. Furthermore, studies have revealed that generally, when it is your turn to speak, you should speak no shorter than twenty seconds and no longer than two minutes--at any one time.

TYPICAL QUESTIONS

Following are some typical questions. As you read through them, the comment of Yate (1987, p.153) is particularly relevant: "To some of the toughest questions, there is never a 'right' answer--that's what makes them the toughest--but there is always a right approach."

You'll notice that most of the questions call for more than a mere "yes" or "no" answer. Concentrate on *your* approach to each question. What would make a good response to each? Write your responses in your notebook. *******

1. What makes you think you would be an asset to this agency?

2. When did you first consider joining the police department/private security field?

3. What public service organizations or clubs do you belong to?

4. Do you realize that your previous training will be of little value in the job you are applying for?

5. Why did you choose the police department instead of the fire department?

6. Do you have applications in at other agencies?

7. Are you married? If so, what does your spouse think of your career choice? The odd hours you'll be working?

8. Are any of your friends members of this agency?

9. Do you have any relatives who are members of this agency?

10. When did you first think about becoming a police/security officer?

11. Have you ever taken any tests for law enforcement/private security positions?
12. Have you ever considered the hazardous nature of the work we perform?

13. Have you talked over the conditions, opportunities, and the attitudes of members of this agency with the agency?

14. What are your hobbies?

15. Have you trained for this examination by going to any coaching schools, taken any courses in public schools, or the like?

16. If you are chosen for the job, would you make it your lifetime career?

17. Has the security of the job or the desire for service been your main reason for applying for this position?

18. Have you ever stood around when you saw a crowd gathered about a serious accident or when a police officer was investigating a crime or making an arrest?

19. Do you listen to police calls on short wave radio? If yes, and you hear a call that sounds serious, do you go to where the officers were sent?

20. What is your attitude about unions in police/security fields?

21. You are a member of this agency and a fellow officer has been injured along with civilians. To whom would you give your first attention?

22. You are a member of this agency and you suspect that a fellow officer is committing thefts in the district/office/business while off duty. What action would you take?

23. You are patrolling on the midnight to morning watch and have been walking hours without seeing anyone. Would you find an unoccupied auto and rest?

24. You are off duty and a hold-up man runs past you with the victim in pursuit. What action would you take?

25. You find that your superior drinks to excess and is drunk on the job. The place your superior drinks is on your beat. What action would you take? Would you say anything to the bartender who serves your superior?

26. You receive an order you believe to be in error from your superior. What action would you take?

27. Who would you rather please in your work, your superior officer or the public?

28. Should the police and fire departments be integrated into a single unit known as a public safety department?

29. What kind of job do you feel this agency is doing?

30. Should this agency perform such tasks as letting locked-out people into their homes, escorting single women home at late and unusual hours, removing from

the street debris which has accidentally fallen from moving vehicles?

31. How would you improve the quality of work in this agency after you have been trained?

32. What is this agency's responsibility in respect to juvenile delinquents?

33. What is your present occupation? Do you feel the training you have received will benefit you if selected to join this agency?

34. What do your friends think of you joining this agency?

35. Have you ever had difficulty with any law enforcement agency either as a juvenile or as an adult?

36. Give us a brief idea of what a good law enforcement/private security officer should be in the way of character, knowledge, and physical condition.

37. Under the authority of government you would represent, could you use deadly force against a citizen where your life or the life of someone else threatened? Could you take another person's life under any other circumstances?

38. What are your greatest strengths? Your greatest weaknesses?

39. Where do you expect to be ten or twenty years from now?

40. Why should we hire you?

Guidelines for Replies to Commonly Asked Interview Questions

Having studied these questions and formulated answers, see how close you come to the following "guidelines."

1. Indicate such items as interest in working with people, interest in serving the public, and having completed so many hours of related course work.

2. Frequently the oral board gives great weight to someone who has considered law enforcement/private security as a career for a long time.

3. You might mention Rotary, Lions, Kiwanis, various veteran's organizations, as well as such organizations in high school as Key Club or anything similar.

4. This is a "loaded" question. Politely take exception. All training you have received in citizenship, first aid, governmental organizations, and the like is important. Rifle club memberships are also important. The value lies in understanding the functions of departments, etc.

5. Law enforcement/private security are challenging, interesting, diversified careers with great opportunity for public service and working with people.

6. Answer frankly, but indicate that the agency in question is your first choice.

7. It is hoped that your "significant other" enthusiastically backs your decision.

8. Be able to recall the names of police/security officers you know.

9. Answer truthfully, even if the relationship is extremely remote.

10. Again, the oral board may give great weight to someone who has been considering that particular career over time.

11. Answer frankly. It might be best to indicate that this agency is your first choice.

12. Indicate that you are aware of some of the hazards in dealing with the criminal element and in driving a patrol vehicle, particularly at pursuit speeds, but that you do not consider law enforcement/private security to be any more hazardous than any other occupation. You might indicate that some training you have received and some you experienced in observing police procedures have helped alleviate this hazard.

13. Talk to members of the agency before the interview. Know the agency's salary range and something about the agency itself and the city/industry such as the approximate size, its type of government/management and so on.

14. Organize your thinking so your answer stresses activities related to law enforcement/private security. Among these may be target shooting, skeet shooting, hunting, youth activities such as scouting, or sports, particularly wrestling, boxing, and the martial arts.

15. A good chance to list the related courses you have successfully completed.

16. Answer this question affirmatively.

17. Job security and service to the public are two factors in your decision. There might also be chance for advancement, growth in a professional organization, and the satisfaction of doing a worthwhile job.

18. Be sure your answer does not indicate you have interfered with any police/security activities. Confine your answer to incidents in which you helped by furnishing license numbers, direction of flight of a suspect, pointing out witnesses, identifying participants, and the like.

19. Such activity usually is frowned on by law enforcement/security officers and might indicate that the person is overzealous.

20. Generally professional law enforcement officers do not feel that police unions contribute to professionalization of law enforcement. Be careful, however, a member of the oral board may also be the primary police union representative.

21. The most seriously injured person should get first attention.

22. Recommended action depends on the basis for the suspicion. If you have sufficient evidence to be considered reasonable cause, you have no alternative but to report your facts to a superior. This is for your own sake and the good of law enforcement/private security. Without sufficient facts, severe damage could be done, and the reporting officer could be open to civil damages.

23. Officers are not paid to "rest" on duty. Alternatives might be to stop in a

restaurant for a cup of coffee where you would still be considered on duty and available for assignment.

24. In such instances, an officer is never off duty. Appropriate action should be taken depending on if you and/or the probable hold-up suspect is armed. Officers in plain clothes should identify themselves, probably by pinning their badges on their lapels, etc. At least, get an accurate description of the suspect.

25. The answer depends on the circumstances and how obviously drunk the superior would appear to others and if he or she is known as a police/security officer. Know department policy. If any police/security officer, regardless of rank, indulges in activity that might discredit the agency, it is the officer's responsibility to report the matter to a superior. Be careful to state only facts. Record the time, date, and to whom such a report is made.

26. Follow the order if not seriously in error. An alternative is to call the error to the superior's attention and, after doing so, abide by that decision. Officers who refuse to obey orders do so at their own peril. Officers should refuse any order that involves an illegal act. Short of an illegal act, it would be the superior's responsibility if he/she gave an erroneous order.

27. This question is similar to "have you stopped beating your wife yet?" Chances are the superior's objectives are the same as yours in public service. If pleasing the public means overlooking offenses and violations, this is wrong.

28. Traditionally, both fire and police service are opposed to integration. While the concept has some merit in financial savings, frequently the objectives of the two agencies are so different that it makes the idea impractical.

29. You feel the agency is a good one or you would not be applying. Have some basis for this belief, however, such as conversations with officers, articles in the paper, or conversations with citizens, particularly people who have had some dealing with the agency.

30. Opinions differ considerably as to the responsibility of law enforcement relative to this area. Generally, this kind of public service is good public relations and may have some crime prevention value as well. The public expects help in emergencies.

31. Such things as continued education, home study, and in-service training would help improve the quality of your work after being hired.

32. Since juvenile delinquency is a serious problem in our society, it is a major responsibility of law enforcement officers. There is disagreement as to the amount of rehabilitative activity in which a law enforcement agency should engage. Generally, authorities agree that law enforcement personnel should handle the law and leave rehabilitation to other agencies whose personnel are better qualified.

33. In addition to specialized knowledge, law enforcement/private security officers should know something about a great many things. Therefore, most experiences and training you have had will be of some benefit.

34. Generally, your friends would approve of your joining the agency.

35. Answer frankly.

36. Because of the nature of the work, police and security officers in effect "live in a fishbowl." Therefore, they must make sure their character and activities are beyond reproach. They must maintain excellent physical condition and continue to search for knowledge and education throughout their careers.

37. Answer in the affirmative to the first half of the questions. The answer to the second part would depend on the law, department policy, and procedures and circumstances.

38. Strengths should be very apparent from your resume. Employers are especially interested in such characteristics as leadership, ability to communicate, compassion, loyalty, and the like. Make the weaknesses portion of this question work to your advantage. Do not be negative, but rather pick a strength that you have perhaps carried to extremes, for example, "I sometimes pay too much attention to details." Or "I am a perfectionist."

39. Take your time on this one. You should indicate that you expect to grow and develop professionally and be promoted accordingly.

40. Be prepared to explain what you can contribute to the agency. This is a favorite interview question.

NEGOTIATING

Negotiating is sometimes not possible. The majority of law enforcement jobs are union jobs, or at least are positions that bargain collectively. Therefore, you will have little room to negotiate, particularly at entry-level positions.

Likewise, private security positions generally permit little room for you to make demands. As you work your way upward in either the public or private sector, you may find room to negotiate. At almost all entry-level, and even mid-level lateral movements, you could easily appear too demanding if you want too much. Be realistic. Recognize the limitations of these careers. If you have specific needs, however, pursue them as far as you can.

CLOSING THE INTERVIEW

The final impression you make on your way out is also important. Here is an opportunity to shine as the ideal, enthusiastic candidate. The interview is likely to close with the interviewer asking, "Is there anything you would like to ask?" Every other candidate will say something like, "Well, no, not really."

Boring. Unmemorable. Your strategy should include having several closing questions . . . *if* you want the answers. The questions should *not* be about salary or benefits. Good questions could be about the size of the agency or a starting date.

Show that you can think and communicate. What would you think if you were the employer and an interviewee asked about the number of vacation or sick days or the number and length of the coffee breaks?

Always leave on an assertive, upbeat, energetic note. Regardless of the words you choose, make sure the message comes across loud and clear: *I want this job and I'll be spectacular at it!*

Don't be too brash or boastful. Make your closing statement(s) brief and to the point. Any last minute chance you have will be ruined if you drag it out with question after question or bragging statement after statement. As is true throughout your overall strategy, seek a balance.

FOLLOW UP

Punctuate your interest with follow up. Follow up is an easy way to score points during the hiring process because few applicants have developed a strategy that includes plain old courtesy. At the least send a letter telling the interviewer(s) you appreciate the time and opportunity to meet. Anything in addition, within reason, will probably benefit you.

MAKING A DECISION

Making a decision is something you probably can't imagine would be a problem. Selecting from several jobs would be a great problem, right? If this does become your "problem," take your time before deciding. Usually employers are happy to give you a reasonable time to make a decision.

If you are a final contender in some other agencies, you now have a card to play. There is nothing wrong with contacting these other employers to let them know you would like to work for them, but you have been offered another job elsewhere. Suddenly you have increased your desirability, since someone else wants you too.

At some point you need to decide. Weigh as many factors as you are aware of. Seek input from others, and then take that risk and make your final decision. Even if you are not going to accept a position with an agency, let them know you appreciate them. Who knows, maybe you'll join them in the future.

REFERENCES

Bolles, Richard Nelson. *What Color Is Your Parachute? A Practical Manual for Job-Hunters and Career Changers.* Berkeley, CA: Ten Speed Press, 1987.

Yate, Martin John. *Knock 'em Dead with Great Answers to Tough Interview Questions.* Boston: Bob Adams, 1987.

MIND STRETCHES*******

1. Why would a mass interview put you at a disadvantage? An advantage?

2. What could you do to make the interview process more enjoyable and, in turn, more memorable for an employer?

3. At what point during any phase of the hiring process can you become a pest rather than an impressive, aggressive candidate?

4. How would you maintain an awareness of this and prevent it?

5. What could you do to remain cool during a "stress" interview?

6. What could you do if you really blew an interview--maybe by freezing up or just having a generally bad showing?

7. What if you had trouble with just one question by giving a wrong answer or not knowing the answer?

8. What techniques could you use to deal with the understandable stress and anxiety everyone experiences during interviews?

9. Why is it a good idea to follow up with an employer who you have applied to, even if you take a different job?

10. List your three greatest concerns about being interviewed for a law enforcement or private security position. How can you reduce these concerns?

"You forgot to say 'captain may I.'"

AN INSIDER'S VIEW

YOUR TURN TO STAR

Jim Chaffee
Director of Security
Walt Disney Pictures and Television

BEFORE THE INTERVIEW

I would suggest that you type all correspondence, including your application. One of my greatest "turn offs" is to receive an application that is not typed. This is not to say I won't look at it, but when you are in competition with a hundred other candidates, every little edge will help.

I don't mean to suggest that if you type all correspondence that's all you need worry about. The correspondence should be neat and organized and *should not* contain spelling errors or noticeably improper grammar. Some people will have their resumes professionally done which looks very nice and can be impressive. A resume does not have to be done professionally, however. With today's computer capabilities, a professional looking resume can be done with little effort.

Do not include a poorly typed cover letter to go with a professional resume. This only points out in a glaring fashion that the resume was done professionally and for obvious reasons.

When responding to a job announcement, try to include in the cover letter all your attributes that mesh with what was indicated in the ad. For instance, if the ad listed "map reading" as a desirable trait, be sure to highlight your qualifications and/or experience in map reading. As a general rule, the cover letter should not be more than one page long and should cover what the announcement asked for.

THE ORAL INTERVIEW

There is not a lot you can do to prepare for an oral interview. Unless you know the type of interview and the questions being asked, you are going in blind, so to speak. *Don't* worry about being nervous. Everyone is. Try not to be overly nervous though, where your voice cracks and breaks and you perspire profusely.

On the other hand, *don't* be too relaxed and nonchalant. It does not look good in the interview process to sit back with your legs crossed and your arm draped over the back of the chair. *Remember* that the interviewers are not only listening to what you have to say, but they are surveying your mannerisms, posture, dress, grooming, and the like. The interviewers may not have ever seen you before, and first impressions are lasting impressions.

Absolutely be on time. If you are late for an interview, it is almost like a kiss of death for that particular job. There may always be a reasonable excuse that caused your tardiness, but the burden will be squarely on you to show why you were late. Some examples of reasonable excuses are: "I was robbed, beat-up, and sent to the hospital on my way over here," or "I was caught in a flood where several people were swept away, and I ended up saving all of them." If you *do* have a reasonable excuse for your tardiness, if at all possible telephone and try to let someone know. If you flat out miss the interview and don't call and explain why, you have just indicated your desire not to continue in the selection process.

Do dress appropriately. That does not always mean a suit or sport coat and tie, but it almost always does. Wear conservative clothing without any loud colors or patterns. A white shirt, neutral tie, and dark suit (gray, black, or dark blue) is most appropriate. *Do not* forget about your shoes and socks. You are being evaluated in totality which includes your shoes and socks. Make sure your shoes are shined and your socks match whatever you are wearing. Try to make sure that your entire outfit is color coordinate and pleasing to the eye. *Do* make sure you are neatly groomed, e.g., hair is combed and not too long.

Women should not have an overabundance of makeup or perfume. And please stress perfume. There is nothing worse (of course, there is) than being in a small interview room permeated with the smell of Chanel #5 which happens to clash with the after-shave or perfume of one of the interviewers.

ANSWERING QUESTIONS

Do *not* attempt to answer a question when you clearly do not know the answer. It is OK to ask to have the question repeated or to ask for clarification. Look the interviewer in the eyes, but not aggressively. If there are several interviewers, look at them also while answering the question. Try not to fidget.

TRICKS OF THE TRADE

When being introduced to the panel, repeat each interviewer's name. For example, "Hi, Lt. Adams. Pleased to meet you." Doing this should help you remember each interviewer's name as you go through the process. It is impressive when you can repeat the interviewer's name some time during the interview. For example, you may need the second part of a question re-read, and you could say, "I'm sorry, Lt. Adams, but I did not understand the second part of the question." Try to work in each interviewer's name some time during the process, but don't do it unless it sounds natural.

Be prepared for trick questions that may or may not have anything to do with the job. Sometimes a question may be thrown in just to see what your reaction is. Sometimes it will be a humorous type of question, but be sure that it *is* before you laugh.

Also, be prepared for the unexpected. During one interview session we placed a lone chair way out in the middle of the room for the applicant to sit in. This very definitely causes stress to the interviewee. We were trying to see how the person coped with the situation. Some sat in the chair very appropriately, and others were obviously very nervous. We even had several drag the chair up to the interview table before sitting down. One candidate just stood and would not, or could not, sit in the chair. Some candidates appeared really perplexed when trying to decide the appropriate action to take regarding the chair.

Always follow up your interview with thank-you letters to the interview panel.

SECTION FOUR
YOUR FUTURE AND THAT OF
YOUR CHOSEN PROFESSION

Once you've landed your "dream job," another challenge begins. How do you not only make certain you keep the job, but also make certain you excel? Chapter Thirteen addresses this major challenge. The book ends with Chapter Fourteen and a return to the future of law enforcement and private security and what it will require in the decades ahead. Only those who are open to, who in fact embrace, change are likely to excel in law enforcement and private security in the twenty-first century.

Preparation for the future is critical because that's where you'll be spending the rest of your life!

CHAPTER 13

AT LAST! YOU'VE GOT THE JOB!

CONGRATULATIONS!!!

When you are making a success of something, it's not work. It's a way of life. You enjoy yourself because you are making your contribution to the world.--Andy Granatelli.

Do You Know:

   * How successful candidates may lose the sought-after job within a week?

   * How to play politics?

   * How to be "appropriate" on the job?

   * Why keeping a job can be harder on you than not getting it?

   * How dangerous "knowing it all" can be?

   * What questions are appropriate?

   * Why it can be so easy to succumb to peer pressure on the job?

   * How to wait until you are asked?

   * Why you should not play "games" on the job?

   * Why being yourself is critically important?

INTRODUCTION

By the time you get to this chapter, you will have covered an exceptional amount of material that should give you a genuine edge during your job search. You have taken a look at where to find jobs, how to write a resume, how to best present yourself, how to interview, how to follow up, and even how to deal with those inevitable rejections. Hopefully you were able to assimilate all this information and emerge victorious.

Hold everything! The race is not over yet. In a sense, it is just beginning. The only thing expected of the unsuccessful candidate is to be a good loser. But for the successful job seeker, the ultimate challenge is just ahead. Getting a job brings a whole new set of problems, especially in law enforcement where you usually face a six-month to one-year probationary period.

Entry-level employees, in particular, are subject to a multitude of unwritten rules. Because law enforcement and private security are fields traditionally closed to outsiders, you have no basis to understand the expectations. You'll learn all too soon that the expectations are extremely high.

Starting a new job is like going to court. It doesn't happen all that often, but when it does, officers are expected to know what to do without having to be told ahead of time. To make an error could be very serious. The same with getting the job. Do you act like the old-timers? Do you act like the rookies? It is imperative that you have at least some idea of what to expect. Call it learning from others' mistakes.

What a bitter disappointment it must be to be successful in the pursuit of that dream job--only to lose it because you don't know what these circumstances demand. While many job applicants who could probably do the job just fine never get the chance because they cannot interview adequately, the opposite is true as well--many people who cannot perform adequately get the job because they came across very well during the interview. You have to balance this situation. Here's what needs to be done once you get the job:

* Keep trying
* Be appropriate
* Know nothing
* Wait until you are asked
* Understand politics
* Be yourself

KEEP TRYING

Do not stop putting forth your best effort just because you have the job. If anything, make even greater attempts to fit into the new job than you did to get it. As Abraham Lincoln was fond of saying: "Things may come to those who wait, but only the things left by those who hustle." This is particularly true for individuals who either have not had a job or a professional-type job before. Law enforcement and private security jobs are demanding, both in expectations and workload. You will be expected to perform as a professional, even at an entry-level position. Most employers expect you to know the basics. They seldom take time to ask if you do.

It's a far greater error to *not* ask questions than to, for whatever reasons, be afraid to ask and then make a mistake. It is far better to ask a "dumb" question than to make a dumb mistake. No one likes to appear unintelligent. But any employer knows that no one knows it all. Employers want to have employees who are intelligent enough to direct themselves while knowing enough to stop and ask for help when needed. In effect, there are no dumb questions.

BE APPROPRIATE

This aspect of easing into your new job may seem terribly simplistic, but it's not. The job you have landed is a far cry from most other entry-level jobs such as working at a fast food restaurant, washing cars, or bagging groceries. The usual horseplay and immature attitudes frequently found at such jobs are simply not tolerated in any law enforcement or security job. When you think about it, it is easy to understand that anything short of professional behavior is not good enough. These fields are constantly seeking to prove their professional image and must demand employees who will help in this mission.

A major difficulty is that it is hard for new employees to know just what *is* appropriate behavior, unless you have been a police explorer, a reserve officer, or had some other association with a department. Few outsiders know what goes on "inside." Particularly for a newly hired individual, a conservative, low-key, quiet approach is not only appropriate, it's key to survival.

The best way to discover what behavior is appropriate is to simply assume a laid-back approach and take the necessary time to observe what is happening around you. You will see what behavior is approved of and disapproved of. A quiet approach for a new employee is always appreciated, while giving you a chance to ease into an admittedly uncomfortable new role.

Particularly younger people who have had little experience in the job world are susceptible to starting out with some rather "extreme" behavior. An overconfident, "cocky," attitude is often a cover-up for some very natural feelings of discomfort, self-doubt, and personal reservations. Coming on too strong, however, can be very abrasive to fellow workers. Such an attitude tends to keep people at a distance when you really need them to welcome you to your new job reassuringly.

KNOW NOTHING

It is frequently easy to tell who the new kids on the block are. They are often overbearing and brash, seeming to go out of their way to show the world they know it all--or at least *think* they know it all. Actually, the more experienced officers become, the more those officers acknowledge that there is always more to learn.

Fact: a hierarchy exists in every police department and security corporation. Entry-level employees, especially *new* entry-level employees, are at the bottom of the ladder. You may never recover from the damage unintentionally done by telling anyone above your bottom level position how *they* should be doing something. Many rookies destroy relationships with senior officers (maybe senior by only a year) by advising them on a better holster to carry, or a safer way to make a traffic stop, or which lights to use on the squad car during a motorist assist.

Chances are the rookie was correct. Rookies usually have received up-to-date training that reflects better ways of doing things and have not had time to develop bad habits. *This is not the point.* You will have plenty of time to do it your own way. Irritate anyone early on and word will spread that you are a "know it all."

Make a point to *know nothing* to avoid being labeled in a way that, at best, will delay being accepted. This is definitely not advice to "play stupid." If you are asked for an opinion, give it as best you can. If you have to make a decision, make it as best you can. Make a good impression.

Show interest and a desire to learn. It may be difficult to admit to yourself and others that you *are* new and really *do* not *know it all*. But pretend that you do, and you have shot yourself in the foot. Not only will others not think you are dumb if you ask questions, they will appreciate the fact that you really want to learn.

WAIT UNTIL ASKED

This is a continuation of "know nothing." Officers in law enforcement or private security are in positions of respect. They tend to expect it and generally receive it. Particularly as a new employee, you will get more respect from other employees if you show respect for them. They deserve it. They have passed those difficult early stages of the job. They are now "regulars" and have a great deal to offer you as a newcomer. Give them the opportunity to share their wisdom with you.

Do not tell others at work all you know. Show respect, and make it very clear that you know considerably less than you think. This should not keep you from asking questions. You have a unique opportunity to learn, so take advantage of it. Do not, however, ask questions that are personally or professionally challenging to the individual (for example, "Why would you wear a holster everyone *knows* is dangerous *and* ugly?"). A better way might be to ask what equipment the officer would suggest you consider when you purchase your gear.

It will not make a positive impression to say to an officer you are riding with, "My instructor told us that you should tag such a violator for _____, why didn't you?" Rather, you might ask what other violations could have been written or how the officer decided what to write on that particular stop.

Many officers feel their own department does not adequately recognize them for their knowledge and ability. To have someone new ride with them and ask well-thought-out, inquisitive questions is flattering to that officer. We all like to be able to "strut our stuff." Your presence can be a positive experience for both of you *if* you take full advantage of it.

Keep in mind that people working in law enforcement and security make their living getting B.S.'d by the best. Do not pretend to be interested or ask questions to "set up" the officer to tell you something for an alternative purpose. You will be spotted before you get the question completed, and you are again off to a terrible start.

Is it possible to ask *too many* questions? This is difficult to answer. Determine this on your own. Teachers *want* students to ask appropriate questions, but also come to cringe at those always-present students who chronically ask questions for the sake of hearing themselves talk.

UNDERSTAND POLITICS

To understand politics, you need to understand that politics are impossible to understand. This is an area to be particularly careful of. Even seasoned veterans can easily fall prey to internal politics. Politics can be a deadly game and should particularly be avoided by the new hiree.

Every organization has its own politics. Webster's defines *politics* as: "competition between competing interest groups or individuals for power and leadership in a government or other group." That is a fitting definition, but the complexities are so deep you can be caught in the political web before ever being aware of its existence.

The biggest problem for newcomers is they do not know where the political lines are drawn. While certain people tend to be more than willing to give advice, such advice may not turn out to be at all sound. Eventually you will learn who you can talk openly to. Some people are willing to share helpful insights; others may well set you up for a fall. Some things you might innocently say may offend someone. *You just do not know*, so don't take a chance. For example, if someone talks negatively about another employee, don't get involved. You may want to nod or grunt appropriately, but if you also start making comments about others, you will quickly expose yourself as a gossip.

Experienced officers learn that it is best to never write anything they do not want to show up because it inevitably will surface. Similarly, it is a good practice to never say things you don't want heard because statements always seem to get repeated.

People will tell you things in confidence. An eight-hour shift in a squad car or on security duty lends itself to sharing a lot of thoughts and ideas. Should you make the mistake of telling others what was told to you, particularly in the wee hours of the morning or late at night, you may cause some serious relationship problems for yourself and others. Never say anything you do not want repeated and never repeat what is told to you in confidence.

Do not play politics. Do not try to understand politics. Do not get yourself drawn into politics--important advice for anyone on the job, but absolutely crucial for a newly hired individual.

BE YOURSELF

This advice is last because it is probably most important. You managed to get the job by being yourself, and you will succeed by being yourself. Recognize from the start that it is very uncomfortable to start a new job, particularly in a field you are not used to. That is just another "job fact," so don't fight it. Accept it, and do not get down on yourself because you are nervous, afraid, feeling inadequate, and all those other feelings all of us have had whenever we start new jobs. The first few weeks *are* going to be rough. Draw energy from it rather than allowing it to exhaust you.

Police and security officers make their livings dealing with people who are trying to run scams on them. Many of these individuals are very good and may be able to fool the professionals at first. You will not be able to. Trying to do so will only result in your being labeled as someone trying to be someone you are not. Officers must be honest!

An important part of "yourself" that you bring to law enforcement or private security is honesty and integrity. These fields demand nothing less. An employee in such work who is caught lying or stealing has few, if any, second chances. This is not only the way it must be, but the way it should be. Develop these important parts of yourself, and do not, under any circumstances, engage in behavior that will not only ruin this job, but probably your career. These professions earn respect, but if you fall from their grace, you earn a label difficult to get rid of.

Peer pressure is always difficult to cope with. As a rookie, you will be expected to do as you are told. If you are unfortunate enough to get drawn into a bad group of fellow employees, you will be faced with some tough decisions. Do not engage in police brutality. Use only the minimum force necessary under the circumstances to accomplish the objective. Do not let peer pressure cause you to violate this important principle. Also recognize that to stand by and watch unethical, possibly illegal, behavior is only slightly less devious than actually participating. If you don't think you can resist the temptations from within or without, get out now.

If you are not happy, do something about it. These jobs are *not* for everyone. If you are not happy at it, or if you can foresee problems for whatever reason, admit this to yourself as soon as you become aware of it. It is sad to see people suffer through the years at jobs they dislike--especially those in jobs that provide the individual with a great deal of power and authority.

Perhaps certain officers "go bad" by becoming terribly abusive or sarcastic, and perpetuate the stereotype that the profession has because the job is just no longer right for that person . . . and it shows. Further, consider that professionals who dislike the work do not have the necessary concentration to be safe. A lot of horrible things can result from remaining in a job "too long."

Do not become cynical because of the nature of the work, the cliental, or opinions expressed by fellow officers. Watch out for "burn out." Use R&R time effectively to relieve stress. Do not become a "mooch," sponging off cooperative retailers, which usually begins with free coffee. Remember the concept of *quid pro quo*, that is *those who give usually expect something in return*.

The longer you remain in a job, any job, the harder it is to let go of the benefits. You will be much further ahead to be honest with yourself and leave if the work does not suit you.

Similarly, the work may suit you just fine, but the job may not. For a variety of reasons, not every employment opportunity will fit everyone. If you know you want to be a police or security officer, but personalities or any other factors make this particular job less than satisfying, do *not* stay around. It is unlikely that things will improve. There *is* a job out there for you. Your job is to find it.

CONCLUSION

Congratulations! You've got the job! These words will, and should, be a deserved conclusion to a significant amount of work. Relish in them. You are well on your way to professional career fulfillment. Don't let your guard down, and don't give up pursuing excellence. Set exceptional goals for yourself, and you will be exceptional.

Work in law enforcement, security, and related fields is important. It is satisfying. It says something about you that people working in other fields cannot boast. Congratulations on choosing these fields to pursue employment in and for making the effort to do it well.

YOUR GAME PLAN FOR EXCELLING ON THE JOB

Take time *now* to write out, on a *separate* piece of paper, three goals to help you excel in your new position. Put the paper someplace you will see it often. Let these goals guide you as you embark on your exciting new career. And again, congratulations!

MIND STRETCHES*****

1. Have you ever been "too enthusiastic" at a new job? Why do you think you were? Did it hurt you?

2. What behaviors have you observed in people in uncomfortable situations (like in a new job)?

3. Why do you think important people often seem so "down to earth"? Conversely, why do you think many "not-so-important" people act so brash?

4. How long does it take to "fit in" at a new job? What helps you fit in?

5. Have you ever felt pressured at a job to behave in a way you did not feel comfortable? How did you handle this situation?

6. Why do you think people, particularly officers, seem to like to complain or be negative? What traps can this create for new employees?

7. What dangers are there in "taking sides" in an office dispute? How can you avoid becoming involved?

8. Can people who work together get along "too well"? Are "office romances" good or bad? Can they be avoided, or do they "just happen"?

9. How would you handle a situation in which you knew a co-worker was doing something illegal, immoral, or unethical? Would you respond differently if the person was a peer or your supervisor?

10. At what point do you think people stop growing and developing professionally? What opportunities exist to help you maintain your own personal and professional vitality?

"Now that I got this job I'm gonna tell those old guys where to get off."

AN INSIDER'S VIEW

SERVING PROBATION

Linda Miller
Sergeant
Bloomington Police Department

Now that you have landed that job, you probably think you can relax. Think again. You are about to undergo a period of the most intense scrutiny you've ever experienced. It's called *probation*. Usually a period of six months to a year, it gives the department a chance to see you in action and to evaluate your work, your judgment, and your style of relating to others. You don't have that job wrapped until you "make probation."

Think of this period as a time to apply what you've learned in school and what you will learn on the job. Advice from veteran officers as you begin your probationary period would surely include the following:

* Don't be a know-it-all. You may have been the star of the academy, but keep it to yourself or you may alienate your colleagues.

* Learn the basics well. Fancy shooting or exotic defensive tactics moves won't be of much help to you unless you can also write a good report and make a proper car stop.

* Don't be a "gadget" person. One can often tell a rookie by the surprising number of pieces of equipment hanging from the gunbelt.

* Concentrate on report writing. Carry a pocket dictionary if you are not a good speller.

* Watch respected veteran officers do their job and learn from them. Do not, however, adopt their "bad" work habits.

* Don't take short cuts. These are for veterans willing to live with the consequences. You can't afford it.

* Don't get a reputation for being too aggressive. You want to be a willing worker, very interested in doing your job, but not a crusader chosen to rid the world of criminals.

* Treat the public and your co-workers with respect. Displaying your personal prejudices can be detrimental to your continued employment. Do not make derogatory racial or sexual remarks, even if you hear others doing so.

* Try to develop a reputation of being cooperative and nonargumentative. Be a team player.

* You may be in social situations with co-workers where alcohol is served. Drink conservatively. You can be sure that what you say and do under the influence of alcohol will be the talk of the department by the next day at the latest. Alcohol abuse is a serious problem in this society and in law enforcement. Most departments will not be impressed with a rookie who displays even a hint of alcohol abuse.

* The same goes for sexual behavior. Keep your personal life personal. Above all, don't sleep around with fellow employees.

Remember, your training officer and the department's supervisors have your future in their hands. In many departments, probationary employees can be let go for *any* reason. With a little forethought, you can avoid providing a reason.

You have what it takes for the job or you wouldn't have been hired. And the department wants you to "make it" too. They have invested time and money in your hiring and training. They need you to assure them they've made the right choice.

CHAPTER 14
THE FUTURE REVISITED

If you can dream it, you can do it.--Walt Disney

Do You Know:

* Why history is important in challenging the future?

* What changes Americans can anticipate in our immediate future?

* How these factors will affect law enforcement and security?

* What new challenges our aging population will present?

* What changes technological advancements in our world will have on law enforcement?

* Why the profession of law enforcement is said to have changed little in centuries?

* What interaction public law enforcement and private security will be likely to have in the future? Why?

* What two courses futurist, Alvin Toffler, says law enforcement can take?

* What advanced training could prove beneficial to law enforcement and security officers?

* Whether speciality training and education are the wave of the criminal justice future?

INTRODUCTION

You began this book with a look at employment trends in law enforcement and private security. You have looked at these fields in depth and know how to go about entering them. Now take another look at just what the future might hold.

It has been said that the best way to know where you are going is to look at where you have been. Private security and law enforcement have deep roots in our past. Be it the Code of Hammurabi (2200 B.C.), the Justinian Code (A.D. 527), Leges Henrici (A.D. 1100s), the Magna Carta, the United States Constitution, or the world A.C.--after computers--law enforcement/private security has played an extraordinary role in the development of civilization. Whether the system was that of a Hue and Cry (A.D. 800s), a Watch and Ward (1200s), or one of the more modern approaches to enforcing the law such as constables, Bow Street Runners (first detectives in London), Bobbies, deputies, marshals, and police officers have been available as valuable societal resources.

For those who have been involved in law enforcement and security, "job security" is not an issue. No matter what social policies are in place, no matter what resources are available, the law will need to be enforced, and people will continue to call for help.

While our technology may become increasingly sophisticated and our society itself more complex, a certain segment of our population will prey upon the weak. Similarly, there will continue to be individuals who, for whatever reason, are unable to care for themselves. The equipment may change, but the challenge will remain-- *to protect and to serve.*

A BRIEF HISTORY

You may be familiar with futurist Toffler's "three waves" theory, using the comparison of waves of the ocean and sweeping major changes in society:

> * The Agricultural Revolution
> * The Industrial Revolution
> * The Technological Revolution

Toffler suggests that the Agricultural Revolution occurred about 8,000 B.C., sweeping aside 45,000 years of cave dwelling. The second wave came around 1760, turning our landscape from that of "amber waves of grain" and "fruited plains" to that of smokestacks. This second wave was not without its resistors. A group of workers, called Luddites, systematically destroyed machinery they saw as a threat to manual laborers. But the wave engulfed America, forcing many farmers to become blue collar workers.

The third wave, the Technological Revolution, began in the mid-fifties and again changed the face of the American work place. Brains rather than brawn became important, and white collar workers began displacing blue collar workers. Again, resistance has occurred. Many people, similar to the Luddites, rebelled against computers, fax machines, voice mail systems. But the third wave *is* here.

Tafoya (1990, p.15) shows how Toffler's wave analogy can be used to describe changes in law enforcement. The first wave was the Metropolitan Police Act of 1829, the first major reform in law enforcement, bringing order and a military model to law enforcement:

> A century later in the 1930s, August Vollmer and O.W.Wilson, two American police pioneers, advanced the goal of "professionalizing" law enforcement. Their efforts ushered in the "second wave" of major law enforcement reform. Standardization, specialization, synchronization, concentration, maximization, and centralization dominated law enforcement during this era.

The third wave began with the civil unrest of the 1960s and 70s. Law enforcement professionals began questioning the military model and the bureaucracy associated with policing. In the past the majority of law enforcement and private security officers had a military background and were used to accepting orders without question. This is no longer true of today's more highly educated young workers who are used to thinking for themselves. Tafoya (p.15) suggests that:

> Today, there is ample evidence to indicate that insofar as dealing with people is concerned, the good ole days may best serve as memories, not models for future personnel practices.

According to Tafoya (p.13), almost a decade ago Toffler spoke to a group of law enforcement executives at the FBI Academy and:

> suggested that because change was taking place so rapidly, tremendous social pressures were occurring and will continue to ferment and explode unless opportunities were created to relieve those pressures.

> According to Toffler, law enforcement, like society, has two possible courses of action. The first is to cling to the status quo; the second to facilitate social change.

Our criminal justice system has a rich history. The fact that the field is so historically based and tends to be so conservative may help to explain why more reliance may have been placed on past tradition than on future advancement. Some believe that other than technologically, the professions of law enforcement and private security and their delivery have actually changed little for literally centuries.

But this book is not about the history of criminal justice, or even about past employment trends. It is about getting the job you want and the future of these professions--*your future*. The best way to know where you are going is to see where your chosen profession has been, and is. Start by looking at who is doing what, where, and how. This will be a general look at the world of work with an examination of what the future may hold for the professions of law enforcement and security and those who choose to be a part of it.

OUR CHANGING WORLD

The Tofflers (1990, pp.2-5) suggest: "We are witnessing the massive breakdown of America as we knew it and the emergence of a strange, new 21st-century America whose basic institutional structures have yet to be formed." They point out that in the past, immigrants who spoke little or no English and poor, uneducated Americans were able to fit into the mainstream because jobs required musclepower rather than mindpower. This is no longer true. Those "on the bottom rung" are more likely to stay there. They caution that:

> It is simple-minded to blame crime on poverty. There are plenty of societies in which poverty does *not* produce crime. But it is equally witless to assume that millions of poor, jobless young people--not part of the work-world culture and bursting with energy and anger--are going to stay off the streets and join knitting clubs.

More importantly, say the Tofflers, as social disapproval has less and less power, "law enforcement must take over." In other words, the role of law enforcement and security will be even more critical in the years ahead. Trojanowicz and Carter (1990, pp.6-12) point out several other changes that will occur in the next century:

* White dominance of the United States will end.
* American will grow "grayer."

* Illegal immigrants will flood into the country.
* Minorities and women will make significant gains.

Change *always* creates a tension. Here the tension is between professions very much rooted in history and tradition and a society always on the move. As recently as the past decade, law enforcement and security have become recognized as professions. New responses to new challenges are sure to emerge.

OUR CHANGING PROFESSIONS

Brown (1991, p.21) notes:

> Police administrators must recognize and address the unique challenges precipitated by the monumental changes occurring both in this country and around the world. The key to meeting these challenges is strong leadership. Without it, police administrators are likely to flounder as the dynamics of change sweep over them, leaving in their wake old and ineffective ways of dealing with a rapidly changing society. . . .
>
> Perpetual change will be the byword of the 1990s.

One of *the* most important changes is the flood of immigrants, legal and illegal, presenting a tremendous challenge to law enforcement and private security. Why? As noted by Trojanowicz and Carter (pp.8-9) these immigrants "cluster together in poor neighborhoods with high crime rates" so we must "guard against stereotyping."

In addition, many immigrants come from cultures where uniformed officers are feared, not respected. Further, many will become victims because they do not know our laws or our customs and are "easy targets for all kinds of predators."

No one can argue that our world is changing, perhaps faster than we can keep up with. Technologically speaking, it seems that the "good guys" are always racing just to keep up with the firepower of the criminal element. Imagine that while the bad guys have been using semi-automatic weapons for years, many police agencies in the United States are still using revolvers. Further, prisons and jails, for the most part, are full and overflowing, and the courts are requiring more correctional authorities to either build more facilities or release more prisoners. The release of unrehabilitated prisoners will certainly affect most police agencies and their personnel in the near future.

An even greater problem may be the increasing significance of the subculture of the illegal drug world and the spinoffs that are adversely affecting more and more people and their organizations (including families) in this country. This problem permeates our society and presents a challenge to both public and private officers.

Even as the makeup of our community is changing, the majority of police agencies still provide the same style of law enforcement service they always have. If law enforcement and the entire criminal justice system are to keep up with the developing needs of society, then it is likely that the way that such services are provided will need to be re-examined. One of the biggest changes that immediately comes to mind is the increasing requirement of police to be educated.

As the profession of law enforcement is considered to be a true profession, the need for education has increased. Police must keep up with the times and with the expectations of the community they serve.

Another important change is in the makeup of those entering law enforcement/security and their expectations. There was a time that these professions were jobs that *men* did upon returning from military service, perhaps because they had no other skills or abilities. In some jurisdictions an individual can still get hired as an officer, without any necessary prior training, and be handed a badge and a gun and expected to enforce the law--or businesses regulations. Such agencies are facing extinction, however.

PUBLIC/PRIVATE COOPERATION

"Private security has emerged as a major player in the safeguarding of Americans and their property," according to Mangan and Shanahan (1990, p.18). They note that (p.19):

> Police have traditionally viewed private security employees as inadequately trained and ill-paid individuals who could not find other work but were nevertheless allowed to carry a gun . . .

> While the 1960s were characterized as a period of indifference toward private security and the 1970s as one of changing perceptions and some mistrust of the industry, the 1980s and 1990s will most likely be regarded as the era of collaboration and joint ventures between public law enforcement and private security.

As our increasing aging and business populations are likely to continue their inhabitation of high-rise buildings, their reliance on private security will also increase. The traditional "police officer" patrolling public roads or a beat officer on foot cannot practically be expected to patrol such structures. Unlike public police officers, private security officers can and do patrol specific buildings, even specific floors or rooms within buildings. It can be anticipated that the fields of public law enforcement and private security may tend to blend together as society recognizes the need for each and as these professions themselves learn how they can best work together--to the benefit of all.

OFFICERS OF THE FUTURE

As the needs of our society change, so will the professions of law enforcement and private security, and the expectations of those entering or remaining in these fields.

Education will continue to be viewed as important, including very specialized education. Applicants with special skills in foreign language or special experiences with different groups such as juveniles or those from different cultures, or those with handicaps, will be sought. These skills will make applicants particularly attractive to employers. Technical skills such as ability with computers will, no doubt, look attractive to employers as well.

Anything you can do to set yourself positively apart from others is important. If you have the chance to acquire specialized skills, take that chance.

Society is changing, and our profession is changing. To meet the increasing demands of our world, people are having to become specialists. Attorneys specialize in certain areas of law. Physicians specialize within the medical field. And more and more, those in law enforcement, private security, and related fields are specializing.

While most officers do, and possibly should, begin their careers as generalists, most upwardly mobile, successful professional police and security officers will specialize: juvenile specialists, crime prevention specialists, polygraph specialists, the list goes on. As technology continues to develop, specialists in these areas will be sought. As our society changes, becomes older, more diverse in demographic and cultural makeup, other needed specialities will emerge as well.

This does not mean that the day of the "generalist" police or security officer on patrol is nearing an end. It is highly likely that patrol officers will continue as the backbone of any law enforcement or security agency. The fact is, every aspect of our world is becoming more complex and specialized. Those who are successful today recognized a decade or two ago, what the future would need. The people who are going to put themselves in a good position for future advancement will be able to successfully work toward the future. Looking toward the future may be as general as obtaining a generalized advanced education to effectively interact with those of similar educational levels in other professions. It may be acknowledging the increasing cultural diversity and continuing interest that people have in moving to the United States and learning a foreign language or two.

It may be acquiring a management degree, a law degree, a degree in computer science, or in public relations, a degree in the sciences or psychology. Our world is complex and no doubt will require significantly more of law enforcement and security professionals than in the past. It's your call. Don't merely keep up with the others. Take advantage of the myriad of opportunities available to meet the challenge and forge ahead.

REFERENCES

Brown, Lee P. "Policing in the '90s. Responding to a Changing Environment," *The Police Chief*, March 1991, pp.20-23.

Mangan, Terence J. and Shanahan, Michael G. "Public Law Enforcement/Private Security: A New Partnership?" *FBI Law Enforcement Bulletin*, January 1990, pp.18-22.

McCord, Rob and Wicker, Elaine. "Tomorrow's America: Law Enforcement's Coming Challenge," *FBI Law Enforcement Bulletin*, January 1990, pp.28-32.

Tafoya, William L. "The Future of Policing," *FBI Law Enforcement Bulletin*, January 1990, pp.13-17.

Toffler, Alvin and Heidi. "The Future of Law Enforcement: Dangerous and Different," *FBI Law Enforcement Bulletin*, January 1990, pp.2-5.

Trojanowicz, Robert C. and Carter, David L. "The Changing Face of America," *FBI Law Enforcement Bulletin*, January 1990, pp.6-11.

MIND STRETCHES*******

1. Is your community changing? How? What about neighboring communities?

2. What effect is this having on law enforcement and private security?

3. Do you see law enforcement and private security
   changing to respond to new challenges?

4. Why would the criminal justice system be slow to change?

5. What special training or education can you anticipate would make you a better
   law enforcement or security professional?

6. Why do you think more people don't pursue advanced education or specialized
   training? Are these reasons legitimate?

7. Can law enforcement continue as it has been in serving communities, or is some
   change inevitable? What change do you foresee, if any? What can you begin
   doing right now to meet the challenge?

8. What role will private security have in the future?

9. How will this affect law enforcement?

10. How will the professions of law enforcement and private security meet the
    increasing demands of the future to maintain very high professional standards?

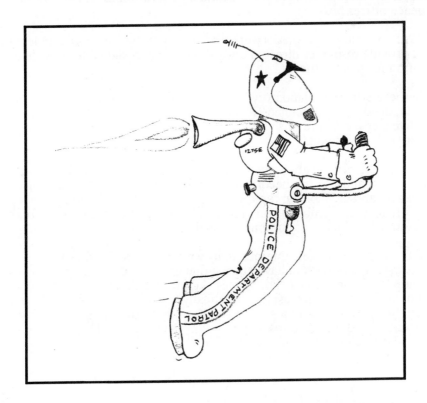

AN INSIDER'S VIEW

WHAT YOU'LL NEED TO SUCCEED

IN THE 21ST CENTURY

Timothy E. Erickson
Education Coordinator
Minnesota Board of Peace Officer Standards and Training

In the early 1900's August Vollmer, Chief of Police in Berkeley, California, had a vision which included a place for college-educated peace officers within the field of law enforcement.

Since the days of Vollmer, this vision has been re-visited periodically in the form of such events as the *Wickersham Report* of the 1930's and the *President's Commission on Law Enforcement and Administration of Justice* in the 1960's. In fact, the cry for college-educated peace officers has come from several quarters within this century, but until rather recently, few real efforts have occurred to make this vision a reality.

During the 1970's substantial amounts of money were spent by the federal government in the form of LEAA grants to help working peace officers attain post-secondary education. In 1977 Minnesota became the first state to require as a state standard, a minimum level of post-secondary education as an entry requirement for the peace officer position.

In 1989 two separate proposals were introduced at the congressional level which would provide resources directed toward programs designed to provide college-level education for peace officers.

While these efforts are laudatory, the law enforcement profession has only been slowly nudged to the precipice. It is time for individual practitioners to take proactive steps to insure this vision for themselves. In other words, peace officers need to "fish or cut bait."

The increasing complexity of the issues in our society, issues individual peace officer's must address, has become an incredible burden. Rapid advances in theory, knowledge, and technology; rapidly changing demographics; and newly developing and evolving social problems ranging from ecology to global political realities--all point toward the need for continual growth in peace officer education.

In addition, peace officers interact daily with other professionals in the criminal justice system, all of whom have at least one undergraduate degree. Most have graduate level educational experiences. Add to this the fact that the educational level of all citizens is increasing dramatically (approximately 40 to 60 percent of current high school graduates will go on to some form of post-secondary education experience), and it is clear that if peace officer education does not at least keep pace with these changes, individual officers will be "left in the dust."

All of the preceding information aside, individuals entering law enforcement professions owe it to themselves to aspire to higher educational levels and to make the commitment to the process of life-long learning. This is important for several reasons.

First, broadly based, post-secondary liberal arts education prepares individuals for a wide range of professional opportunities both within and outside of the law enforcement profession. Recent research indicates that most adults will have the opportunity to make major career changes anywhere from three to six times during their lifespans. It would be tragic if those choosing law enforcement as one of their careers were not in a position to have similar opportunities.

Second, although no scientific or empirical evidence indicates that increased education results in increased performance levels of peace officers, numerous recent perceptual studies report that citizens have more confidence in and esteem for more highly educated officers.

Third, law enforcement executives are constantly expressing the need for more officers who have:

> * Well-developed verbal and written communication skills.
> * Excellent critical thinking and decision-making skills.
> * Highly developed ethical and moral standards.
> * The ability to analyze complex public policy issues and social trends.

Such attributes are developed in the broad-based, interdisciplinary liberal arts curriculum available through post-secondary educational experiences.

Finally, and perhaps most important, post-secondary education will prepare peace officers to grow personally. If allowed to, the law enforcement environment can become a narrow, isolated, cynical place, not unlike a prison. Post-secondary education, continuing education, commitment to life-long learning, and an appreciation for diversity can help peace officers keep the walls from closing in on them.

We in law enforcement do not have the luxury to wait for our agencies or our governments to provide education for us. We must recognize that education is as important to our "officer survival skills" as our firearms and other weapons training. Education does not need to be a state mandate or a department policy. It can be our individual choice, a gift to ourselves. No group of professionals is more deserving.

APPENDIXES

A Resume Worksheets

B Sample Resumes

C Sample Cover Letters and Follow-Up Letters

D Sources of Employment Information

E Sample Application Forms

F Equal Employment Opportunity (EEO) Guidelines

RESUME WORKSHEETS

Name:_____

Current Address:_____

_____

Permanent Address: _____

_____

Phone Number(s):_____

Colleges:_____

_____

Professional Schools:_____

_____

_____

_____

Certificates Held:_____

_____

_____

_____

Other Educational Experiences:_____

_____

_____

High School: _____

_____

EMPLOYMENT HISTORY
(Note: Make as many copies of this form as you have had jobs so you can complete one form for each job you've had.)

Dates Employed: From _____ to _____

Employer: _____

  Address: _____

          _____

  Phone: _____

  Supervisor: _____

Position/Title: _____

Responsibilities: _____

_____

_____

_____

_____

Skills Acquired: _____

_____

_____

_____

_____

Achievements/Awards: _____

_____

_____

_____

Salary (NOT included in resume): _____

Reason for Change: (NOT included in resume): _____

_____

_____

Position Desired/Employment Objective: _____

_____

_____

Other information that may be put in your resume includes the following:

Birthdate: _____

Height: _____

Weight: _____

Health: _____

Travel: _____
  (Willing to travel?)

Location: _____
  (Willing to relocate?)

Military: _____
  (Service, dates, rank, honorable discharge)

_____

_____

  Reserve status: _____

Professional Memberships: _____
  (Committees served on, awards)

_____

_____

_____

_____

Foreign Languages: _____
  (Read, write, speak fluently)

Foreign Travel: _____

_____

_____

Awards: _____

_____

_____

Publications: _____

_____

_____

Community Service/Involvement: _____
   (Organizations, offices held, etc.)

_____

_____

_____

Interests/Hobbies: _____
   (Avocations, non-business pursuits)

_____

_____

_____

Availability: _____
   (Immediate or extent of "notice" required)

Present Employer Contact: _____
   (Is present employer aware of your prospective job change?
    May the employer be contacted?)

Salary Desired: _____
   (NOT included in resume, but know what you'd expect.)

BUSINESS/PROFESSIONAL/ACADEMIC REFERENCES:

Full Name: _____

Position: _____

Address: _____

_____

Phone: _____

Full Name: _____

Position: _____

Address: _____

_____

Phone: _____

Full Name: _____

Position: _____

Address: _____

_____

Phone: _____

PERSONAL REFERENCE:

Full Name: _____

Relationship: _____
(Neighbor, teammate, etc.)

Address: _____

_____

Phone: _____

RESUME EVALUATION CHECKLIST

CATEGORY	Excellent	Average	Poor	How to Improve
APPEARANCE				
Is the format clean?				
Is it easy to follow?				
Are headings effective?				
Does it make the reader want to read it?				
CONTENT				
Do my qualifications stand out?				
Is the language clear and understandable?				
Have I used short phrases?				
Have I used verbs (action words)?				
Is it brief and to the point?				
Are all important skills and qualifications included?				
Does it create a true picture of me?				
Is irrelevant personal information left out?				
PROOFREADING				
Is it error free?				
Spelling?				
Punctuation?				

APPENDIX B

SAMPLE RESUMES

Historical/Chronological Resume

TERRY A. SMITH
101 South First Street
Minneapolis, MN 55404

Home Phone: (612) 827-5650
Work Phone: (612) 339-9123

PERSONAL   Date of Birth: 6/3/69, 6'0", 175 lbs. Will relocate.

EDUCATION

1987-91   NORMANDALE COMMUNITY COLLEGE
                 Bloomington, Minnesota
                 Associate Arts Degree and Law Enforcement Certificate.
                        Member of football team.
                        Photographer for school paper.

1987   BLOOMINGTON HIGH SCHOOL
                 Bloomington, Minnesota
                 High school diploma. Honor student.
                        Member of football team.

WORK EXPERIENCE

1988 to present   SECURITY OFFICER
                  Dayton's Department Store
                  Minneapolis, Minnesota
                  Hired as store detective. Duties include plainclothes observation of retail sales area to observe and arrest shoplifters. Assist in loss prevention seminars for store employees.

1985-1988   CASHIER
                  Burger King
                  Bloomington, Minnesota
                  Hired as dishwasher. Promoted to busboy and then to cashier. Duties as cashier included, taking customers' orders, determining, the amount due, making change, and filling the orders. Also responsible for totalling up register at end of shift.

References available on request.

Functional Resume

WILLIAM L. SMITH
10 South First Street
Minneapolis, MN 55404
Home Phone: (612) 339-9123

Personal Data, Date of Birth: 6-3-62, 6' 0", 175 lbs. Single

Objective:

Position as a law enforcement officer.

Work History

1987 - present

Southdale Shopping Center, Inc.,
Edina, Minnesota,

Security Officer:
Security

❏ Hired as uniformed security officer. Duties include patron assistance, emergency first-aid response, enforcement of property rules and statutes. Assist in training new employees by providing presentations on company rules and state criminal statutes. Frequently appear as witness in court cases resulting from my position. Work with the area law enforcement officers hired to assist during holiday seasons. Act as company representative to Minnesota Loss Control Society.

1985 - 1987

Kenny's Market, Inc.,
Bloomington, Minnesota

Office Worker:
Administration

❏ Hired as assistant to the vice-president. Duties included typing, filing, and telephone reception. In charge of confidential employee records. Assisted in organizing the company's first loss prevention program.

Education

1985 - 1987

☞ B.A., University of Minnesota, Minneapolis, Minnesota.

1983 - 1985.

☞ A.A., Law Enforcement Certification, Normandale Community College, Bloomington, Minnesota.

1986

❏ Emergency Medical Technical Technician Registration, Hennepin County Vo-Tech, Eden Prairie, Minnesota.

references on request.

WILLETT L. SMITH
10 South First Street
Minneapolis, MN 55404
Home Phone: (612) 827-5650
Work Phone: (612) 339-9123

Job Objective: Apply my proven ability in loss prevention.

Qualifications Retail Security:
Have developed knowledge and skills in the profession while employed as loss prevention officer for several retail stores. In addition to providing undercover and plainclothes loss prevention services as a store detective, have provided extensive training on the subject to store employees. Excellent performance reviews at each position. Continued increases in apprehension statistics. Received "Employee of the Month" award six times for excellent work as a security officer.

Supervisory Skills:

Promoted to supervisor of 17 loss prevention officers at most recent position. Duties included training, delegating duties, and scheduling. Performance statistics for the crew increased significantly.

Organizational Skills: All jobs have required detailed activity reports. Hands-on-experience using computers to organize data. Often provided oral reports to supervisors.

Employers

1983 - present	Donaldson's Department Store, Edina, MN
1982 - 1983	Tom Thumb Stores, Inc., St. Paul, MN
1980 - 82	Automobile Club of America, St. Louis Park, MN

Education

1983	Associate of Arts and Private Security Certificate Normandale Community College Bloomington, MN

Other

1984	Participated in organization of 1984 American Industrial Security Association National Convention.

References available on request.

APPENDIX C

SAMPLE COVER LETTER AND FOLLOW-UP LETTER

Sample Cover Letter

1234 Second Avenue
Los Angeles, CA 90017
September 5, 199_

Mytown Police Department
1234 First Avenue
Denver, CO 80203

Dear Lt. Jones:

Could your department use a well-educated, highly trained, enthusiastic officer?   With an A.A. degree in law enforcement and three years' experience as a reserve officer with the Los Angeles Police Department, I am ready to enter your profession and hope it will be with your department.

I am enclosing a resume highlighting my background, qualifications, and experience. I will call you the week of September 15th to arrange for a personal interview.

I will look forward to talking with you.

Sincerely,

Jane Smith

Encl. Resume

Sample Follow-Up Letter

1234 Second Avenue
Boulder, CO 23456
September 21, 19

Protection Plus Security
1234 First Avenue
Denver, CO 12345

Attn: Mr. Ronald Smith,
     President

Dear Mr. Smith:

Thank you for the opportunity to participate in the
hiring process for the position of security officer.
I delivered my resume to your office yesterday and
am sorry to have missed you.

I remain extremely interested in the position and
look forward to the possibility of being considered
for the job. Please call if you need any further
information.

Very sincerely,

Scott Anderson

APPENDIX D

JOB INFORMATION SOURCES

HELPFUL HINTS FOR GETTING A JOB

From: Job Search. Career Information Series. Job Service, Minnesota Department of Employment Services.

From among the many sources of job information, you will have to select those most appropriate for you. The ones you choose will depend on the type of job you want, where you want to live and want to work, and the demand in your field. Some sources of job information are listed below. Brief comments on their characteristics may help you choose the ones best suited to your needs.

STATE JOB SERVICE. It has more job listings in more occupational categories than any other single source. Using a computer, job openings in the entire State are compiled for use by placement specialists. This job listing, known as the Job Bank, is updated and distributed daily to more than 50 State Job Service facilities located throughout Minnesota. Employment counseling and career consultation is also available. All services are provided free of charge.

FRIENDS AND RELATIVES. Through their work or social and business contacts, they may know of opportunities not listed by regular sources. But, of course, their knowledge is likely to be limited to their own, and perhaps a few other places of employment. If you're on good terms with a banker, insurance agent, or others that have a lot of contact with people, check with them for possible leads.

LIBRARY. Librarians can show you various business directories, membership rosters of various trade associations, purchasing guides, professional journals, etc. They can help you zero in on companies that utilize your particular skills.

SCHOOL OR COLLEGE PLACEMENT SERVICE. This may be a productive source, but is generally available only to students and alumni.

WANT ADS IN NEWSPAPERS, PROFESSIONAL JOURNALS, AND TRADE MAGAZINES. These provide a broad range of definite openings. A large share of listings in publications devoted to your field are likely to be for jobs you are qualified to fill. Analysis of the ads provides information about the extent of employment activity in your field throughout the area.

INDUSTRIAL AND CRAFT UNIONS. This is a productive source for members, particularly those with seniority. They may have exclusive hiring authority for some firms.

GOVERNMENT CIVIL SERVICE DEPARTMENTS. Federal, state, county, and city civil service departments fill jobs in a wide variety of professional, technical, clerical, craft, and other occupations.

some collect fees from employers. If you use a private agency, observe the following advice: (1) Be sure it is licensed by the State; (2) check its reputation with the Better Business Bureau, large employers, and friends; (3) before you sign a contract, be sure you understand it (ask if you may take it home to check it out); and (4) fees vary considerably, so make sure you understand what you must pay.

YELLOW PAGES OF TELEPHONE DIRECTORY, INDUSTRIAL DIRECTORIES, AND CHAMBER OF COMMERCE LISTS. These provide names of firms that employ workers in your field and other useful information.

HOW TO GET MORE INFORMATION

From *Criminal Justice Careers Guidebook.* U.S. Department of Labor. Raymond J. Donovan, Secretary. Employment and Training Administration. 1982.

The following is a list of agencies and organizations that can supply information about careers in the criminal justice system. In cases where specific listings of names and addresses cannot be given, other means of obtaining information are suggested. Although this listing of sources is not all inclusive, it does provide a base from which to start gathering career information.

LAW ENFORCEMENT

Federal Level

Bureau of Alcohol, Tobacco, and Firearms
U.S. Treasury Department
1111 Constitution Avenue, N.W.
Washington, D.C. 20220

Drug Enforcement Administration
U.S. Department of Justice
1405 I Street, N.W.
Washington, D.C. 20537

Federal Bureau of Investigation
U.S. Department of Justice
9th Street and Pennsylvania Avenue, N.W.
Washington, D.C. 20535

General Services Administration
Office of Federal Protective Service
   Management
18th and F Streets, N.W.
Washington, D.C. 20405

Immigration and Naturalization Service
U.S. Department of Justice
425 I Street, N.W.
Washington, D.C. 20536

Internal Revenue Service
Criminal Investigation Division
U.S. Treasury Department
1111 Constitution Avenue, N.W.
Washington, D.C. 20220

Internal Revenue Service
Internal Security Division
Career Development Section
U.S. Treasury Department
1111 Constitution Avenue, N.W.
Washington, D.C. 20220

United States Civil Service Commission
1900 E Street, N.W.
Washington, D.C. 20415

United States Customs Service
1301 Constitution Avenue, N.W.
Washington, D.C. 20229

United States Department of Agriculture
14th Street and Independence Avenue, S.W.
Washington, D.C. 20250

United States Department of Defense
The Pentagon
Washington, D.C. 20301

United States Department of Health
and Human Services
200 Independence Avenue, S.W.
Washington, D.C. 20201

United States Department of the Interior
C Street between 18th and 19th Streets, N.W.
Washington, D.C. 20240

United States Department of Labor
200 Constitution Avenue, N.W.
Washington, D.C. 20210

United States Department of Transportation
400 7th Street, S.W.
Washington, D.C. 20590

United States Marshals Service
One Tysons Corner Center
McLean, Virginia 22102

United States Postal Service
Chief Postal Inspector
475 L'Enfant Plaza, S.W.
Washington, D.C. 20260

United States Secret Service
Personnel Division
U.S. Treasury Department
1800 G Street, N.W.
Washington, D.C. 20223

Federal Job Information Centers

Information about federal employment can also be obtained by contacting the nearest Job Information Center in your area. Some Job Information Centers also provide information about jobs in other jurisdictions (local, county, and State) and are identified in the list below by an asterisk (*).

Alabama
Huntsville
Southerland Building
806 Governor's Drive, N.W. 35801

Alaska
Anchorage
Federal Bldg. and U.S. Courthouse
701 C St., P.O. Box 22. 99513

Arizona
Phoenix
552 N. Central Ave. 85004

Arkansas
Little Rock
Federal Bldg. Room 1319
700 West Capital Ave. 72201

California
Los Angeles
Linder Bldg.
845 S. Figueroa. 90017

Sacramento
Federal Bldg.
650 Capitol Mall. 95814

San Diego
880 Front St. 92188

San Francisco
Federal Bldg., Rm. 1001
450 Golden Ave. 94102

Colorado
*Denver
1845 Sherman St. 80203

Connecticut
Hartford
Federal Bldg., Rm. 717
450 Main St. 06103

Delaware
*Wilmington
Federal Bldg.
844 King St. 19801

District of Columbia
Metro Area
1900 E Street, N.W. 20415

Florida
*Miami
1000 Brickell Ave.
Suite 660. 33131

*Orlando
80 N. Hughey Ave. 32801

Georgia
Atlanta
Richard B. Russell Federal Bldg.
75 Spring St., S.W. 30303

Guam
Agana
238 O'Hara St.
Room 308. 96910

Hawaii
Honolulu (and island of Oahu)
Federal Bldg., Rm. 1310
300 Ala Moana Blvd. 96850

Idaho
Boise
Box 035, Federal Bldg. 83637

Illinois
Chicago
Dirksen Bldg., Rm. 1322
219 S. Dearborn St. 60604

Indiana
Indianapolis
46 East Ohio Street
Room 123. 46204

Iowa
Des Moines
210 Walnut St.
Rm. 191. 50309

Kansas
Wichita
One-Twenty Bldg., Room 101
120 S. Market St. 67202

Kentucky
Louisville
Federal Building
600 Federal Pl. 40202

Louisiana
New Orleans
F. Edward Hebert Building
610 South St., Rm. 103. 70130

Maine
Augusta
Federal Bldg., Rm. 611
Sewall St. and Western Ave. 04330

Maryland
Baltimore
Garmatz Federal Building
101 W. Lombard St. 21201

DC Metro Area
1900 E Street, N.W. 20415

Massachusetts
Boston
3 Center Plaza. 02108

Michigan
Detroit
477 Michigan Ave.
Rm. 595. 48226

Minnesota
Twin Cities
Federal Bldg.
Ft. Snelling, Twin Cities. 55111

Mississippi
Jackson
100 W. Capitol St. (Suite 102). 39201

Missouri
Kansas City
Federal Bldg., Rm. 129
601 E. 12th St. 64106

St. Louis
Federal Bldg., Rm. 1712
1520 Market St. 63103

Montana
Helena
Federal Bldg. and Courthouse
310 S. Park, Rm. 153, 59601

Nebraska
Omaha
U.S. Courthouse and Post Office Bldg.
Rm. 1014, 215 N. 17th St. 68102

Nevada
*Reno
Mill and S. Virginia Streets
P.O. Box 3296. 89505

New Hampshire
Portsmouth
Federal Bldg., Rm. 104
Daniel and Penhallow Streets. 03801

Pennsylvania
*Harrisburg
Federal Bldg., Rm. 168. 17108

Philadelphia
Wm. J. Green, Jr. Fed. Bldg.
600 Arch Street.19106

Pittsburgh
Fed. Bldg. 1000 Liberty Ave. 15222

Puerto Rico
San Juan
Federico Degetau Federal Bldg.
Carlos E. Chardon St.
Hato Rey, P.R. 00918

Rhode Island
Providence
Federal and P.O. Bldg., Rm. 310
Kennedy Plaza. 02903

South Carolina
Charleston
Federal Bldg.
334 Meeting St. 29403

South Dakota
Rapid City
Rm. 201, Federal Building
U.S. Court House, 515 9th St. 57701

Tennessee
Memphis
Federal Bldg., 176 N. Main St. 38103

Texas
Dallas
Rm. 1042, 1100 Commerce St. 75242

El Paso
Property Trust Bldg.-Suite N302
2211 E. Missouri Ave. 79903

Houston
702 Caroline St. 77002

San Antonio
643 E. Durango Blvd. 78205

Utah
Salt Lake City
350 South Main St., Rm. 484. 84101

New Jersey
Newark
Federal Bldg.
970 Broad St. 07102

New Mexico
Albuquerque
Federal Bldg.
421 Gold Ave., S.W. 87102

New York
Bronx
590 Grand Concourse. 10451

Buffalo
111 W. Huron St., Rm. 35. 14202

Jamaica
90-04 161st St., Rm. 200. 11432

New York City
Federal Bldg., 26 Federal Plaza. 10007

Syracuse
100 S. Clinton St. 13260

North Carolina
Raleigh
Federal Bldg.
310 New Bern Ave.
P.O. Box 25069. 27611

North Dakota
Fargo
Federal Bldg., Rm. 202
657 Second Ave. N. 58102

Ohio
Cleveland
Federal Bldg.
1240 E. 9th St. 44199

Dayton
Federal Building Lobby
200 W. 2nd St. 45402

Oklahoma
Oklahoma City
200 NW Fifth St. 73102

Oregon
Portland
Federal Bldg., Lobby (North)
1220 SW Third St. 97204

Vermont
Burlington
Federal Bldg., Rm. 614
P.O. Box 489
Elmwood Ave. and Pearl St. 05402

Virginia
Norfolk
Federal Bldg., Rm. 220
200 Granby Mall. 23510

D.C. Metro Area
1900 E Street N.W. 20415

Washington
*Seattle
Federal Bldg.
915 Second Ave. 98174

West Virginia
*Charleston
Federal Bldg.
500 Bldg., 500 Quarrier St. 25301

Wisconsin
Milwaukee
Plankinton Bldg., Rm. 205
161 W. Wisconsin Ave. 53203

Wyoming
Cheyenne
2120 Capital Ave., Rm. 304
P.O. Box 967. 82001

STATE LEVEL

Patrol Division
Department of Public Safety
Chief
Coliseum Boulevard
Montgomery, Alabama 36109

State Troopers Division
Department of Public Safety
State Office Building
Juneau, Alaska 99801

Arizona Highway Patrol
Department of Public Safety
Chief
2010 West Encanto Boulevard
Phoenix, Arizona 85009

Police Services Division
Department of Public Safety
3701 West Roosevelt
Little Rock, Arkansas 72204

California Highway Patrol
Commissioner
2611 26th Street
Sacramento, California 95814

California State Police
Chief
915 Capitol Mall
Office Building #1
Sacramento, California 95814

Colorado State Patrol
Chief
4201 East Ark Avenue
Denver, Colorado 80222

Connecticut State Police
Commissioner
100 Washington Street
Hartford, Connecticut 06106

State Police Division
Superintendent
P.O. Box 151
Dover, Delaware 19901

Florida Highway Patrol
State Police
Neil Kirkman Building
Tallahassee, Florida 32304

Georgia State Police
Department of Public Safety
Supervisor
959 East Confederate Avenue, S.E.
Atlanta, Georgia 30301

Department of the Attorney General
Sheriff
State Capitol Building
Honolulu, Hawaii 96813

State Police
Department of Law Enforcement
Superintendent
3211 State Street
Boise, Idaho 83703

State Highway Police
Director
Armory Building
Springfield, Illinois 62706

Indiana State Police
Superintendent
100 North Senate Avenue
Indianapolis, Indiana 46204

State Capitol Police
Chief
State Capitol Building
Des Moines, Iowa 50309

State Highway Patrol
Superintendent
1st Floor Office Building
Topeka, Kansas 66612

Division of State Police
Director
Department of Public Safety
New York Office Building
Frankfort, Kentucky 40601

State Police Division
Department of Public Safety
P.O. Box 1791
Baton Rouge, Louisiana 70821

Maine State Police
Chief
36 Hospital Street
Augusta, Maine 04330

Maryland State Police
Superintendent
1201 Reistertown Road
Pikesville, Maryland 21208

Massachusetts State Police
Superintendent
1010 Commonwealth Avenue
Boston, Massachusetts 02215

Michigan State Police
Director
714 South Harrison Road
East Lansing, Michigan 48823

Minnesota Highway Patrol
Chief
State Highway Building
St. Paul, Minnesota 55101

Mississippi Highway Patrol
Public Safety Department
Commissioner
P.O. Box 958
Jackson, Mississippi 39205

State Highway Patrol
Superintendent
1710 Elm Street
Jefferson City, Missouri 65101

Montana Highway Patrol
Director
Hustad Center
Helena, Montana 59601

State Patrol
Superintendent
14th and Burnham
Lincoln, Nebraska 68509

Nevada State Highway Patrol
Division of Law Enforcement Director
555 Wrightsway
Carson City, Nevada 89701

State Police Division
New Hampshire Department of Safety
Superintendent
85 Loudon Road
Concord, New Hampshire 03301

State Police Division
Superintendent
Route 29
West Trenton, New Jersey 08628

New Mexico State Police
Superintendent
P.O. Box 1628
Santa Fe, New Mexico 87501

Division of State Police
Superintendent
State Campus, Building 22
Albany, New York 12226

Highway Patrol
Department of Motor Vehicles
Director
New Bern Avenue
Raleigh, North Carolina 27602

North Dakota Highway Patrol
Superintendent
State Capitol
Bismarck, North Dakota 58501

State Highway Patrol
Superintendent
660 East Main Street
Columbus, Ohio 43205

Highway Patrol
Department of Public Safety
Box 11415
Oklahoma City, Oklahoma 73111

Department of State Police
Commander
Public Service Building
Salem, Oregon 97301

Pennsylvania State Police
Commissioner
617 Highway Safety Building
Harrisburg, Pennsylvania 17120

Rhode Island State Police
Superintendent
P.O. Box 185
North Scituate, Rhode Island 02857

Highway Patrol
State Highway Department
Director
1100 Senate Street
Columbia, South Carolina 29201

South Dakota Highway Patrol
Superintendent
Highway Office Building
Pierre, South Dakota 57501

Highway Patrol Division
Department of Safety
Superintendent
Cordell Hull Building
Nashville, Tennessee 37219

Texas Rangers
Department of Public Safety
Superintendent
Box 4087 North Austin Station
Austin, Texas 78751

Highway Patrol
Department of Public Safety
Superintendent
State Office Building
Salt Lake City, Utah 84101

Vermont State Police
Public Safety Department
Superintendent
Bailey Avenue Extension
Montpelier, Vermont 05602

Department of State Police
Superintendent
P.O. Box 1299
Richmond, Virginia 23210

Washington State Patrol
Superintendent
Headquarters General Administration Building
Olympia, Washington 98501

West Virginia State Police
Superintendent
Capitol Building
Charleston, West Virginia 25305

State Patrol
District I Headquarters
4845 East Washington
Madison, Wisconsin 53700

Highway Patrol
Wyoming Highway Department
P.O. Box 1708
Cheyenne, Wyoming 82001

Information about jobs at the state level can also be obtained by contacting a representative of the nearest State civil service commission.

Local and County Levels

International Association of Chiefs of Police
11 Firstfield Road
Gaithersburg, Maryland 20760

National Sheriffs' Association
1250 Connecticut Avenue, Suite 320
Washington, D.C. 20036

American Society of Criminology
1314 Kinnear Road
Columbus, Ohio 43212

Specific information about job opportunities at these levels can be obtained by contacting a representative of the nearest local and/or county civil service commission, or the recruitment or personnel office at the local and/or county police department.

THE JUDICIARY

Administrative Office of the U.S. Courts
Division of Personnel
Supreme Court Building
Washington, D.C. 20544

Administrative Office of the State Courts
Division of Personnel
(In the 50 States, American Samoa, Guam, and Puerto Rico, these offices are usually located in the capital or principal city.)

American Bar Association
1155 East 60th Street
Chicago, Illinois 60637

American Library Association
50 East Huron Street
Chicago, Illinois 60611

American Polygraph Association
P.O. Box 74
Linthicum Heights, Maryland 21090

Institute of Judicial Administration
1 Washington Square Village
New York, New York 10012

National Association of Legal Secretaries
3005 East Skelley Drive, Suite 120
Tulsa, Oklahoma 74105

National Association of Para-Legal Personnel
188 West Randolph Street
Chicago, Illinois 60601

National Business Education Association
1906 Association Drive
Reston, Virginia 22091

National Center for State Courts
300 Newport Avenue
Williamsburg, Virginia 23185

National Council on Crime and Delinquency
411 Hackensack Avenue
Hackensack, New Jersey 07601

National Shorthand Reporters Association
2361 South Jefferson Davis Highway
Arlington, Virginia 22202

Specific information about job opportunities can be obtained by contacting a representative of the nearest local, county, and/or state civil service commission office, Federal Job Information Center.

CORRECTIONS AND REHABILITATION

Federal Level

To find out more about correction occupations or general information on corrections at the federal level, write to any of the offices listed below:

Federal Bureau of Prisons
Central Office
Washington, D.C. 20534

South Central Regional Office
3883 Turtle Creek Boulevard
Dallas, Texas 75219

Southeast Regional Office
3500 Greenbriar Parkway, S.W.
Atlanta, Georgia 30331

North Central Regional Office
8800 Northwest 112th Street
K.C.I. Bank Building
Kansas City, Missouri 64153

Northeast Regional Office
Scott Plaza II
Industrial Highway
Philadelphia, Pennsylvania 19113

Western Regional Office
330 Primrose Road - Fifth Floor
Crocker Financial Center Building
San Francisco, California 94010

State Level

To obtain information about occupations, or general information about corrections at the state level, write to the agency in the capital city of the state in which you reside or wish to work.

Local and County Levels

To find out more about correctional programs in your community, get in touch with your city or county civil service commission, or apply directly to the program center.

APPENDIX E

SAMPLE APPLICATION FORM

minneapolis
city of lakes

PERSONNEL DEPARTMENT
CIVIL SERVICE COMMISSION
312 3RD AVENUE SOUTH
MINNEAPOLIS, MINNESOTA 55415

IMPORTANT EMPLOYMENT APPLICATION INSTRUCTIONS - PLEASE READ

1. **Read the Job Announcement** carefully to be sure that you meet all of the requirements.

2. **Type or print** in ink.

3. **Be sure to include** with your application all requested proofs of education, licenses, veteran's eligibility, etc. (such as trade licenses, drivers license, transcripts, etc).

4. Your application **must be completely** filled out and copies of all required documents must be included. Applications which are not complete will not **be processed.**

TITLE OF JOB:	EXAM NUMBER:

1 | LAST NAME: | FIRST NAME: | MIDDLE NAME: |

2 | PRESENT ADDRESS: | APARTMENT NO: | CITY: | STATE: | ZIP CODE: |

NOTE: If you should move after applying for this position, please notify the Personnel Department Office in writing immediately of your change of address.

3 | PRESENT HOME TELEPHONE NUMBER: AREA CODE - | PRESENT WORK TELEPHONE NUMBER: AREA CODE - | **4** | SOCIAL SECURITY NUMBER: |

5	CIRCLE THE LAST GRADE OF SCHOOL COMPLETED 5 6 7 8 9 10 11 12 GED	DID YOU GRADUATE (NOT MANDATORY)	DATE OF GRADUATION	NAME OF LAST ELEMENTARY OR HIGH SCHOOL ATTENDED	CITY OR POST OFFICE	STATE

6	ADDITIONAL EDUCATION AND TRAINING (include names and locations of Colleges, Universities, Trade, Vocational or other schools attended)	DATES ATTENDED FROM	TO	CERT OR DEGREE	DATE REC'VD	MAJOR/MINOR SUBJECT(S)

OTHER APPLICANT INFORMATION

AN AFFIRMATIVE ACTION-EQUAL OPPORTUNITY EMPLOYER, the City of Minneapolis will hire and promote without regard to such non-job related distinctions as race, creed, color, age, religion, sex (except when sex is a BFOQ), ancestry, marital status, status with regard to public assistance, national origin, physical or mental disability or affectional preference.

DATA PRIVACY: Except for requested race/ethnic data, the information on this application including social security number, is necessary to identify you and to determine your suitability for this position. You **must** supply this information in order to be considered for City employment. Racial/ethnic data is used by the Minneapolis Personnel and Affirmative Action Departments to monitor employment opportunities for protected classes. While we encourage you to provide this information, it is not required.

CS-1606 Rev. 10/89

| 7 | EMPLOYMENT RECORD: | List all your work history for at least the past ten years. Start with your PRESENT or MOST RECENT Job. Include both paid and job-related unpaid or volunteer experience. | | | | |

EMPLOYER:		ADDRESS:	CITY:	STATE:	ZIP CODE:

SUPERVISORS NAME:		PHONE NUMBER:	DATES EMPLOYED (MONTH AND YEAR ONLY): FROM: TO:	HOURS PER WEEK:	IS THIS VOLUNTEER WORK? ☐ YES ☐ NO
YOUR JOB TITLE:			REASON FOR LEAVING:		

Your Job Duties (include examples of the type of paid or volunteer work you performed): _____

If you are currently working, may we contact your PRESENT employer about your work?   ☐ YES   ☐ NO

PRIOR EMPLOYER

EMPLOYER:		ADDRESS:	CITY:	STATE:	ZIP CODE:

SUPERVISORS NAME:		PHONE NUMBER:	DATES EMPLOYED (MONTH AND YEAR ONLY): FROM: TO:	HOURS PER WEEK:	IS THIS VOLUNTEER WORK? ☐ YES ☐ NO
YOUR JOB TITLE:			REASON FOR LEAVING:		

Your Job Duties (include examples of the type of paid or volunteer work you performed): _____

PRIOR EMPLOYER

EMPLOYER:		ADDRESS:	CITY:	STATE:	ZIP CODE:

SUPERVISORS NAME:		PHONE NUMBER:	DATES EMPLOYED (MONTH AND YEAR ONLY): FROM: TO:	HOURS PER WEEK:	IS THIS VOLUNTEER WORK? ☐ YES ☐ NO
YOUR JOB TITLE:			REASON FOR LEAVING:		

Your Job Duties (include examples of the type of paid or volunteer work you performed): _____

IMPORTANT NOTICE

If you need more space, enclose or attach additional sheets, including, for each job, all information requested above.

YOU MUST COMPLETE THIS APPLICATION FORM FULLY, however, you may also include a resume or other related documentation relevant to this position.

8 Give dates and reasons, excluding disabilities, for any time in the last ten (10) years that is not accounted for in your employment history (e.g, unemployment, education, etc): _____

_____
_____
_____
_____

9 Have you ever been discharged or asked to resign from any position for misconduct or unsatisfactory service? ☐ NO ☐ YES
If yes, please describe the situation. Use the back of this application if you need more space: _____

_____
_____
_____

10 Would you, in any of your listed education or experience, be known **only** under another name? ☐ NO ☐ YES
If yes, under what name: _____

11 Have you ever been convicted of any violation of the law (other than parking tickets)? ☐ NO ☐ YES - If yes, list **all convictions within the last seven years**. Do not list juvenile (under 18 years of age) convictions unless you were tried as an adult. The Minneapolis Civil Service Commission **does not** automatically reject applicants who have conviction records.

| DATE | | PLACE | | NATURE OF OFFENSE | RESULT |
MONTH	YEAR	CITY	STATE		

PERSONAL EXPERIENCE

12 City of Minneapolis employees serve the public. Please describe any work, volunteer or personal experience which is relevant to this position and in which you worked with persons of different races, sexes or ages or with a person with a disability? _____

_____
_____
_____
_____
_____
_____
_____
_____
_____

13 Do you have any other personal experience (hobbies, other volunteer or training experiences, other coursework, etc.) which you feel may help you qualify for this position? _____

_____
_____
_____
_____
_____
_____
_____
_____
_____
_____

PLEASE BE SURE TO SIGN THIS APPLICATION, AND READ THE FOLLOWING STATEMENTS CAREFULLY

1. I certify that all the information I have provided on this application is true and complete to the best of my knowledge. I understand that giving false information or omitting requested information could result in rejection of my application or dismissal if I am hired.
2. I authorize the City of Minneapolis Civil Service Commission to verify this information to determine whether or not I am qualified for the position for which I am applying.
3. I hereby authorize all current and previous employers to release job-related information upon the written request of the Minneapolis Civil Service Commission. However, I understand that if, in the Employment Record Section, I have answered "No" to the question, "May we contact your present employer?" contact with my current employer will not be made without my specific authorization.

PRINTED NAME:	SIGNATURE:	DATE SIGNED:

PLEASE COMPLETE A VETERAN'S PREFERENCE FORM (103A) IF YOU ARE A VETERAN OF THE U.S. ARMED FORCES.

CONFIDENTIAL DATA FORM - To be separated from application immediately upon receipt in the Personnel Office.

To be completed by applicant: The City of Minneapolis has an equal employment opportunity/affirmative action policy. Knowledge of your race, sex, age, handicap and medical status is necessary for monitoring the effectiveness of the program. Although you are not required to provide the information requested on this form, your cooperation is appreciated. Persons referred for employment may be required to verify race and citizenship.

LAST NAME:	FIRST NAME:	MIDDLE NAME:

TITLE OF JOB APPLYING FOR:	EXAM NUMBER:	SEX: ☐ MALE ☐ FEMALE	DATE OF BIRTH:

RACE

☐ 1. **WHITE:** All persons having origins in any of the peoples of Europe (including Spain), North Africa or the Middle East.

☐ 2. **BLACK:** All persons having origins in any of the Black racial groups of Africa.

☐ 3. **HISPANIC:** All persons of Mexican, Puerto Rican, Cuban, Central or South American or other non-European Spanish culture or origin (regardless of race) who retain cultural identification through name, community recognition, language and/or activities.

☐ 4. **ASIAN OR PACIFIC ISLANDERS:** All persons having origins in any of the original peoples of the Far East, Southeast Asia, the Indian subcontinent or the Pacific Islands. This area includes, for example, China, Japan, Korea, the Phillipine Islands and Samoa.

☐ 5. **AMERICAN INDIAN OR ALASKAN NATIVE:** All persons having origins in any of the original peoples of North America and who maintain cultural identification through tribal affiliation or community recognition.

WHERE DID YOU LEARN THAT THIS POSITION WAS OPEN FOR APPLICATION?

☐ Minneapolis Personnel Department (Civil Service)

☐ Hot Line 348-MPLS

☐ Minneapolis Star and Tribune

☐ State Job Bank

☐ City Employee

☐ Friend

☐ School - which one: _____

☐ Community Newspaper - which one: _____

☐ Community Agency - which one: _____

☐ TV Announcement - which station: _____

☐ City Department - which one: _____

☐ Radio Announcement - which station: _____

☐ Other: _____

FOR OFFICE USE ONLY

P-#:	F:	NSO-NSW-NST:	CODE:	DNA:	R:

. . . . CONTINUED ON REVERSE SIDE . . . .

CLAIM FOR VETERAN'S PREFERENCE

ELIGIBILITY: A person who is eligible to receive a monthly veteran's pension based on length of service will not qualify for preference. To qualify for preference for a **competitive exam** you must have been separated under honorable conditions from any branch of the armed forces of the United States after having served on active duty for 181 consecutive days or by reason of disability incurred while serving on active duty and be a United States citizen or resident alien; or be the spouse of a deceased veteran; or be the spouse of a disabled veteran who because of such disability is unable to qualify or earn a living. To qualify for preference on a **promotional exam** you must be entitled to disability compensation for a permanent service connected disability rated at 50 percent or more; or be the spouse of a veteran who is rated as 100 percent disabled and who because of such disability is unable to qualify or earn a living. Persons eligible for such preference may use it only for the 1st promotion after securing public employment.

NOTE: If you do not meet the eligibility requirements outlined above, do not complete this section.

Name of Veteran (Last, First, Middle): _____ Date of Birth: _____

Did you serve on active military duty without interruption for 181 days or more (does not include Active Duty for Training (ADT) in the Reserve or National Guard . . . . ☐ Yes ☐ No

Are you a U.S. citizen or resident alien . . . . ☐ Yes ☐ No

Date of entry into active duty: _____ Date of release from active duty: _____

Branch: _____

Type of separation (for verification purposes, furnish a copy of your DD-214, WD AG053-55, NAC. PERS., or other separation papers . . . . ☐ Honorable ☐ Medical ☐ Honorable release from active duty and transfer to reserves

Are you now receiving or are you eligible to receive a monthly veteran's pension based on length of military service . . . . ☐ Yes ☐ No

Disability claim number: ☐☐☐☐☐☐☐

Be sure this number is correct. If not available, put service serial number here _____

Percent of service connected disability _____ Currently existing: ☐ Yes ☐ No

Date and **amount** of most recent disability payment: Month - _____ Day - _____ Year - _____ $ _____

State in which filed _____

If not Minnesota, have records since been transferred to Fort Snelling: ☐ Yes ☐ No Where _____

Have you ever been promoted in the City service: ☐ Yes ☐ No

FOR SPOUSES OF DECEASED VETERANS		FOR SPOUSES OF DISABLED VETERANS	
DATE OF DEATH:	HAVE YOU REMARRIED: ☐ YES ☐ NO	VETERAN'S PRESENT OCCUPATION:	VETERAN'S TOTAL EARNINGS FROM EMPLOY-MENT FOR PAST 12 MONTHS: $

I hereby claim veteran's preference for this examination and (swear/affirm) that the information given on this document is true and correct. I also authorize the release of necessary information by the Veteran's Administration to the City of Minneapolis Personnel Department.

SOCIAL SECURITY NO: _____

SIGNATURE: _____   DATE: _____

PART 2: CONFIDENTIAL DATA FORM - To be separated from application immediately upon receipt in Personnel Office.

The information requested below will **NOT** be stored with your employment application. Providing this information is voluntary and, by not doing so, you will not hurt your chances for employment. The City is requesting this information solely to track and improve the effectiveness of its Affirmative Action recruitment and testing efforts. This information will not be accessable to City personnel involved in the selection process. Such access would violate the Minnesota Human Rights Act.

For the purposes of this section, a disability is defined as a condition which limits one or more major life activities such as employment opportunities, access or testing.

Do you consider yourself to have any of the following disabilities, handicaps, or medical conditions?

☐ 8. No
☐ A. Joint Disability
☐ E. Post Polio Disability
☐ G. Speech Disability
☐ I. Hearing Disability
☐ J. Mental/Emotional Disability
☐ O. Back Injury or Disability
☐ L. Diabetes or Related Disability
☐ H. Communicative/Learning Disability

☐ B. Amputated or impaired limb
☐ C. Paraplegia, Quadriplegia or Hemiplegia
☐ D. Neuro Muscular Disability (Cerebral Palsy, Muscular Dystrophy, Multiple Sclerosis, etc.)
☐ F. Visual Disability (does not include corrected vision.)
☐ K. Epilepsy or other Seizure Disability
☐ Z. Other Medical Disability which limits employment opportunities and/or ability to perform all job tasks. If yes, explain: _____
_____
_____

If you have checked one or more of the disabilities above, it may be possible to arrange alternative testing accommodations. Do you need any alternative testing accommodations? ☐ NO ☐ *YES - If yes, please explain _____
_____
_____
_____
_____

If you have a question about alternative testing, call 348-2292 or TDD 348-2157.

*If necessary, you will be contacted by the Personnel Office to make alternative testing arrangements.

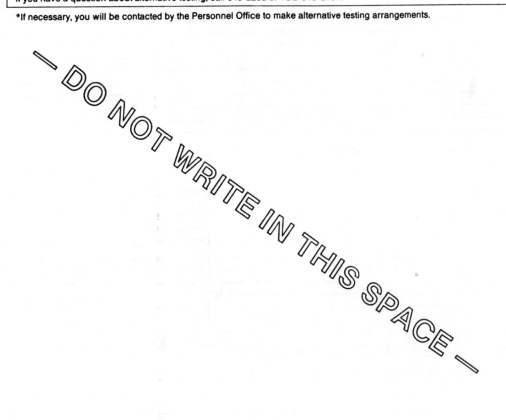

238

DO NOT WRITE BELOW THIS LINE

APPROVAL:		DATE:	INITIALS:
INCOMPLETE (REASON):		DATE:	INITIALS:
WITHDRAWAL (DATE):	INITIALS:	REJECTION (DATE):	INITIALS:

REMARKS: _____

ACTION	DATE	BY
Application Indexed		
Rejection Notice		
NST-NSO-NSW		
Fail Notice		
Written Notice		
Oral Notice		
Practical Notice		
References Sent		
Other		
Final Results		

Final Average: _____ Rank: _____

NECESSARY PROOFS	DATE PRESENTED	RECEIVED BY	ITEM

APPENDIX F

EQUAL EMPLOYMENT OPPORTUNITY (EE0) GUIDELINES

Topic	Permitted Inquiries	Prohibited Inquiries
AGE	Whether candidate meets minimum age requirements or is under 65. Requirement that candidate submit proof of age after hired. Whether candidate can meet terms and conditions of job.	Age, birth certificate. Any inquiry for purpose of excluding persons between 40 and 70. Inquiries as to date of graduation from college or high school to determine age should also be avoided.
ARRESTS	None.	Any inquiry relating to arrest.
CONVICTIONS	Inquiries about actual convictions which relate reasonably to performing a particular job.	Inquiries regarding convictions that do not relate to performing the particular job under consideration.
CREDIT RATING	Inquiries about credit rating, charge accounts, etc., that relate reasonably to performing the particular job in question.	Any inquiries concerning charge accounts, credit rating, etc., that do not relate to performing the particular job under consideration.
DRIVER'S LICENSE	If required for the job, may ask if applicant possess a valid license.	Not permitted to ask applicant to produce or show a license.
EDUCATION	Inquiries regarding degrees or equivalent experience. Information regarding courses relevant to a particular job.	Disqualification of a candidate who does not have a particular degree unless employer has proven that the specific degree is the only way to measure a candidate's ability to perform the job in question.
HANDICAPS	Whether candidate has any disabilities which would prevent him or her from performing the job. Whether there are any types of jobs for which candidate should not be considered because of a handicap or health condition.	General inquiries that would elicit information about handicaps or health conditions which do not relate to job performance.
HEIGHT & WEIGHT	Inquiries regarding ability to perform a particular job. However, being a specific height or weight will not be considered a requirement unless the employer can show no employee with ineligible height or weight could do the work.	Inquiries are prohibited if they are not based on actual job requirements.
MARITAL & FAMILY STATUS	Whether candidate can meet work schedule or job. Whether candidate has activities, responsibilities, or commitments that may hinder meeting attendance requirements. (Should be asked of candidates of both sexes.)	Childcare problems, unwed motherhood, contraceptive practices, spouses' preferences regarding job conditions. Inquiries indicating marital status, number of children, pregnancies. Any questions directly or indirectly resulting in limitation of job opportunity in any way.

Topic	Permitted Inquiries	Prohibited Inquiries
MILITARY RECORD	Type of experience and education in service as it relates to a particular job.	Discharge status, unless it is the result of a military conviction.
NAME	Whether candidate has ever worked under a different name.	Inquiries to determine national origin, ancestry, or prior marital status.
NATIONAL ORIGIN	Whether candidate is legally eligible to work in the United States.	Lineage, ancestry, descent, mother tongue, birthplace, citizenship. National origin of spouse or parents.
NOTICE IN CASE OF EMERGENCY	Permitted after time of hire.	Not permitted before hire.
ORGANIZATIONS	Inquiries which do not elicit discriminatory information.	Inquiries about membership to determine the race, color, religion, sex, national origin, or age of candidates.
PHOTOGRAPHS	Photos may be requested after hiring for identification purposes.	Requests for photos at any time before hiring.
PREGNANCY	Inquiries re: duration of stay on the job or anticipated absences which are made to males and females alike.	All questions re: pregnancy and related medical history.
RACE OR COLOR	None.	Complexion, color skin, hair, eyes, etc.
RELATIVES	Relatives' names already employed by the company or by a competitor.	No other inquiries re: relatives permitted.
RELIGION	Whether candidate can meet work schedules ·of job with reasonable accommodation by employer if necessary.	Religious preference, affiliations, denomination.
RESIDENCE	Applicant's address with regard to being able to contact him during the selection process.	Owning or renting a home. Names or relationships of people residing with applicant.
SEXUAL PREFERENCE	None.	Number of male vs. female friends, roommates, living arrangements, etc.
WORK EXPERIENCE	Candidate's previous job-related experience.	None.

INDEX